# RECOVERING INEQUALITY

# THE KATRINA BOOKSHELF

*Kai Erikson, Series Editor*

In 2005 Hurricane Katrina crashed into the Gulf Coast and precipitated the flooding of New Orleans. It was a towering catastrophe by any standard. Some 1,800 persons were killed outright. More than a million were forced to relocate, many for the remainder of their lives. A city of five hundred thousand was nearly emptied of life. The storm stripped away the surface of our social structure and showed us what lies beneath—a grim picture of race, class, and gender in these United States.

It is crucial to get this story straight so that we may learn from it and be ready for that stark inevitability, *the next time*. When seen through a social science lens, Katrina informs us of the real human costs of a disaster and helps prepare us for the events that we know are lurking just over the horizon. The Katrina Bookshelf is the result of a national effort to bring experts together in a collaborative program of research on the human costs of the disaster. The program was supported by the Ford, Gates, MacArthur, Rockefeller, and Russell Sage Foundations and sponsored by the Social Science Research Council. This is the most comprehensive social science coverage of a disaster to be found anywhere in the literature. It is also a deeply human story.

# RECOVERING INEQUALITY

## HURRICANE KATRINA, THE SAN FRANCISCO EARTHQUAKE OF 1906, AND THE AFTERMATH OF DISASTER

STEVE KROLL-SMITH

*University of Texas Press*

AUSTIN

Requests for permission to reproduce material from this work should be sent to:
Permissions
University of Texas Press
P.O. Box 7819
Austin, TX 78713-7819
utpress.utexas.edu/rp-form

♾ The paper used in this book meets the minimum requirements of
ANSI/NISO Z39.48-1992 (R1997) (Permanence of Paper).

LIBRARY OF CONGRESS CATALOGING-IN-PUBLICATION DATA
Names: Kroll-Smith, J. Stephen, 1947– author.
Title: Recovering inequality : Hurricane Katrina, the San Francisco
Earthquake of 1906, and the aftermath of disaster / Steve Kroll-Smith.
Other titles: Katrina bookshelf.
Description: First edition. | Austin : University of Texas Press, 2018. |
Series: Katrina bookshelf | Includes bibliographical references and index.
Identifiers: LCCN 2017036828
ISBN 978-1-4773-1610-8 (cloth : alk. paper)
ISBN 978-1-4773-1611-5 (pbk. : alk. paper)
ISBN 978-1-4773-1612-2 (library e-book)
ISBN 978-1-4773-1613-9 (non-library e-book)
Subjects: LCSH: Emergency management—United States. | Disaster relief—Social
aspects—United States. | Equality—United States. | United States—Race relations. |
United States—Social conditions. | Hurricane Katrina, 2005—Social aspects. |
San Francisco Earthquake and Fire, Calif., 1906—Social aspects.
Classification: LCC HV551.3 K76 2018 | DDC 363.34/80973—dc23
LC record available at https://lccn.loc.gov/2017036828
doi:10.7560/316108

*To*
*Emma Kroll-Smith*
*who at twenty-one years of age*
*continues to teach me much about myself and the world,*
*Love you, Dad*

# CONTENTS

# ACKNOWLEDGMENTS

Most books are coauthored, even those, like this one, that list but one author. This book would not be around at all were it not for Kai Erikson's inspiration and critical editing. Carol Stack read and commented presciently on several chapters. Vern Baxter, Art Murphy, and Pam Jenkins also offered numerous helpful suggestions along the way.

I want to thank Evan Holtz, whose early work gathering data on the United States and San Francisco at the turn of the twentieth century proved invaluable to this study. Joyce Clapp also collected important data on the use of labor to rebuild San Francisco. Jessica Priesmeyer (now Priesmeyer Gibbs), wrote a compelling master's thesis on disaster and looting. I draw from it, and the book is the better for it. Andrew Bynum, a former undergraduate honors student at the University of North Carolina at Greensboro, now at Columbia University, wrote a commendable study on the militarization of disaster that I cite liberally in chapter 4. Rachel Madsen also added some original insights and data to this chapter. Shelly Brown-Jeffy helped me think through many of the issues raised in chapter 6. Anelise Dar helped with the details of the endnotes and other pesky but critical editing tasks. A special thanks is due Debbie Wauford, who met with aplomb my many requests for copies of this or that chapter.

Finally, to Susan Kroll-Smith, thanks for hanging in there with me. I could not do this and so much more without you. And to my cousin, the honorable Jerry VandeWalle, a remarkable man whose resilience and wisdom I carry with me, thank you.

# FOREWORD: CRISIS AND CAPITAL
## THE DARK SIDE OF RECOVERY

The immediate aftermath of disaster is frequently portrayed as a time of great solidarity, often across all the traditional lines, such as race and class, that divide people in complex societies. Disaster is also framed as the opportunity for change, to "build back better," to improve the lives of the victims, to address those features of a community that rendered people vulnerable to hazards. As many disaster chroniclers have noted, Dickens's ringing phrase "It was the best of times, it was the worst of times" could not be more apt. We do see the best in human beings and communities in immediate aftermaths. Moments of great courage, generosity, and nobility express the deep roots of human sociability.

That period of intense social solidarity, however, tends to be fragile and short-lived. The arrival of aid and the beginning of debates about the direction and form of reconstruction tend to dissipate the altruism of the early moments of post-impact solidarity. Entrenched interests soon emerge to restore their advantages temporarily suspended in the wake of catastrophe. In fact, much post-disaster reconstruction restores many of the social features that render people vulnerable to hazard onset. In a market society, as Steve Kroll-Smith notes, "How could it be otherwise?"

There is no lack of that irony in the compelling narratives and analyses of the 1906 San Francisco earthquake-fire and Hurricane Katrina at the turn of the twenty-first century in New Orleans that Steve Kroll-Smith skillfully weaves together in *Recovering Inequality*. He explores and demonstrates that the two cities, both lauded for their beauty and the wealth and diversity of their cultures, both situated within extremely exposed environments, privileged the accumulation of wealth over anything approaching basic security for their inhabitants.

The chapters roughly follow the trajectory of the catastrophes in both cities from the moments of impact and the stories of people helping people to the inevitable hysteria around looting, from the wicked capital-inspired algorithms of disaster assistance to the opportunistic efforts of elites and politicians in both cities to engage in "ethnic cleansing," seeking to rid themselves of social groups that were seen as inferior and consequently less deserving of assistance in the aftermath. Throughout, Kroll-Smith takes us on side trips through history that help elucidate the processes set in motion as the needs of the market easily outmaneuver empathy and fairness.

In this study of two iconic American cities and the aftermath of disaster, Kroll-Smith masterfully reveals how the process of post-disaster re-construction reflects and expresses the fundamental tensions and contra-dictions in our social, economic, and environmental relations. Moreover, the narratives reveal the essential continuities between late-nineteenth-century laissez-faire economics and early-twenty-first-century neoliberal-ism that inform the process of reconstruction to privilege accumulation by certain sectors of society over others.

Thus, neoliberal market logics and the eradication of most structural regulations or constraints today guide the decisions and choices made by governments, businesses, and now even nongovernmental organizations (NGOs) involved in recovery. In this context, human interests and market interests rarely coincide. The frequently chanted trope "Build back better" is far more a rhetorical gloss on the realpolitik of setting aright those pillars of inequality knocked about by disaster.

As I write, neoliberal versions of social and environmental relations are ubiquitous in current discourses, making alternative understandings ex-tremely difficult to deploy, much less empower. Neoliberalism, as a model for relations between human beings and between human beings and the environment, is presented today as if designed by nature. Under such con-ditions it is reasonable to ask how any process of recovery can be socially just and environmentally secure.

"But it is ironic, is it not," Kroll-Smith observes at one point in the book, "that the human labor done in the name of disaster relief too often cre-ates a suffering, a cruelty, that equals or exceeds that wrought by nature?" *Recovering Inequality: Hurricane Katrina, the San Francisco Earthquake of 1906, and the Aftermath of Disaster* throws a bright light on just this irony.

ANTHONY OLIVER-SMITH
Professor Emeritus of Anthropology at the University of Florida

# FROM WHENCE RECOVERY?
## A PRELUDE

*There is much to learn about ourselves
and the worlds we fashion
when all hell breaks loose*

W. LLOYD WARNER, *THE SOCIAL SYSTEM
OF THE MODERN FACTORY* (1947)

More than twelve years ago, a catastrophic flood inundated a celebrated American city. On August 29, 2005, we watched from afar as levees fell like dominoes and the bowl that is New Orleans filled with the waters of Lake Pontchartrain, Lake Borgne, and the Industrial Canal. But more than levees collapsed in the heat of that fate-filled summer; a widespread, if self-serving, belief also buckled. Most of us want, perhaps need, to believe that in the face of a totalizing disaster like Hurricane Katrina, this society is committed to protecting and assisting all of its citizens.

But that conviction could not bear the weight of the endless video scanning the bewildered faces of thousands of people left on rooftops, bridges, and highways. It could not stand against the sickening photographs of bloated bodies floating facedown in the dark waters of the city. It had no defense against the inhumane housing of US citizens under armed guards or their transfer by buses and planes to points hundreds or thousands of miles from New Orleans, only to be dropped off abruptly without a return ticket.

What happened in New Orleans in late August 2005 invites a larger, more complex, question. Ron Eyerman poses this question in the provocative title of his book on Katrina, *Is This America?*[1] Was this an aberrant outcome of catastrophe in America? Or was this painful glimpse of inhumanity more illustrative of a unique place with a unique history? After all, New Orleans past and present is deeply intertwined with many shades of skin color bound in complex relationships with historical and contemporary class privilege. On the other hand, perhaps it is less New Orleans and more the result of gross ineptness on the part of the Federal Emergency Management Agency (FEMA), a famously disorganized unit at the time of the disaster. But it might conceivably be something else.

Is the horrific tale of Hurricane Katrina and New Orleans intimately connected to the very tissue of American society, something close to our social skeleton? I have a suspicion that it is, and if so, we should find a likeness of sorts between this calamity and other historic American disasters. It is in pursuit of this hunch that I bring together two unforgettable calamities in one narrative account.

A close-up look at Hurricane Katrina and the flooding of New Orleans in 2005 and the San Francisco earthquake and fire in 1906 invites us to consider whether disruptions of this kind expose what is hidden in humdrum, day-to-day life. San Francisco minutes before the first trembler struck and New Orleans moments before the flood were urban spaces where socially fashioned categories of people lived aside, atop, and beneath one another in uneven and unequal circumstances. My point of departure in this inquiry is simple: in both disasters, it is this order that was disordered, and it is the reclaiming or refashioning of this arrangement that knowingly and unknowingly shaped the work of recovery in 1906 and 2005.

This project disputes the conventional meaning of disaster recovery. It recalls Lewis Carroll, who has Alice debating Humpty Dumpty on the meaning of words. "The question is," said Alice, "whether you can make words mean so many different things." "The question is," parries Humpty Dumpty, "which is to be Master—that's all." Following Mr. Dumpty's mischievous lead: What if we approach recovery not from the starting point of the indomitable human or community spirit to revive, heal, and push on but from a more divisive point of departure, one that concedes, as William Dean Howells knew well, that "inequality is as dear to the American heart as liberty"?[2]

# AN INTRODUCTION

# "THE EARTH DRAGON"
# AND "MISS KATRINA"

*Cities have always been condensations of their civilizations.*
*If their density distorts, so it also reveals.*

IRA KATZNELSON, *MARXISM AND THE CITY*

City of many hills overlooking bay and ocean, guardian of the Sierra gold
and holder of the keys to unlock Cathay, to thee in this hour of need I
pledge my troth and offer this humble tribute. . . . Earthquake-rocked and
fire-devastated, thy marts and dwelling-places swept to nothingness in
three brief days, thou standest shelterless but unafraid. Thy fair hillslopes
are strewn with miles of destruction, thy children have faced hunger and
death, thy homes of yesterday are no more.[1]

At 5:12 a.m. on April 18, 1906, a foreshock rocked the city of San Francisco,
a brief portent of something imminent and far worse on its way. Seconds
later, the San Andreas Fault opened its craggy face, fracturing the surface of
the earth up and down the California coast. Its speed as it shot underground
is estimated to have been seven thousand miles an hour. Within thirty seconds, with a force greater than all of the explosives used in World War II,
the quake ripped through the city.[2]

The undulating earth limned, if only for a moment, the pitch of the sea.
Vulnerable structures, brick and stone walls with no interior frames, simply
collapsed. Wood- and steel-frame structures fared far better. Fires broke
out around the doomed city. The fires would burn for three days, aided
by the imprudent, some might say reckless, use of black powder to dynamite buildings ahead of the blaze. The idea behind the willful destruction
of houses and buildings was to create dead zones in front of the advancing
flames. When the fires reached the zones, they would—it was thought—
burn themselves out. This thinking proved faulty. A witness to the cataclysm, Fred J. Hewitt, wrote:

**1.1.** San Francisco, Market Street, 1900

It is impossible to judge the length of that shock. To me it seemed an eternity. I was thrown prone on my back and the pavement pulsated like a living thing. Then an unnatural light dimmed the rising sun and the word went forth from every throat: "The city is ablaze. We will all be burned. This must be the end of this wicked world." From down south of Market Street the glare grew and grew. The flames show heavenward and licked the sky. It looked as if the end of the world was surely at hand.[3]

When the last fires were extinguished on April 21, three days later, 514 city blocks, approximately 4 square miles, were incinerated. More than twenty-nine thousand houses and businesses were destroyed. In all, 80 percent of the city's 4.7 square miles was toppled or burned to the ground. A survivor wrote a few months after the last fires were extinguished:

Think of this enormous city with not a single hotel, every factory and wholesale and retail shop destroyed, all the markets gone, every office building and business black, nine hospitals, every theatre and half or more of the homes destroyed.[4]

The savage destruction of the fires suggested to many in the Chinese community that the dreaded "Earth Dragon" had been let loose among them.[5] The charred and broken remnants of what was once San Francisco mocked the claims of those who saw the city as the imperial outpost of America's western expansion. Daguerreotypes, Kodak Brownie photographs, the occasional landscape painting, and fallible memories were all that remained of the cityscape.[6]

Estimates put the number of urban homeless at approximately three hundred thousand people, almost three-quarters of the city's entire population.[7] Upwards of 75 percent of the city's four hundred thousand residents evacuated, many carrying only what they could throw in a bag or trunk. Estimated deaths have varied widely over the years, but it is now generally acknowledged that at least three thousand people perished.[8] Many died from the seismic jolt and aftershocks that leveled poorly constructed houses and hotels. The dead were disproportionately from the working class and the poor, those who lived in poorly constructed shacks, houses, and tenement hotels, buildings defenseless against the subterranean power of an earthquake.

**1.2.** Approximately 80 percent of San Francisco was destroyed or damaged by the earthquake and subsequent fires. Arnold Genthe, Library of Congress Prints and Photographs Division

As the seismic jolt coursed its way beneath the earth's surface, Jack London and his wife, Charmaine, were shaken from their beds in Glen Ellen, California, some forty miles from San Francisco. The force of the temblor was reason enough to saddle their horses and ride in haste to the city. But London had another reason: he was born near Market Street, close to the city's heart. Approaching from the east, the couple was shocked by the destructive scene on the horizon. Gazing at the ruin, London confided to his wife, "I'll never write about this for anybody, no, I'll never write a word about it. What use trying? Only could one string big words together and curse the futility of them."[9]

In the end, London would write about what he saw on that day in April 1906. In serious debt, he would accept a lucrative offer from *Collier's* to pen an eyewitness account of the disaster. *Collier's* published London's twenty-five-hundred-word essay, "The Story of an Eyewitness," on May 5, seventeen days after the cataclysm. In lean and unsparing prose, London enumerates the obliteration of the cityscape:

> On Wednesday morning . . . came the earthquake. A minute later the flames were leaping upward. In a dozen different quarters south of Market Street, in the working-class ghetto, and in the factories, fires started. There was no opposing the flames. . . . All the cunning adjustments of a twentieth century city had been smashed by the earthquake.
>
> Not in history has a modern imperial city been so completely destroyed. San Francisco is gone. Nothing remains of it but memories and a fringe of dwelling-houses on its outskirts. Its industrial section is wiped out. Its business section is wiped out. Its social and residential section is wiped out. The factories and warehouses, the great stores and newspaper buildings, the hotels and the palaces of the nabobs, are all gone. I urged a man to seek safety in flight. He was all but hemmed in by several conflagrations. He was an old man and he was on crutches. Said he "Today is my birthday . . . and all I own are these crutches." I convinced him of his danger and started him limping on his way.

With a studied eye for the intersection of humans and topography, London was struck by the "caravan of trunks" moving about the broken streets of the city:

**1.3.** Dragging trunks down Van Ness Avenue, April 19, 1906.
C. L. Nelson, US Geological Survey

Before the flames, throughout the night, fled tens of thousands of homeless ones. Some were wrapped in blankets. Others carried bundles of bedding and dear household treasures. Sometimes a whole family was harnessed to a carriage or delivery wagon that was weighted down with their possessions. Baby buggies, toy wagons, and go-carts were used as trucks, while every other person was dragging a trunk. Yet everybody was gracious. The most perfect courtesy obtained. Never in all San Francisco's history, were her people so kind and courteous as on this night of terror. . . . They held on longest to their trunks, and over these trunks many a strong man broke his heart that night. The hills of San Francisco are steep, and up these hills, mile after mile, were the trunks dragged. . . . Often, after surmounting a heart-breaking hill, they would find another wall of flame . . . and be compelled to change anew their line of retreat. . . . Everywhere were trunks with across them lying their exhausted owners, men and women.[10]

Others would follow London, telling their stories of the great San Francisco earthquake and firestorms in dozens of books and hundreds of newspaper and magazine articles. In a 2006 PBS documentary, historian David McCullough referred to this catastrophe as "the worst disaster in American history."[11] There are some who would dispute this assessment. Ninety-nine

**1.4.** Streetcar at the corner of Canal and Royal Streets, New Orleans, 2004.
Nicolas Larchet, Wikimedia Commons

years and four months after the San Francisco earthquake, another disaster laid waste to another unparalleled American city.

> Marshy spillover is first to flood: where water
> first met sand and pilings lost all anchor.
> Where nothing rose above the surge, that wall
> of black, black water. Where houses buckled, crumbled. . . .
> The levees overfilled, broke open. And I came home to see
> the city grieving.[12]

At 11:00 a.m. on August 24, 2005, Tropical Depression 12 was upgraded to Tropical Storm Katrina. As if seeking greater notoriety, Katrina's winds quickly exceeded 75 miles per hour, and the tropical storm was upgraded to a hurricane at 5:00 p.m. on August 25. Two days later, Hurricane Katrina was a Category 3 storm. By August 27, she reached Category 5 intensity, with winds topping 175 miles an hour.

Early in the morning on August 29, Hurricane Katrina came ashore near the village of Buras, little more than an hour's drive from New Orleans. Laying waste to lower Plaquemines Parish, the storm veered a bit east, sparing the city a direct hit. It appeared, for a brief while, like another near miss. But as the winds blew eastward, the water surged, racing through Breton Sound to Lake Pontchartrain and that devilish US Army Corps project known locally as MRGO, the Mississippi River Gulf Outlet. The rushing water scoured the bottoms of levees that simply laid down, as if bowing to the deluge.

Other levees stood their ground as walls of water washed over them. By 9:00 a.m. on Monday, August 29, a storm surge destroyed the ramparts separating New Orleans residents from the Industrial Canal. By day's end, upwards of fifty or more levees were breached. By the evening of the twenty-ninth, 80 percent of the city lay beneath three to twelve feet of brown fetid water.

Kevin L. remembers:

We had water up to our waist, up to our neck. By the time I got out of there, it was up to my neck. I'm six feet even. My mom couldn't [stand] it was already over her head. . . . The people were drowning in their homes. They couldn't get out of their houses. By that time, the water was at the roof and the attic, and they were trying to get on top of the roof. You can't get a seventy-year-old woman on top of a roof. That's kind of hard. So a lot of people didn't make it.[13]

Without working pumps to flush the floodwaters from the city, most of which sits at or below sea level, it would be two weeks before they re-treated, leaving a wake of unimaginable destruction. Close to 80 percent of New Orleans's roughly 460,000 residents evacuated to higher ground, but roughly 100,000 residents, many with no means to leave the city, remained in harm's way. Hundreds of people drowned. Hundreds more died from heat exhaustion and inadequate medical care; perhaps some were killed intentionally to prevent further misery.

The demography of death was anything but democratic. Jolinda Johnson, a lifelong resident of the city, put it this way: "You plain didn't want to be poor when 'Miss Katrina'"—as she had come to call this hurricane—"came to town."[14] She might well have said the same about the coming of "the Earth Dragon." In New Orleans, as in San Francisco one hundred years earlier, it was the poor, the elderly, and the medically infirm who perished.

**1.5.** Water everywhere, New Orleans, August 30, 2005.
National Oceanic and Atmospheric Administration

## "THE SITUATION AT THE LAFAYETTE SCHOOL"

Dietmar Felber did not evacuate ahead of the flood. An instructor in the Department of Germanic and Slavic Studies at Tulane University, Dietmar made the decision to ride out the hurricane. After all, his second-floor apartment did sit behind the stoutest levee, protecting the city's wealthier residents from the waters of the Mississippi River. How could he know that the levees shielding other parts of the city from industrial waters to the east and Lake Pontchartrain to the north would not withstand the tidal surge of a comparatively weak hurricane? He could also not have known what he was to discover about a city, a disaster, and himself.

Dietmar waited patiently for the water that filled the city to subside. But on the fourth day, the waters washed to and fro, much like they did on the first day. Water or no water, it was time to leave his apartment. Fortunately, he had a canoe.

I launch the canoe from the front steps of the house and paddle up Short Street. My task this September morning a few days after the levees broke is, first, to check on my friends Lisa and Mulry, whose house is not far from mine, and then to go on from there to Lafayette School, another two blocks away. We have seen helicopters land on the roof of the school to evacuate people trapped in the flooded city. . . . The water in the streets is not going down, and its smell is rapidly becoming intolerable.

I see a white-bearded old man wading haltingly toward me, sounding out the water before him with a cane. "I want to go back to Rampart Street," he declares. I tell him that Rampart Street is too far and the water too high everywhere, but he does not seem to understand. "My house is near Rampart Street," he insists. As I look at him more closely, I spot a blue plastic band inscribed with letters or numbers on his right wrist. I ask him where he is coming from. "From the hospital," he replies. . . . "Near my house, a corpse is floating in the water; according to a woman living on Short St., the police said to throw the body in a dumpster for now."

Schools, hospitals, hotels and other multi-storied buildings quickly became destination points for those seeking to escape the waters and find adequate shelter and perhaps food and just maybe some way to evacuate the city.

I am going to scout out the situation at the Lafayette School. . . . The canoe glides silently toward the front steps rising out of the water until it bumps into them with a thud. . . . The stairs leading up into the school are wet and slimy. On the second floor, a little girl with ribbons in her hair is waiting for the helicopter with her grandfather. She doesn't know where her mother is, she tells me. "You'll see her soon," I try to reassure her. I sincerely hope I am right.

. . . [T]wo members of the Coast Guard in orange wet suits bolt down the stairs from the third floor and head toward me. . . . "Can you help us?" one of them asks me. "Those who can walk need to go up to the roof; those who can't walk we take out to the boats." They try to communicate with a disheveled, massively overweight woman reclining in a wheelchair, but she does not respond. . . . The two Guardsmen plan to carry her down the front steps. A giant in green National Guard camouflage joins the three of us, and we get ready. As I grab the frame of the chair, I notice it: the woman's feet have been amputated, and the stumps of her legs dangle from the seat like the limbs of a wooden puppet.

After she is ferried away . . . I return to the top of the stairs on the second floor. A dignified elderly woman with graying hair is waiting there to begin her journey. To get down to the boats from the second floor, she will have to master the flight of stairs down to the entrance and then the remaining steps outside the building down to the water. . . . [W]alking down stairs on her own is out of the question. I take her walker to the bottom of the stairs and run back up. Her son and I support her on each side as she makes her way.

Her descent is painstakingly slow: in this instance, the pain is literal. . . . [T]he stairs . . . seem altogether too steep . . . designed for children . . . not for elderly women with walkers trying to leave a flooded city. The woman's left hand tightly clasps my right forearm, and I feel the imprint of her fingers on my skin.

Dietmar connects this moment of human touch to the chronicle of social neglect that is woven tight to our collective past:

Minutes go by and I feel time . . . looping back across the ages in order to hook up with other moments of exclusion or abandonment in history.[15]

## "WHAT IS WORTH STUDYING?"

In 1906, at the western edge of the United States, a calamity laid waste to a unique and irreplaceable American city. San Francisco, sometimes called the "Paris of the Pacific," lay in ruins. Parts of the city were leveled by seismic force, and the remainder was burned beyond recognition. Ninety-nine years later, in 2005, at a precarious sliver of land betwixt a mighty river and a massive lake, a quite different disaster engulfed another of America's matchless cities. Within hours of the levee breaches, New Orleans, called by some the "Paris of the South," lay submerged, a nightmarish Atlantis.

Two disasters, two cities, separated by almost a century. What sense can we make of this medley? What is the purpose of our comparative venture? "Not every comparison," Lucien Febvre cautions us, "is valuable in itself." Febvre has a point. But so does Nietzsche, who makes a provocative case for examining two. Fond of the aphorism, he writes, "One is always wrong, but with two, truth begins."[16] I am not convinced that *one* need always be mistaken; there is a good deal of truth to be found by burrowing deep into the single case study. But Nietzsche's insight into ways that *two* can help us see what we might well miss in pursuit of *one* is my point of departure for this inquiry.

These, of course, are not just two commonplace cases. They are nothing less than the most catastrophic urban disasters in American history. These two colossal collisions between nature and society exceed the means we possess to make comprehensive sense of either calamity, much less both together. Faced with what Baudrillard would call an "excess of reality," we are left with telling but a part of the story.[17] Mine is not an inclusive history of either disaster, if such a history could be written. By the sheer magnitude of both calamities, much will be left out.[18]

With this caveat in mind, we turn to Elizabeth Clemens, who rightly asks of historical sociology, "What is worth studying?" Charles Tilly complicates this question, reminding us that those who study history are obliged to walk "a narrow road between randomness and teleology."[19] Captured in this cryptic remark is the need to find in the disparate and seemingly contingent events and circumstances of not one but two historical moments an intelligible meaning, a convincing story—one worth telling. One place to begin is by noting key points of convergence between these two calamities.

For years leading up to Hurricane Katrina, sociologists and others were parsing the various meanings of disaster and catastrophe. "Even two decades ago," Enrico Quarantelli notes, "some researchers were saying that there were 'disasters' and that there were 'disasters' that were beyond typical disasters. The latter came to be called 'catastrophes.'" After Katrina the Federal Emergency Management Agency adopted Quarantelli's distinction, defining a catastrophe as "any natural or manmade incident, including terrorism, that results in extraordinary levels of mass casualties, damage, or disruption severely affecting the population, infrastructure, environment, economy, national morale, and/or government functions."[20]

If Hurricane Katrina in 2005 was a "catastrophe," so too was the 1906 earthquake and firestorm in San Francisco. While we will use the words *disaster, catastrophe,* and their cognates throughout this book, it is worth remembering that each city experienced what researchers and the federal government now call the most extreme disruption and destruction wrought by nature or humankind or both. It is to the etiology of these two catastrophes that we now turn.

Destruction of the built environments of both cities totaled somewhere close to 80 percent, itself a suggestive comparison. But of more interest, it was not acts of nature that destroyed these two cities but a mix of reckless human actions and inherently flawed human construction. The tremor of forty seconds or so that shook San Francisco in 1906 caused some structural damage, particularly in the poorer tenement areas. But it was the firestorms, by and large human caused, raging unchecked through the city, that would reduce this urban landscape to charred rubble. It was known at the time that dynamite could be used—in an extreme emergency—to create dead zones, preventing fires from advancing. The city had little dynamite on hand. The unfortunate replacement was volatile black powder, deployed by men with no real experience in fighting fires. With each explosion, incendiary rubble blew across streets and city blocks to start yet more fires.[21]

As if the fates were plotting against San Francisco, Dennis Sullivan, the city's chief fire engineer, was killed before the ill-fated decision was made to use combustible powder to snuff out the blaze. Sullivan died when a chimney attached to a firehouse collapsed shortly after the quake, falling atop the chief's house that sat adjacent to it. For three years before the earthquake, Sullivan had warned San Francisco's board of supervisors that the water system in place to fight fires was dated and in dire need of repair. He was repeatedly rebuffed. When the earth moved, the water mains burst.[22] Between General Frederick Funston's misuse of black powder to prevent the fires from advancing and the penny-pinching responses to Sullivan's demands to plumb the water supply, San Francisco was allowed to burn. "Only after the earthquake," Andrea Rees Davies observes, dryly, "did the city engineer admit that city water pipes were not suited for extensive fire-fighting."[23]

Like San Francisco's earthquake, the Category 3 hurricane that brushed the east side of New Orleans a century later caused comparatively little damage to the city. In an ironic twist, Brian Handwerk reports, "Until the day before Katrina's arrival, New Orleans' 350 miles (560 kilometers) of levees were undergoing a feasibility study to examine the possibility of upgrading them to withstand a Category Four or Five storm." The engineers conducting the study apparently did not know that this expansive levee network could not withstand a Category 3 hurricane, much less a Category 4's or 5's winds. By early morning on August 30, in Douglas Brinkley's colorful words, "The city's flood walls were exposed as ugly monuments to shoddy engineering. Once they cracked open, a monstrous spell engulfed New Orleans." In *Catastrophe in the Making: The Engineering of Katrina and the Disasters of Tomorrow*, William Freudenburg and colleagues document a history of efforts to expand New Orleans with little regard for the quality of the complex levee system necessary to protect a city that, by and large, sits at or below sea level. Urban development was of more immediate concern than urban safety.[24]

In short, the two most devastating urban catastrophes in US history could—with foresight—have been prevented. The technological know-how was available, the risks, in both cases, knowable. But the political and market urge to grow, the allure of investing in capital enterprises at the expense of infrastructure, was—at both moments in time—greater than the will to reduce the hazards that beset these two signature cities.

The totality of loss experienced by San Francisco and New Orleans and the human-caused origins of both catastrophes might be reason enough to launch a comparative inquiry into these calamities. But I want to shift our attention from the amount and kind of destruction that overwhelmed both cities to yet another juncture where these two moments in time come together. If we take a close look at the work to return to those urban arrangements that existed prior to impact, both cases challenge the normal social science approach to disaster recovery. It is this challenge that will mark my path down Tilly's "narrow road."

Of the seemingly countless places where a comparison might be drawn, I have chosen those points of contrast and similarity that light up the idea that, like Nietzsche's "eternal recurrence," recovering from catastrophe in a market society is always, in part, reanimating those market-friendly arrangements temporarily suspended in the mayhem of the moment when things could well be otherwise.[25] In the massive destruction of two American cities separated by a century, we can begin to discern the ways recovery eschews the otherwise, the fleeting grasp of something new, and becomes all too predictably the recovery of inequality. If some of the many ways inequality can be recovered are found in these two calamities separated by an expansive stretch of time, we have reason to have some faith in this counterintuitive turn of phrase.[26]

A simple, graceful allegory of this tie between an abstraction and the all too real events that beset 1906 San Francisco and New Orleans in 2005 is found in a short fictional story. The unreal, after all, can often teach us something about the real. Imagine for a moment you are standing on a rise in rural Mississippi in the waning years of the 1920s.

### "OVER ALL HUNG A FIRST-DAY STRANGENESS"

In his short story "Down by the Riverside," Richard Wright—a native of Natchez—describes a black family's return to their water-ravaged home during what came, with time, to be called the "Great Mississippi Flood" of 1927. In his gift for social portraiture, Wright summons to life two critical moments in the aftermath of disaster:

At last the flood waters had receded. A black father, a black mother, and a black child tramped through muddy fields, leading a tired cow by a thin bit of rope. They stopped on a hilltop. . . . As far as they could see the ground was covered with flood silt. The little girl lifted a skinny finger and pointed to a mudcaked cabin. "Look, Pa! Ain tha our home?" Without moving a muscle, scarcely moving his lips, he said: "Yeah."

The flood waters had been more than eight feet high here. Every tree, blade of grass, and stray stick had its flood mark; cakey, yellow mud. It clung to the ground, cracking thinly here and there in spider web fashion. Over the stark fields came a gusty spring wind. . . . Over all hung a first-day strangeness.[27]

The idea of a "first-day strangeness" gestures to the transformation in landscape and the human connection to it. With strangeness comes the possibility of starting anew, perhaps in another place. In the late 1920s, this idea could not have been far from the minds of many black tenant farmers in the Deep South. This epic flood created the opportunity to imagine life elsewhere. Perhaps now was the moment to pack up family and possessions and head north to Chicago or Detroit, to get out from under what W. E. B. DuBois called the "second slavery."[28]

As the family considered the misery that lay about them, they noticed someone approaching in a buggy:

"Look! Here comes somebody!" "Thas Mistah Burgess now!" A mud-caked buggy rolled up. The shaggy horse was splattered all over. Burgess leaned his white face out of the buggy and spat. "Well, I see you're back." "Yessuh." "How things look?" "They don look so good, Mistah." "What seems to be the trouble?" "Waal. Ah ain got no hoss, no grub, nothing. The only thing Ah got is tha ol cow there . . ."

"You owe eight hundred dollahs down at the store, Tom." "Yessuh, Ah know. But, Mistah Burgess, can't yuh knock something off tha, seein as how Ahm down n out now?" "You ate that grub, and I got to pay for it, Tom." "Yessuh, ah know." "It's going to be a little tough, Tom. But you got to go through with it. Two of the boys tried to run away this morning and dodge their debts, and I had to have the sheriff pick em up. I wasn't looking for no trouble out of you, Tom . . . The rest of the families are going back."[29]

Captured in Wright's prose are the disordering and reordering moments of disaster. A family returns after a massive flood to ponder their fate. Witnessing all that is laid to waste, they might well begin to think that the old way is no more. Now, they might ask, could life be different, perhaps a bit more just and equitable? This massive flood begged the question, might a tenant farmer escape his fate? Perhaps this disaster is an opportunity to start anew some other place where a poor black family might find life a little more evenhanded and just. This imaginative moment is quickly replaced, however, by the arrival of a white man who speaks about debt, responsibility, and dire consequences if Tom and his family do anything other than rebuild and continue life as it was before the flood.

It is a solitary encounter, though we can imagine similar encounters occurring up and down the Mississippi's riverine corridor. This exchange between a well-off plantation owner and a poor black family underlines a certain truism about humans and the worlds we create: call it a penchant for categorical order. To borrow from Clifford Geertz, who wrote tellingly of such matters, humans demonstrate an inclination to arrange themselves into "categories, some hierarchic, some coordinate, but all clear-cut, in which matters out-of-category disturb the entire structure and must be either corrected or effaced."[30]

It is not hard to picture Tom and his family gazing at all they have lost and pondering a new future in a northern state free of the shackles of tenant farming. Should they make that decision, the family would in effect efface the categorical distinction between them and the southern tenant-farming culture. DuBois was among the first to note that the exodus to the cities occurring since 1880 in the Deep South was the effort to escape a life of "forced labor practically without wages."[31]

Mistah Burgess, however, has other plans. While the flood might well threaten to disturb the categorical inequality of the white southerner and the black tenant farmer, Burgess takes this opportunity to make a small correction in that disturbance by reminding Tom that he is obliged to recommit himself to tenancy and all that accompanies it. In this short vignette, Wright captures disorder and a few moments of hope quickly eclipsed by reorder and a return to customary inequality. As a literary caricature of durable human inequality, Tom and his family would go back to tenant farming and life in the second slavery.

In Wright's story, a brief encounter between two quite different categories of people reminds us that more than lives and property are damaged and destroyed by catastrophic floods, hurricanes, earthquakes, and similar agents of destruction; damaged also are the geographic, social, and racial partitions that work in concert to create and sustain a stable, enduring inequality. In the immediate wake of the Great Mississippi Flood, the old order of tenant farming was disordered as people were uprooted and set adrift. The economic and territorial arrangement of the Deep South—rooted in racism and the exploitation of black labor—was endangered.

Imagine this sudden disordering as a wilderness, a wild, uncultivated space. Here the relational patterns of inequality are suspended, and the idea of something new, something different, seems more than a remote possibility. Like madness, Ken Hewitt points out, disaster "challenges our notions of order" and does so, he might have added, in the very derivation of the words *disorder* and *disaster*.[32]

The Latin root of *disaster* is *astrum*, or "star."[33] The Latin prefix *dis* means "apart," "separate," or "take-apart." Today the prefix *dis* is applied to the word *order* when we want to signal a breakdown or collapse of organization and regulation. Adding the star, or *astrum*, *disaster* is literally "a disordered star," a kind of celestial mayhem—as in "The stars are against us"—that wreaks havoc on human communities. The idea of disaster is appropriate to those sudden moments when order—at least the conventional order—is radically disordered.

Samuel Henry Prince, a minister turned sociologist, describes life in Halifax shortly after the 1917 explosion that almost leveled the city: "Life becomes like molten metal. Old customs crumble, and instability rules." Philip Fradkin is less lyrical but more to the point in his conclusion that disaster exposes "an underlying fear that the dominant class will be overthrown during a period of chaos." The stark visibility of the now mobile *vulgus* begs many questions, among them the following: Where will we go? What will we do? Who will ensure our safety and property? "In the moment of disaster," Rebecca Solnit writes, with a hint of hyperbole, "the old order no longer exists."[34]

Disasters do indeed create dramatic moments of openness and indeterminacy. The old order suddenly appears vulnerable. Hierarchies are deranged; social categories lose their customary power to organize day-to-day life. The boundary between public and private is blurred, if not effaced. And perhaps most jarring, the last shall finally, if not become the first, at least escape the authority of the first. But Richard Wright's story chides those who worry that a post-disaster world will be unrecognizable. Tom and his family return to their pre-flood way of life. By returning, they teach us—in at least one fundamental way—that for all the mayhem they create, disasters are not transformative.

If we peer with a critical eye through Wright's rich description, we might see a door into disaster and the momentary unmaking followed quickly by the remaking of social inequality. Our story takes us through this door to the remarkable events that unfolded in San Francisco in 1906 and New Orleans a century later. In compelling and complex ways, each catastrophe dramatizes in its own way a simple truth revealed in the brief encounter between Tom and Mistah Burgess on the flooded lowlands of rural Mississippi—to wit, disaster recovery and the rebounding of a resilient inequality are inseparable. In Wright's story, the economics of sharecropping fashioned recovery; market forces of a different kind, as we will see, were more or less in control of the recovery of both San Francisco and New Orleans. Like the illusion of the faces hidden in the goblet, the recovery of inequality is not hard to see once it is pointed out. Richard Wright situates his story in the rural South. Our story takes us to the city.

### THE CITY AS MIRROR

In his epigraph at the head of this chapter, Ira Katznelson notes, incisively, that the thickness and mass of the modern city might well distort but may also disclose. David Harvey identifies the city as the optimal location for examining key dynamics "operating in society as a whole—it becomes, as it were, a mirror in which other aspects of society can be reflected."[35] The social and market forces set in motion in the recovery from urban catastrophes become, for those who care to look, windows into the deeper ruling abstractions that organize city life. Richard Wright sets his story in the rural South in the 1920s, directing our attention to the one-off encounter between a black sharecropper and a white plantation owner. Catastrophes that leave our great cities in ruins are occasions to observe a broader and more complex materialist stage upon which the making of social inequality is plainly visible.

Charles Dickens anticipates Harvey, seeing in the city a reflection of the complexity of human arrangements. Our inquiry into 1906 San Francisco and New Orleans in 2005 echoes a few of the central motifs in Dickens's fabled *A Tale of Two Cities*.[36] In his story, London and Paris are juxtaposed as two iconic urban centers. In this tale, two iconic American cities are placed side by side. In telling his story, Dickens employs a doubling motif to carry the narrative forward. I too make use of doubling, dividing our discussions and analyses to reveal parallels and continuities but also to draw opposition and difference.

But where Dickens sets his novel in the years immediately before and after the French Revolution, my story spans a century. The century interval between the San Francisco earthquake and fires in 1906 and the 2005 flooding of New Orleans ensures that this telling will need to make some sense of the significant alterations in the social, political, and economic landscapes between the beginning of one century and the start of another.

The strong undercurrent that carries Dickens's tale is the staggering inequities between peasants and aristocracy. That undercurrent, now in its modern guise of capital, class, and race, also carries this story. If we are "goaded by the spirit of hierarchy," as Kenneth Burke thinks we are, it is arguably in cities like London, Paris, San Francisco, and New Orleans where our penchant for human inequality is most vividly evident.[37] And, we might add, when "challenged by crisis," this embrace of disparity is likely to be on dramatic display.[38]

This book is intended as an irreverent critique of what happens to people after the shock of disaster, during that protracted period we optimistically call "recovery." We will move back and forth in time to put critical social, economic, and political forces in historical perspective. Taking these occasional brief detours will reveal the ways that the twists and turns of the past are always shaping the present. Our journey will take us from order to disorder to reorder as we move through the continuum of calamity. Each chapter in its own fashion will toggle between two unparalleled American catastrophes, highlighting the conjunctures, contingencies, and variations between them, as each city reclaims its version of social and economic disparity.

## A PREVIEW

Drawing on histories of early-twentieth- and early-twenty-first-century America, combined with insights from the early Chicago school of urban sociology, we begin with a thick account of the social, cultural, and political life of early-nineteenth-century San Francisco, on the one hand, and early-twenty-first-century New Orleans, on the other. Chapter 2, "Geographies of Inequality: A Sketch of Two Cities Spanning a Century," elaborates several ideas introduced in chapter 1 in an ambitious effort to describe the unique configuration of geography, race, and class in these two urban milieus. Chapters 1 and 2 set the stage for the four chapters to follow.

In part 2, "Deranging and Rekindling," chapters 3 and 4 explore in some detail two contiguous moments in each calamity. Chapter 3 is organized around the classic narrative of the therapeutic community, the comparatively brief moment of shared compassion that emerges in the immediate wake of catastrophe. A monstrous earthquake and ensuing fire in 1906 and a devastating flood in 2005 muddled the more or less tidy market orders of these two unforgettable cities. Amid this disorder, a dramatic, short-lived new order, one based on a leveling of hierarchies and stressing an ethic of mutual aid, emerges. "The Great Derangements" portrays this fragile configuration, one that could not survive the militarization of both disasters.

Chapter 4 picks up the narrative of chaos and crime that quickly eclipses the story of communal kindness. "Fashioning 'the Looter': Rekindling Racial and Class Kinds" is an account of the emergence of the fictive "looter" in both cities. Examined as a social kind, making up "the looter" sets in motion the recovery of categorical distinctions. These distinctions, as we will see, begin the recovery of inequality in both disasters.

Part 3, "Rebooting Inequality, The Road to Recovery," is a close-up look at the administration of disaster relief, the mixed efforts of city elites to accumulate valuable urban real estate following each calamity, and the historical forces in play that shaped the uneven recoveries of the two cities themselves. Chapter 5, "Disaster Relief: Parsing the Vernaculars of Worthiness," examines in considerable detail the administration of disaster aid following the earthquake and fire in 1906 San Francisco and the flooding of New Orleans in 2005. While each relief effort was administered in quite different ways, both efforts relied on what we might call an algorithm of market worthiness to determine who received what and why. The tortured social logic deployed to allocate disaster relief in both cities ensured the restoration of that categorical inequality necessary to a market-organized society.

Chapter 6, "Spatial Accumulation by Dispossession: Two Attempts to Rob the Marginal," narrates the dramatic story of the struggles of Chinese immigrants to maintain residency in their famed Chinatown, all but destroyed by the earthquake and fire. Likewise, though with quite different results, this chapter examines the clash between residents of public housing in New Orleans and the concerted efforts of powerful stakeholders to demolish these historic urban residential complexes.

The final chapter, "One City Necessary, One City Expendable," tracks the quite different destinies of San Francisco and New Orleans following their catastrophic destructions. The impressive efforts at the local, state, and federal levels to rebuild San Francisco phoenixlike from its literal ashes stand in stark contrast to the fortunes of New Orleans after the waters retreated. The remarkable differences in the trajectories of these two urban recoveries illuminate both the significance of the historical moment when disaster strikes and the always peripatetic path of capital as it retreats here and moves there.

## A NOTE ON THE DATA

Data for this study come from many different sources, as is clearly seen in the many and varied references found in the endnotes. Among the primary data on the San Francisco disaster are letters, newspapers, diaries, and novels from the early decades of the twentieth century. A substantial amount of primary material on the San Francisco earthquake and fire is found in a remarkably informative virtual library available to anyone with access to the Internet. Secondary data originate with dissertations, theses, and academic papers, accompanied by journalistic and historical analyses of the catastrophe.

Primary data on the twenty-first-century flooding of New Orleans are found in the University of New Orleans Oral History Project, local newspapers, and interviews collected while I was working with Vern Baxter and Pam Jenkins on *Left to Chance: A Story of Two New Orleans Neighborhoods*.[39] Please note, the names provided in the personal interview descriptions drawn from *Left to Chance* are pseudonyms. I also draw on city, state, and federal agency reports as well as personal accounts of the flooding posted on the Internet. Among the secondary data used in this project are the Brookings Institution's periodic reports on the city, government documents, magazine and academic journal publications, and various histories of the city.

# GEOGRAPHIES OF INEQUALITY
## A SKETCH OF TWO CITIES
## SPANNING A CENTURY

*In every city the people are divided into three sorts:*
*the very rich, the very poor, and those who are between them.*

ARISTOTLE, BOOK 4 OF *A TREATISE ON GOVERNMENT*

At the beginning of the twentieth century and then again at the dawn of the twenty-first century, two of America's most prominent cities are virtually destroyed by the capricious forces of nature in collaboration with a parade of human foibles. We may be tempted to search for a cosmic meaning in these striking coincidences. What should we make of the fact that each city is often called the "Paris" of its region? By what cosmic design are the "Paris of the Pacific" and the "Paris of the South" visited by totalizing calamities occurring a century apart?

But it is less that the two events were somewhere "in the stars," a kind of celestial certainty, and more the fact that both cities are located on high-risk landscapes that just happen to provide immeasurable value to enterprising people who developed the market potential of both geographies. In his early-nineteenth-century *Notes on a Journey in America*, Morris Birkbeck fairly cries out, "Gain! Gain! Gain! is the beginning, the middle and the end, the *alpha* and *omega* of the founders of American Towns."[1]

Birkbeck was witness to a dynamic set in motion in the first decade of the seventeenth century. In April 1606, James I charted the Virginia Company, a joint-stock venture to acquire gold and precious metals. Nine months later, Christopher Newport set sail with orders to establish a commercial enterprise in what would become Jamestown, Virginia, the first permanent English colony in America. The joint-stock company was the prototype of today's modern corporation. Moneyed investors bankrolled the expedition. They risked their capital with an eye to reaping high rates of return once ships sailed back loaded with the hidden wealth of the new continent.[2]

Venture capital, in short, was the prime mover in creating America's first human settlement. By the beginning of the nineteenth century, the American city was becoming a simile for the market society. By century's end, for good or for ill, in DuBois's memorable words, "the habit [was] formed of interpreting the world in dollars."[3]

## "GOOD SITUATIONS BOTH, BUT DREADFUL SITES"

San Francisco sits on a volatile hotbed of seismic energy. The city is sandwiched between two "fault zones," the famed San Andreas that sits just to its west, running north and south, and the lesser-known, but perhaps the more potentially destructive, Hayward Fault, whose north-to-south boundary slices through the East San Francisco Bay.[4] Sitting between the Pacific on one side and a bay fifty miles long and thirteen miles wide on the other, San Francisco is also subject to capricious winds and damp, miasmic fog.[5] One geographer found this Far West city "an eccentric location and a rough site."[6] But if it was nature that fashioned this coarse site, the humans who inhabited it also roughed it up a bit.

It was but a year after San Francisco was officially founded in 1847 that gold was discovered in the Sierra Madre, east of the city. Ships carrying men filled with hope that a fortune was near were abandoned in the bay as crews and passengers alike made their way to the Sierra foothills. The population of San Francisco grew exponentially in response to the gold rush. To make room for the thousands of newcomers and the waste a burgeoning city produces, dozens of these ships were sunk, tons of human detritus piled on them, and all of it topped off with a bit of soil. A semblance of land, subject to flooding and liquefaction, expanded the city several blocks into what was the San Francisco Bay.[7]

Adding to this assemblage of risks, nineteenth- and early-twentieth-century San Francisco, like all cities of this era, was prone to fire. From its incorporation as a city on June 11, 1856, to a half century later in 1906, San Francisco had burned to the ground on six separate occasions.[8] City officials sitting on an urban tinderbox ready with little provocation to burst into flames would, reason suggests, marshal the latest and best firefighting equipment and construct adequate mains to distribute water in the event of fire; in this case, however, reason would be mistaken. Writing in 1905, the National Board of Fire Underwriters appears to have forgotten the past six conflagrations, noting that "San Francisco has violated all underwriting traditions . . . by not burning up."[9]

The almost complete breakdown of the main water piping system following the earthquake was particularly evident "where streets crossed filled ground and particularly, where such filled ground covered former deep swamps."[10] In the intersection of artificial land, earthquakes, water mains, and fires, we begin to see how vulnerability is fashioned by both imperfect human creations and the quirky temperament of nature.

New Orleans too is tethered to water. In 1718 the colorful Jean-Baptiste Le Moyne de Bienville founded what would become New Orleans not far from what is now known as the Vieux Carré, or French Quarter. Standing on this patch of "high" ground with the Mississippi River on one side and swamp draining into a massive lake on the other, Bienville presciently called this dry land surrounded by water "L'isle de La Nouvelle Orléans."[11] Roughly one half of present-day New Orleans sits above sea level and one half below. Approximately 10 square miles of the city rest level with the sea.[12]

During the eighteenth and most of the nineteenth centuries, what was then New Orleans sat atop its natural levee along the Mississippi River. But like its sister city to the west, as New Orleans's population expanded, more land was needed. As people began to move into the wetlands that lay between the settlement and Lake Pontchartrain, the surface water sitting atop this sagging soil was drained, creating a damp sediment, optimistically called "land." By the mid-twentieth century, New Orleans had expanded from the Vieux Carré to Lake Pontchartrain, becoming, in Lawrence Powell's colorful words, an "accidental city."[13]

Sandwiched between the Mississippi River and Lake Pontchartrain, much of it sitting at or below sea level, and hemmed in by 350 miles of levees, New Orleans looks, topographically, like a bowl. Add to this mix an annual rainfall that often exceeds sixty-two inches, and we might say New Orleans is, in a fundamental way, synonymous with water.[14] By the year 2000, the city could boast of 148 drainage pumps. Rainfall above one half inch per hour, however, often exceeded the pumps' collective capacity, resulting in periodic flooding, particularly in low-lying areas.[15] Once water gets into the bowl, getting it out can be a long and tedious process.

Geographers draw a useful distinction when writing about cities. The "site" of a city is the actual geographic niche it occupies. A city's "situation," on the other hand, is the practical or, more to the point, the market value of that site.[16] Considering the cities together, a geographer might reasonably say of San Francisco and New Orleans: "good situations both, but dreadful sites." It is not too much of a stretch to claim that no two urban settlements in the United States are as vulnerable to cataclysmic destruction as these two iconic cities.[17] Each, in its own way, affirms Ken Hewitt's discerning observation: "Most . . . disasters are characteristic rather than accidental features of places and societies where they occur."[18]

In spite, or perhaps, in part, because, of their fragile settings, both cities, over the course of their respective histories, have played outsize roles in connecting North America with world trade. San Francisco Bay provides a natural harbor for shipping to and from Asia, a key resource in North America's ambitious trade-based commerce. New Orleans sits aside a vast, navigable inland waterway, the great Mississippi River, that transverses the central region of the United States from what is now Minnesota to Louisiana and from the Pelican State to the Gulf Coast. With both cities integral to trade and markets, their fortunes are linked to the fortunes of the nation-state and global economic trends. The close tie between these two cities and historical shifts in both the relative place of America in world affairs and the morphing modes of capital accumulation help to account for some of the variations in their post-disaster histories, as we will see.

If the needs of the market are paramount, each city is well situated. But if the principal concern is locating a human settlement on a reasonably sound piece of real estate, both San Francisco and New Orleans are high-risk places. From 1836 to 1898, the Bay Area was struck by six earthquakes, ranging in magnitude from 6.5 to 7, roughly one every decade. Prior to 2005, New Orleans had weathered thirty-six hurricanes in 136 years. This old French city is "brushed" or "hit" by a hurricane every 3.78 years.[19]

To paraphrase Peirce Lewis, who was writing specifically about New Orleans but might well have had San Francisco in mind: What other cities have such illogical and dangerous sites but insouciantly go about their mixed business of commerce and fun in defiance of the threats? Above all, what other cities are so extravagantly charming?[20] Each is amiable and appealing in its own fashion, but each in its own way is also an ordered configuration of class and race inequality.

### THE PARIS OF THE PACIFIC AT THE DAWN OF THE TWENTIETH CENTURY

In the first sentence of his "The Gospel of Wealth," published in 1900, Andrew Carnegie acknowledged the dilemma created by the absence of parity in a market society founded on the Enlightenment ideas of universal human worth: "The problem of our age is the proper administration of wealth, that the ties of brotherhood may still bind together the rich and poor in harmonious relationship."[21] In Gilded Age America, inequality was inescapable. Carnegie's dilemma, and the dilemma of the moneyed-propertied class writ large, was how to manage wealth in such a way as to keep the poor relatively contented with this arrangement.

For Carnegie, the answer, in part, was philanthropy, a political economic strategy informed by a belief in the power of paternalism toward those deemed worthy. The fashioning of consent among commoners, however, also relied heavily on the splayed fingers of social reform, actively promoted by an emerging middle class, reaching into and molding a moral temper of hard work and individual responsibility consistent with the goal of capital accumulation.

At the turn of the twentieth century, San Francisco's population was just under 343,000, making it America's eighth-largest city.[22] Whites made up slightly more than 325,000 residents. The second-largest group was the Chinese, totaling just fewer than 14,000. Approximately 1,800 Japanese and somewhere between 1,600 and 1,700 blacks, or "Negroes," lived in the municipality. San Francisco's black population was not segregated from whites and lived in various places throughout the city. By 1900 a virulent racism supported by city, state, and federal legislation had pushed the Chinese and most Japanese into six square blocks, creating a dense and vibrant Asian quarter.[23] "San Franciscans," Issel and Cherny write, "sorted themselves into class, ethnic, and regional groupings [that] contributed to the creation of a complex social mosaic."[24]

By 1906 San Francisco was the leading West Coast city for US banking, manufacturing, and shipping interests.[25] The city's most arresting physical feature, its famed bay, was host to a "great multitude of boats and ships crowded along its waterfront and extending far out into" its waters.[26] Arguably, its most striking social and political feature was the visible role of labor and labor unions in the day-to-day life of the city.[27]

San Francisco in 1900 was a union town. In *Barons of Labor*, Michael Kazin quotes muckraker Ray Stannard Baker, who wrote, "In San Francisco we have a new kind of industrial peace, a condition, perhaps, without precedent, in which the ancient master, the employer, has been hopelessly defeated and unionism reigns supreme."[28] In seeming endorsement of Baker's legislative tone, in July 1906, just two months after the disaster, unionized plumbers struck for higher wages.[29] (This noted muckraker would draw on a markedly different vocabulary—as we will see—to describe the aftermath of the San Francisco earthquake and firestorms.)

Slightly more than four thousand manufacturing businesses employed more than forty-two thousand workers,[30] and this number does not represent the large number of seasonal workers who flocked to the city to labor in the many fish-processing plants that dotted the wharves. In addition, thousands of people drifted in and out of town, working in the booming construction businesses that offered temporary employment. While the economy of San Francisco was based in part on finance, city revenue and taxes were based primarily on manual jobs, including skilled building trades and unskilled trades such as cannery workers and transit operators.[31]

At the turn of the twentieth century, an emerging middle class was finding its collective voice.[32] Though a diverse lot, members of this nascent demographic were aware of themselves as somewhere betwixt and between the gilded affluent and what were tellingly called "the deserving" and "the undeserving poor," a parsing of people that would surface with a vengeance in San Francisco in the spring and summer of 1906.[33] Many among the middle class acted as if their destinies were tied to moderating the radical and volatile tendencies of labor, on the one hand, and persuading the industrial elite, the "upper ten" or the "Leisure Class," to act in a manner that would benefit all of society and not just the privileged few, on the other.[34] Like most cities in the early 1900s, the "City by the Bay" was in the grip of progressive social reform.

In his essay "What Makes a Life Significant?" William James pokes a little fun at progressivism while noting the middle-class concern with parity and fairness: "You have culture, you have kindness, you have cheapness, you have equality. . . . You have, in short, a . . . middle-class paradise."[35] The progressivism of this betwixt-and-between class, however, was not fueled solely by a spirit of justice and fellow feeling. By the beginning of the twentieth century, the middle class feared "an unprecedented crisis of alienation amid the extremes of wealth and poverty."[36] While it worried about the "upper ten," actually about 1 or 2 percent of the US population of seventy-six million, the middle class was far more anxious about the working class and the poor. The fear of working-class violence was the primary motive behind progressive activism.[37]

Behind the lively presence of unions and the reformist politics of the middle class was a growing and robust class of prosperous business owners, manufacturers, stockbrokers, bankers, importers, and similarly situated men.[38] By the middle of the nineteenth century, less than 5 percent of the city's "male labor force . . . owned between 75 and 80 percent of personal and real property."[39] As tectonic plates deep within the earth chafed one against the other, generating unimaginable physical force, market forces in tandem with categorical distinctions were organizing San Francisco by geography, race, and class.

While labor could not keep up with the increasing market power of a rising middle class in early-twentieth-century America, it still had some agency and the workingman and -woman had some reason to be hopeful about the future. By the beginning of the twenty-first century, however, that agency and hope were all but gone, seemingly for good. In David Harvey's memorable description, "The figure of the 'disposable worker' emerges prototypical upon the world stage."[40]

Between the turn of the twentieth century and a hundred years later at the dawn of the twenty-first century, capital had found a way to reproduce without manufacturing; money was now making money. Labor is economically redundant—beside the point—in a post-industrial, finance-driven Western market. Adopting a strident tone, Britain's prime minister Margaret Thatcher alerted the British public to an internal foe. "We had to fight the enemy without in the Falklands. We always have to be aware of the enemy within, which is much more difficult to fight and more dangerous to liberty." She was referring, of course, to labor unions.[41]

Her counterpart in the United States, Ronald Reagan, a former president of the Screen Actors Guild, was less conspiratorial in his public comments on unions but no less committed to weakening the role of organized labor. A year after he took office, he used provisions in the Taft-Hartley Act to fire more than 11,000 striking air-traffic controllers. "They are in violation of the law," he intoned, "and if they do not report for work within 48 hours they have forfeited their jobs and will be terminated."[42] The air-traffic controllers were striking for better working conditions and a pay raise. The fortunes of New Orleans were tied, of course, to these historic market changes.

In 1840 New Orleans was the third-largest city in the United States, behind New York and Baltimore. By 1880 New Orleans was America's tenth-largest city, with a population of just over 216,000. With just under 234,000, San Francisco was ranked ninth in the country.[43] By the turn of the twenty-first century, however, New Orleans was America's fiftieth-largest city, with a population of a little more than 484,000.[44]

The 2000 Census counted roughly 70 percent of the city's residents as "Black or African American."[45] Roughly 30 percent were listed as "White." For years before the turn of the century, middle- and working-class whites were abandoning the city for nearby suburbs, leaving New Orleans to those comparatively few who preferred the rich cultural life of the city to the generic tidiness of brick-on-slab neighborhoods.

At the turn of the twenty-first century, forty-seven New Orleans neighborhoods were identified as geographies of "extreme poverty." More than 40 percent of the residents of these neighborhoods lived below the official poverty line. By 2000 New Orleans ranked second only to West Fresno, California, in the rate of concentrated poverty.[46] While cities have always separated the poor from the more affluent, in the early years of the twenty-first century territorial isolation of the poor had become the modus operandi of urban planning in New Orleans.

Irony is most poignant when unintended. On the day the levees failed and the city flooded, the US Census Bureau released a devastating report on poverty in the Crescent City. By August 2005, the report concludes, close to one in four residents of New Orleans lived in poverty. Orleans Parish ranked seventh among 290 US counties in the number of people living without an adequate income. Eighty-four percent of those impoverished New Orleanians were African American.[47]

Amid the contiguous public housing and neighborhoods of poverty that shaped the non-tourist landscape of New Orleans at the turn of the twenty-first century sat what one geographer dubbed the "golden ghettos."[48] From the older "sugar money" mansions of the Garden District to the modern upscale subdivisions along Lake Pontchartrain and some places in between, whites and Creoles, some affluent and some upper and upper middle class, fashioned their enclaves of privilege or, more colorfully, "magnolia curtains."[49] By 2000, Peirce Lewis writes, "New Orleans was more segregated than it had ever been, and the inequities between rich and poor were as extreme as at any time since the legal end of slavery."[50]

Like most cities at the turn of the twenty-first century, New Orleans's economy did not depend on skilled and unskilled labor. If the progressive middle class at the turn of the twentieth century fretted about both the wealthy and the poor, by the beginning of the twenty-first century this class had joined with the more affluent, and both worked in tandem to fend off the threats from below. A city built below sea level whose semblance of order rested on a geography of class and race inequality was always a precarious place. On a late summer day in the first years of a new century, this wobbly arrangement would give way to a historic deluge.

So, here are two port cities, each situated to exploit the market opportunities of their respective waterways, each built on faulty geographies, as if taunting nature to knock down or drown what excessive conceit had constructed. And while it is true that history records the steep price humans pay for messing with Mother Nature, cities, as spaces of capital, are likely to survive disaster.[51] Perhaps this is because market-oriented cities are, historically, sites of capital's first intensity, refracting its power to fashion the mosaic of urban life. Although this may change as capital evolves, since its inception a market economy needs an urban-based market society.

For Karl Polanyi, this "means no less than the running of society as an adjunct to the market. Instead of the economy being embedded in social relations, social relations are embedded in the economy."[52] The power of the market to author society is visually apparent in the many ways capital creates and sustains a mélange of kinds and categories of people, each tied in some fashion to market forces and each distributed spatially about the city.

## "THE EYES OF THE POOR": THE CITY AND THE SOCIAL KIND

In 350 BCE, practicing what is likely the first urban sociology, Aristotle described the city as a predictable location for the display of material distinction. To revisit the epigraph introducing this chapter: "In every city," Aristotle notes, "the people are divided into three sorts: the very rich, the very poor, and those who are between them."[53] Anticipating by millennia the insights of Henri Lefebvre, Walter Benjamin, Robert Park, Ira Katznelson, David Harvey, and others, Aristotle observed how the machinations of relative wealth organized the geographies of everyday urban life. Evoking the transformation of Paris in the middle of the nineteenth century, Charles Baudelaire creates a fleeting moment to remind us that this order is vulnerable, jeopardized by the most innocent of acts, a glance, a look, or an exchange of eyes, for example.

In his poem "The Eyes of the Poor," Baudelaire places a middle-class Parisian couple "in front of a new café that formed the corner of a new boulevard." The street was "littered with rubble," but "the café was dazzling." Smitten with love, the pair stares into each other's eyes; they soon see other eyes staring at them. Looking from the debris-filled street to their cozy table just outside the door of the café are six eyes fixed intently on the couple. An old man, a young son, and a baby dressed in rags gaze transfixed, mouths agape. In this awkward meeting of eyes, Baudelaire captures a primal scene: the fleeting encounter of two quite different urban worlds and the types of people who inhabit them. Aware that he has become self-conscious in this exchange of eyes, the young man turns to his lover: "I turned my eyes to look into yours, dear love, to read my thoughts there." As the couple places the impoverished family outside their field of vision, no longer seeing them, the young woman cannot refrain from complaining, "Those people with their great saucer eyes are unbearable! Can't you go tell the manager to get them away from here?"[54]

In her self-conscious moment, she utters the phrase "Those people," two words freighted with deep meaning. "Those people" don't belong on this newly constructed Parisian boulevard, staring at a proper couple enjoying one another and this "dazzling" café. They are, to paraphrase Mary Douglas, a category out of place.[55] In "The Eyes of the Poor," Baudelaire exposes a momentary breach in the subtle ways social categories work in tandem with spatial segregation to sustain a durable urban order around markedly unequal life chances.

Charles Baudelaire published "Les yeux des pauvres" in 1857. Greater Paris in the 1850s boasted a population of well over a million. It was a city stretching toward modernity. The idea of economic classes and class struggle was very much on the minds of Parisians. From January through October 1850, Karl Marx would publish a series of essays on class conflict in France. This work, Friedrich Engels writes, was Marx's "first attempt to explain a piece of contemporary history by means of his materialist conception." By 1850 Paris was a capitalist city, indistinguishable in many ways from its economy. Paris, as Baudelaire sensed, had become a market society organized around the "allure of gain."[56]

Max and Marianne Weber journeyed to America in 1904. In his journal, Max Weber described what he saw in Chicago:

> By the lake there are a few . . . beautiful residential districts. . . . [R]ight behind them there are little old wooden houses. . . . Then come the "tenements" of the workingmen and absurdly dirty streets. [The houses] are graded in cleanliness according to nationality. . . . There is a mad pell-mell of nationalities: Up and down the streets the Greeks shine the Yankees' shoes. . . . The Germans are their waiters, the Irish take care of their politics, and the Italians of their dirtiest, ditch digging. . . . [P]rostitutes are placed in a show window with electric light and the prices are displayed. . . . Look, this is what modern reality is like.[57]

Baudelaire's verse and Weber's prose evoke the image of a market city as akin to a dance, a gavotte between unequal social kinds distributed spatially within and across the urban landscape. While this dance is always precarious—a mere glance can disturb the choreography—its deep structure is regulated by police, the rule of law, and the generally shared cultural sensibility that human society is an accessory of the market. In short, a city is literally and figuratively a place where socially fashioned kinds of people live aside, atop, and beneath one another in uneven and unequal circumstances.

The sheer numbers of diverse people inhabiting a city militate against developing close and personal ties with all but a few. The rest must be known by only their most elemental or categorical features: skin color, language or dialect, mode of dress, spatial location, and so on. If we are "cognitive misers," as some social psychologists suggest, prone to deploy mental shortcuts and simple rules of thumb to make everyday mundane judgments, surely the urban milieu is one place where we are likely to practice this economy of thought.[58] Here, in this space, we adapt by abstracting from the complexity of humanness. On city sidewalks and streets, stores, and buses, we are likely to "know" most people as social kinds—"those people," not flesh-and-blood persons.

A social kind for Canadian philosopher Ian Hacking—who borrows the idea of "kind making" from American philosopher Nelson Goodman—is *not* an embodied person. There is nothing material about a social kind; it is an idea, a cultural construct. But an idea, Hacking argues, can prove far more influential than a flesh-and-blood person.[59] Social kinds—as ideas about certain sorts of people—do serve a critical taxonomic purpose: they organize thinking about and acting within the always intricate web of urban market life. Public spaces, the macadam of social life, invite the unfamiliar person who, in turn, invites a nomenclature of placement, becoming a kind of person, one we can momentarily abide as we make our way.

At its simplest, if I am in a certain part of the city, I expect to meet a certain kind of person. I will know how to act and respond based on my knowledge and experience of this social kind. Social kinds vary by the geographic spaces of the city. Robert Park referred to this configuration between urban geographic space and social kind by deploying the seemingly ambiguous term *natural area*.[60] Effete, bluenosed people live in this space; working-class stiffs are found over there, tawdry, perhaps dangerous, people reside at that far edge, and so on through the rich and varied panoply of kinds that give urban life its peculiar dynamism and edginess. For the urban dweller, this order can seem—as Park knew—"natural."

Erving Goffman had the orderly city in mind when he wrote, "There are many social settings that persons of a certain status are forbidden to enter." Nineteenth-century London, for example, excluded "certain categories from some parks." The title of Harvey Zorbaugh's classic study of Chicago, *The Gold Coast and the Slum*, captures the intersection of kinds of people and geography in the making of urban order. Ferdinand Toennies anticipated Zorbaugh and Goffman, invoking a distinction between the village, wherein all "dwell together peacefully," and the market city, where all "are essentially separated," where "nobody . . . is inclined to give ungrudgingly to another."[61] Inequality does not breed neighborliness. A communitarian spirit would interfere with the machinations of the market.

In some ways, this modern urban order is a simpler social and spatial arrangement than the pastoral order Goffman found in his dissertation research on that now famed Welsh village. It is not the subtle signs of crofter identity management that organize urban life but something cruder—to wit, a spatially segregated and categorically unequal collage of social types or kinds of people. Cities, in contrast to rural enclaves, place a premium on difference, strangeness, and the real possibility of disorder if these differences are not synchronized in some fashion.

In "The White Space," Elijah Anderson makes a persuasive case for how white people move through the urban landscape with the freedom to avoid or visit black spaces, an advantage that black people do not enjoy. Most black people must traverse white spaces in order to meet basic life needs, including meaningful employment. It is in the city, Ira Katznelson writes, that "key elements of a sociology of differentiation in space are elaborated . . . impersonality, detachment, isolation, segmented friendships, commodification of relationships, and, above all, the significance of boundaries."[62]

But the sorting of urban social kinds does more than help us navigate the city. If cities are places where a variety of kinds of people live, it is, in part, because the uninterrupted pursuit of gain depends on the creation of difference, a difference "not just between capital and labour," writes Cindi Katz, "but within and across class formations. Capitalists and their various agents have been wily . . . in deploying and reinforcing various forms of difference, whether of race, or nation, region or gender, industry or age."[63] The topography of cities, the ways they are spatially arranged, their infrastructures, and their sizable and diverse populations are unique features of each cityscape, yet each city, in its own fashion, is a more or less organized geography of inequality. Local knowledge of the juncture of money, color, and physical location is shared among most inhabitants of any city.[64]

## WARRENS OF SOCIAL KINDS IN TWO AMERICAN CITIES: IMAGINE FOR A MOMENT

Imagine for a moment that you arrive in San Francisco on the Northern Pacific Railroad, a new visitor to this bustling Far West outpost of twentieth-century America. It is early April 1906, a couple of weeks before catastrophe would destroy the city. You find a suitable boardinghouse and make it known to the proprietor that you want to see the "real San Francisco." He sizes you up, determines you are an adventurous sort, and describes the city as it is generally known among locals:

Yes, sir, you are in the Queen City, the Bride of the Pacific, the Paris of the Pacific—we've been called all that and more. But once you get behind the tall talk, San Francisco is just a city of neighborhoods, a crazy quilt of different kinds of people—some good, some bad, some rich, some poor, some white, some yellow, and a few who are black. You're standing in what we call South of Market, a district of mostly boardinghouses. You got your room cheap because people around here don't have a lot of money; mostly unskilled workers live in these buildings, a mean sort, you know, but hardworking. Not that you're poor, lad; you're just on a budget.

South of Market wasn't always this way, though; just a couple of decades ago, this was where the rich lived. But things changed, and the wealthy moved to Nob Hill. "Nob," you know, is short for "nabob," what you might call a snob. So, it's really Snob Hill. There are handsome homes on Russian Hill, too. The wealthy like the hills. They got the money and the pretty views. If you want to see more people with money, walk north of California Street to Pacific Heights. If money could sing, you'd hear one loud choir over there.

Money, money, money—if this city ever caught fire, it would take years to burn through the greenbacks. You know that humorous fella Mark Twain? Well, he lived in this city a long time ago. Wrote a book called *The Gilded Age*. He called it "A Tale of Today" about a society with a few too many rich and far too many poor. My point, you ask? San Francisco is like that, my opinion . . . But I see what I see and know what I know. Money, money, money—listen to me go on. Let's stop talking money. You look like a young man with appetites.

It's with some reserve that I suggest, though I must suggest, you visit Chinatown. Here is our city within a city. Just walk down those moneyed hills and through North Beach, a neighborhood some call Little Italy, where most of our Italian immigrants live; most are working stiffs. Did you know that more than a third of our city people are immigrants? I'm from Ireland myself. Came over with Mum and Dad—bless 'um both. But you can tell from my brogue, hey? Yea, my parents settled in the Mission District, south of downtown. Lots of German and Irish immigrants live in these neighborhoods.

Chinatown begins just the other side of North Beach. It's about six square blocks of gambling, opium, and those women of the night—you know what I mean. Now that's what I hear. I'm a Catholic man with a family, so I don't dabble in vice—well, the occasional whiskey, but no vice, my word. I hear tell those yellow ones, they like their foul drugs and wicked ways. We like them herded up into one spot. Though I hear some businessmen got their eyes on that piece of fine real estate. Why should those slant eyes get to settle in what could be a fine white business area like the Financial District, just east of Chinatown? Some call these streets the "Financial Capital of the West." I don't go there much. The buildings are too tall, and those men in their suits and bowlers—Captains of Industry, they call themselves—look at me like I don't belong. I don't really; give me South of Market any day.

Ah, but laddie, I've saved the best for last. A strapping young man like you must get to the Barbary Coast, also called "Sailor Town." Make your way to the wharves where the ships come in. There you'll find all manner of good times, but it's always good to watch over your shoulder. Some people I know tried to start a hotel just a block from the water, called it Hotel Nymphomania. Whew! But the police said, "No. You can't name a place Hotel Nymphomania." So they called it the Nymphia. But everyone knew what was going on. It was shut down three years ago. A wild area of the city worth seeing, I'd say.

Well, I've kept you long enough. I can tell you're itching to explore. Go see what the city reveals and come back for a rye. I like a good story. Oh, and laddie, leave six bits for the room before you go.

Now, with this ground view of San Francisco in mind, picture yourself a time traveler and fast-forward a century. You find yourself in the Paris of the South. It is August 20, 2005, nine days before the flood walls collapse, the levees fail, and the city fills with water. You arrive at the Louis Armstrong Airport, some nineteen hundred miles southeast of San Francisco, in the deep delta region of the United States. On the taxi ride from the airport to your hotel, a rousing, if somewhat expensive, idea occurs to you. Getting the driver's attention, you ask him to change course and take you on a tour of the city as it is known and experienced by residents. He stops his cab and explains that there are some areas of the city that he, a second-generation Haitian immigrant, will not enter.[65] He offers instead to provide you an oral account of what he calls "New Orleans through my eyes."

You are lucky to meet me today. I consider myself a student of this remarkable city. *Fanmi mwen* came to New Orleans . . . Oh, *fanmi mwen* is Haitian for "my family." *Fanmi mwen* came to New Orleans in 1975. I was born here, but *Mwen se Ayisyen*, I am Haitian. Some people want to say, "I'm Creole," but *Mwen se Ayisyen*, which brings me to my first point.

You can't understand New Orleans as a place without understanding the importance of the color of your skin. In some ways, it is more important than money, though money does appear to prefer some colors over others. I suppose that's true everywhere in the United States, hey? Keep this idea of color and money in mind, and look at my map here.

Let's start at the eastern edge of the city between St. Bernard Parish and what is called the Lower Ninth Ward. What you call a county, we call a parish, a reminder of our collective Catholic heritage. We're in Orleans Parish now. St. Bernard is some 90 percent white working-class folks, solid as they go but not too keen on black people. At the western edge of St. Bernard sits the Lower Ninth Ward, or neighborhood.

Actually, the ward is made up of many neighborhoods. The Lower Nine was among the last New Orleans wards to be developed. The area was just cypress swamp until some folks drained it and built affordable housing for poor working-class families, some black, some white. See that levee over there? That protects all these families from the Industrial Canal. I don't know what kind of shape it's in. Time will tell, I guess.

It didn't take long for the whites to move out of the Lower Nine. Now it's some 98 percent black, so I hear. Proud folks live there, mostly home owners. You might take owning a house for granted; folks in the Lower Nine don't. It's the same scene with the Holy Cross neighborhoods next to the Ninth Ward, home-owning working-class African Americans. A guy I know who cabs for Yellow Cab lives in the Nine. He says folks make about $28,000 a year. Not too shabby.

Now, follow my finger over to what is called Pontchartrain Park. See, it's right next to the lake. It's not like the Lower Nine and Holy Cross. Almost everyone who lives here is black, but these folks are middle class, professional types, teachers, college professors, businessmen and -women—you know what I'm talking about. I know some of 'um personally. They take cabs. One woman I drove to the airport told me the average income in "the Park," as she called it, is $45,000 a year. That's real money.

Now watch my finger. We move just a bit west, and, voilà, here are Lakeshore and Lake Vista neighborhoods, bordered by St. John's Bayou on the east and Pontchartrain Park Boulevard on the west. Almost all white here. Everyone in these places got money, but some folks have more money than time. The local newspaper says people here make more than $111,000 a year. That's middling, so some are making a lot more.

Here see St. John's Bayou, the only natural waterway between the Mississippi River and Lake Pontchartrain. Follow the bayou from the lake toward the Mississippi, and you can see Gentilly on the east side of the waterway. Gentilly is a bit of a rainbow. All shades live here; most are working-class and middle-class families. A regular customer of mine lives on Art Street just over there. He makes about $60,000 a year. He says that's average for Gentilly. Part of this area, Gentilly Ridge, sits on a bit of high ground, meaning it is only a few feet below sea level. Continue on and we come to Mid-City. Originally called "Back of Town," these neighborhoods are a bit of salt and pepper, but mostly pepper. They're working-class folks probably making a little more than those folks in the Lower Nine.

Do you see Carrollton Avenue right here? Follow my finger down going toward the river. To the right of Carrollton is Hollygrove. At the turn of the nineteenth century, this land was part of the McCarty Plantation. It was once a favorite destination of Italian working-class families. Now it is almost all black, working people and, like the people in the Lower Nine, proud of their houses.

Oh, see, now we're at the Audubon neighborhood. It wraps right around the Mississippi River, see? Big houses in the Audubon . . . Lot's of old "sugar money" lives here, families who made their bread from raising cane, if you know what I mean. You look like you could raise a little "cane" yourself. This was once called the "English side of town." It's where the British Isles folks settled to separate themselves from the French. White folks here make some serious change.

Watch my finger as it goes down the Mississippi; hey, are you watching? Looking at the float, are you? They put floats on trucks and drive 'um around to parades. We parade in this city. The City That Care Forgot, we call it. This brings us to the French Quarter, the high ground in New Orleans, the Vieux Carré. Gotta love it. New Orleans was founded right near this spot in 1718. Between the architecture, the food, and the music, this is the heart of the city. Too many tourists around here for me, but you'll like it.

Look here, I've got to show you Iberville. It is just outside the Vieux Carré. Originally, this was called Storyville, the most famous red-light district in America. But along with that sin was born the music we call jazz. Yep, right here, the home of jazz. But I must tell you, don't spend much time here. It is steeped in poverty. I hear the average income of this poor neighborhood is just about $7,300. Who can live on that?

But speaking of poverty, I can't let you go without pointing out our public housing complexes. We've got four of them: C. J. Peete, B. W. Cooper, Lafitte, and St. Bernard. I hear upward of twenty thousand working-class to poor African Americans live in these apartments. Many are single-parent households. My wife was raised in B. W. She thinks fondly of it, but life was hard.

*Ezkize mwen*, excuse me, I've rattled on for some time. But I could go on describing different neighborhoods all day long. New Orleans is a tapestry of neighborhoods, each woven with different threads of color and money. I've given you just a quick tour. Know what? I'm driving you to Tipitina's, no charge. But you can tip if you like. Have a beer, check out the music, and *laissez les bons temps rouler*.

Two folk descriptions, one of San Francisco in 1906 and the other of New Orleans in 2005, suggest how the complex filigree of urban life was visible in the ordered menagerie of color and class. As if summing up the two accounts offered by the hotelier and the cabbie, Sarah Deutsch explains, "In an urban landscape you know who you are by where you are. At the same time, you understand the nature of the terrain by who lives there."[66] The sharp scissors of money and color cut each urban space into warrens of social kinds whose disparate relations to capital accumulation and the privileges of skin shade brought a modicum of both cognitive and social order to the cacophony of urban life.

The outlines of this order are familiar: people are sorted into race and class categories; wages, wealth, and life chances are distributed inequitably across these categories; residential segregation is created and maintained through legal and illegal practices; and a modicum of civility regulates disparate classes and races as they pass by, occasionally nodding to one another in that moment when the human face beckons a response. Douglas Massey and Nancy Denton refer to this durable urban and ordered inequality as "American apartheid."[67] It is this order that was dramatically disordered in response to the blunt force of two catastrophes. It is to this disarray that we now turn.

## II

# DERANGING AND REKINDLING

# THE GREAT DERANGEMENTS

In *Evangeline*, Longfellow brings to life the estrangement from place and the uprooted lives of those French Canadians expelled from Nova Scotia by the English in 1755:

> Meanwhile had spread in the village the tidings of ill,
> and on all sides Wandered, wailing, from house to house
> the women and children . . . and there on the sea-beach
> Piled in confusion lay the household goods of the peasants.

The human uprooting and miseries the poet evokes are remembered historically as *le Grand Dérangement*. Many of those thousands of displaced French settlers found their way to Louisiana, becoming over time the Cajuns who have left an indelible stamp on New Orleans. This historic eviction disordered what was an orderly arrangement of farmers, tradesmen, and townspeople in a small maritime province at the far eastern edge of Canada.[1]

I want to borrow the image of *le Grand Dérangement* to convey how the San Francisco earthquake and fire in 1906 and the flooding of New Orleans a century later muddled the orderly arrangement of those spatial and social enclaves that together make up the modern urban mosaic. In each disaster, nature collaborated with human error and malfeasance to create, at least momentarily, a primeval landscape, a world where people were tossed, some literally, some figuratively, onto the streets and sidewalks, "piled in confusion," with nowhere to go but away from the advancing flames or rising waters.

In its own destructive fashion, each disaster tore gaping holes through the social and spatial walls of these two cities. With the earthquake striking at the break of dawn without advance warning, San Franciscans one and all, the rich, the middling and working classes, and the poor alike, were thrown onto the streets. Terrified and confused, they sought the company of others and safe ground.

Though known far and wide for his photography, Arnold Genthe used words to capture this image of his hometown on April 18, 1906:

> The streets presented a weird appearance, mother and children in their nightgowns, men in pajamas and dinner coat, women scantily dressed with evening wraps hastily thrown over them. Many ludicrous sights met the eye: an old lady carrying a large bird cage with four kittens inside, while the original occupant, the parrot, perched on her hand; a man tenderly holding a pot of calla lilies, muttering to himself; a scrub woman, in one hand a new broom and in the other a large black hat with ostrich plumes; a man in an old-fashioned nightshirt and swallow tails, being startled when a friendly policeman spoke to him, "Say, Mister, I guess you better put on some pants."[2]

Unlike the earthquake and fires that suddenly and unexpectedly consumed the Paris of the Pacific, most people in New Orleans a century later had ample foreknowledge of Hurricane Katrina's path toward the city. Many of them with some discretionary income, credit cards, and roadworthy cars evacuated the city in advance of the storm. Others too poor to afford a road trip or too stubborn to accept the possibility of a worst-case scenario—the massive failure of the levees—remained.

Christiane Charlemaine, in spare, potent prose, summons this primal scene the day after the Paris of the South flooded:

> With water up to our knees, we walked to the school. . . . Luckily we saw a lighted spot with a group of about 30 people sitting on the ground. . . . In the group were two dialysis patients, a woman with Alzheimer's, and a young mother with her newborn baby girl. . . . [The next day] [t]he street was flooded up to our knees, but our spot . . . was dry. . . . [A] young Black boy . . . spent his day going back and forth with a small craft . . . to pick up or locate people trapped in their houses or roofs. In addition, he was the one "shopping" for the group bringing snacks and drinks. . . . [W]e heard that a helicopter would come to pick up the sick and elderly people and the mother and the baby . . . but it never came. Exhausted, we fell asleep on the cement.[3]

Victor Turner was not thinking of disasters when he refashioned Arnold van Gennep's idea of liminality to help us see that hierarchy and structured inequality might on occasion be temporarily replaced by "communitas."[4] But his wife, Edith, would later write of a "communitas of disaster, a powerful force," in her book *Communitas: The Anthropology of Collective Joy*. Victor and Edith Turner's moment of profound togetherness is akin to Jürgen Habermas's idea of "the lifeworld." In this world, lives are made present to one another outside the boundaries of market-organized rationality.[5] Here, people slip the bonds of classifications, customs, and pecuniary habits. Bereft of business, we are left to treat one another in our humanness. Described in Christiane's and others' accounts are spaces alive with a fellow feeling of social equivalence.

For many who remained in both cities, life assumed a communitarian, if freakish, quality. For most of those who fled, life quickly became unpredictable as they passed through the wide expanse that is America. *Charities and the Commons*, a weekly journal published by the Charity Organization Society, reports on those who evacuated San Francisco:

> The extent to which families were scattered is shown by the fact that many children and even babies arrived in Portland unaccompanied and unidentified. [An] advanced guard of the refugees from San Francisco reached New York on Sunday night. . . . The first applicants at the United Hebrew Charities of New York made up a family of man and wife and four children who arrived absolutely penniless and with scant clothing. . . . The family were on the train eight days . . . with varying amounts of food.

The family attempted to leave the train in Chicago, but when a guard discovered that they had once lived in New York, "he pushed him and his family back through the gates and on to an east-bound train. The relief problem . . . thus spread across the entire country in ten days time."[6]

TroyLynn Wilson recounts her journey out of New Orleans and the misery of unforeseen separation:

> The water was rising up near our housing projects so a boat came and rescued us. From the boat, we got on a helicopter. From the helicopter, we got on an airplane and were told we were entering Utah. . . . I don't have my little boy with me. I hope he's alive. . . . He was with his auntie. When I last spoke to her, she said she was going to Alaska. That was the last time I talked to her. We got trapped and didn't know this was going to happen.[7]

The tribulations and triumphs of those displaced by these two urban catastrophes beg a separate inquiry, one beyond the reach of this study.[8] In this chapter we keep our focus on the morphing socialscape, on the massive muddle and confusion that sundered the conventional boundaries of both cities, boundaries that, in normal times, keep the contradictions of class and race if not out of sight at least sufficiently obscure to allow those more comfortable and well-off the presumption that all is fair, or fair enough. Replacing these social and spatial borders was the fleeting promise of a new kind of social arrangement, one based on the felt need to accept help offered by others, often strangers, and to help those others in return. A bit later on, we will see that the utopian promise that things would be otherwise could not survive the onslaught of both the Hobbesian narratives of social breakdown and the criminalization of survival behavior.

## URBAN DERANGEMENT: "RICH AND POOR ALIKE"

When streets broke open, buildings collapsed, and fires raged, when floodwaters swamped streets and houses, moving some off their foundations, when people were tossed out of the ordinary and into makeshift worlds, it was difficult to discern those physical and social boundaries that carved up an urban landscape organized around the algorithm of capital. If, in ordinary times, the middling and upper classes can pretend that the underclass is invisible, urban disasters are likely to make this pretense impossible. "Men in pajamas," "dialysis patients," "an old lady carrying a large bird cage with four kittens inside," "a woman with Alzheimer's," and so many more people were forced from their private worlds onto streets to see and be seen. The private had spilled into the public in ways that sullied the categorical tidiness of both cities.

While the numbers vary—these kinds always do—it is generally accepted that somewhere between 225,000 and 300,000 of San Francisco's estimated 400,000 residents suddenly and quite unexpectedly found themselves on the streets.[9] Some landed there after being literally thrown from their houses to the bricks by the trembler. Others voluntarily abandoned their houses to the advancing flames. Still others were ordered to the streets by soldiers charged with vacating neighborhoods, preparing to dynamite houses in failed attempts to deny the fire flammable material. It is estimated that 90 percent of the infrastructural damage to the city was the result of fires.[10]

The twelve blocks of Chinatown were obliterated by the fire, as the more than 13,000 Chinese fled their ethnic enclave for the surrounding streets and neighborhoods. The "made land" under the area known as South of Market, a neighborhood of tenements housing the poor and working class, liquefied, becoming a pudding-like substance.[11] Buildings collapsed, trapping hundreds of the city's poorer residents. Fires started almost immediately. While the lives of the wealthy were spared, their property did not fare as well. The shock and aftershocks of the earthquake destroyed many of Nob Hill's finest mansions. Many of those still standing were dynamited by army troops ordered to create firebreaks to stop the advance of the flames.

Disaster destroys, but it also creates. The inferno that devoured San Francisco set ablaze the physical and social partitions that brought a certain order to urban life: work here, homes there; vehicular traffic here, foot traffic there; the wealthy here, the middle class there; the poor here and the races tolerably separated—this arrangement could not endure the firestorm that ravaged the cityscape. The social and physical partitions that kept the poor more or less out of sight, shielded the wealthy, and divided the races were gone, replaced by a moving chaos, a varied assortment of people quite unlike one another, trudging through the streets in search of safety.

A prominent member of the San Francisco Hooker family writes:

Rich and poor alike struggled along, side by side. Never was democracy more completely illustrated. On the winding drives in the Presidio reservation the spectacle was indescribable. Destiny had thrown together in that spot all sorts and conditions of human beings. Women of the town sat on the roadside with last night's rouge on their cheeks, holding the babies of poor mothers who tried to hush the crying of other children hardly older. Wealthy travelers, escaped from the hotels with only the clothes they wore, stood dazed among the rabble, and shook their heads to the anxious inquiries of those who were searching in the crowd for relatives or friends. A man who walked wearily along holding a little one by each hand was asked if his children were not tired. "They're not *my* children," he answered, "I guess somebody else is looking after my seven."[12]

A well-heeled member of San Francisco's polite society describes what he saw as the fires raged:

All day long hordes of refugees, mainly Italians, had poured over our hill from what was known as the Latin Quarter, a pitiful crowd, destitute and panic-stricken. Strange sights were to be seen. One distraught Italian mother had a bird-cage in one hand and her little boy led by the other. But she was holding the boy by his leg instead of his hand, and the poor little boy was protecting himself as best he could with his hands. I stopped her, turned the boy right side up, placed his hand in hers, and she went on without comment.[13]

Physician Margaret Mahoney recalled months later:

From the lower section of the town the mass of people were already moving westward. All that day and all that night they passed, the inhabitants of a cosmopolitan city; French, Spanish, Italians, the dark children of African origin; Oriental, Chinese and Japanese. They came pushing trunks, wheeling baby carriages full of household goods, carrying babies, carrying canaries in cages, carrying parrots; pushing sewing machines and trunks until the sickening sound of grating on the concrete entered so deep into my brain that I think it will never leave it.[14]

A certain Bertha wrote her sister in Milwaukee, summoning words to capture her last few minutes in her doomed house:

So at the last moment I picked up some of my little trinkets and filed my dresscase, what victuals I had I put into a little telescope and with that slung over my shoulder like all the rest—rich and poor alike.[15]

Katherine Putnam Hooker, a woman of considerable means, describes an open moment as the fires raged:

Men and women who had lived in wealth and elegance stood in the bread-line with Chinese and Negroes, with street-sweepers and paupers. Rich and poor struggled along, side by side. . . . On the winding drives in the Presidio reservation the spectacle was indescribable. Destiny had thrown together in that spot all sorts and conditions of human beings.[16]

Keenly aware of social position and the importance of rank, perhaps Jack London felt some odd sense of fleeting social parity in this account of a brief rest on the stoop of an abandoned house:

On Thursday morning at a quarter past five, just twenty-four hours after the earthquake I sat on the steps of a small residence on Nob Hill. With me sat Japanese, Italians, Chinese, and negroes—a bit of the cosmopolitan flotsam of the wreck of the city.[17]

**3.1.** Fleeing San Francisco, June 18, 1906. National Archives and Records Administration

Edith H. Rosenshine wrote her account sometime after the last of the fires were extinguished:

> As the City began to burn clouds of smoke could be seen as far as Santa Cruz, a distance of more than fifty miles from San Francisco. The poor hurried out of their cracked houses, leading their children by the hand. They carried what belongings they were able to on their backs or in wheel barrows. One saw little children carrying all that they were able to, or dragging them along. . . . The rich too, rushed out of their homes. They were in the same disarray. These women were also clutching their children and carried their jewel boxes, hats, bird cages and cats. Painted women from the underworld and the ladies who were in the habit of riding in their carriages, walked together and conversed glibly as they wended their way. Unter [*sic*] the stress of the situation, cast and social standing meant nothing.[18]

The following first-person account was written by Emma M. Burke, wife of San Francisco attorney Bart Burke, who lived on Waller Street, near Golden Gate Park, at the time of the earthquake. Emma's words reveal one Victorian woman's nomenclature of human sorting and how all that is properly separated in the mundane life of the city is suddenly mixed together in disaster. She notes:

> We had gathered some unfortunates about us who had lost everything, and I still had the house to draw upon as a base of supply. A wheelbarrow was our table, and about it gathered our family, a fat old lady who had owned a lodging-house, her daughter, a parlor-maid at the St. Francis Hotel, an old Hebrew tailor, penniless and forlorn, a medical fakir with long hair; and—I am afraid, one of the genus Tramp! However, he was hungry as the rest. This list I kept for four days, until my own resources were gone and the generous distribution of supplies was well inaugurated.[19]

Graham Taylor saw a

> truce even in the race war. Chinese merchants contributed their generous share to the general relief fund. Local committees were considerate of the diet preferred by Chinese coolies. Human was the party of the first part, and there was no second part.[20]

Reform-minded journalist Ray Stannard Baker captures the sudden instability of hierarchy following the cataclysm:

> In a single instant it stripped the city bare, it wiped out property, it tore the veil from human vanity of every sort, and it leveled all distinctions, political, social, even racial. For an instant there were neither millionaires nor paupers—just American people.[21]

If Ray Stannard Baker were alive today and describing New Orleans in late August 2005 as the waters breached and toppled the levees, his description would vary, no doubt. Hurricanes are qualitatively different disaster agents. They disturb urban order in their own fashion.

The first signs of an oceanic tempest are identified, and its path is tracked. If the winds become sufficiently concentrated and reach a speed of forty miles per hour, the tempest becomes a tropical depression and is given a name. At wind speeds in excess of seventy-three miles per hour, the named storm is reidentified as a "Category 1 hurricane."[22] In short, residents of a city or coastal area know well in advance that danger is coming. But such foreknowledge does not always translate into a predictable, orderly, and all-inclusive evacuation.

In testimony to the House of Representatives' Select Bipartisan Committee on preparing and responding to Hurricane Katrina, Terrol Williams, a New Orleans resident and evacuee, offered his assessment of the evacuation of the city:

> At the local level, I think the biggest failure was leadership didn't take into account the fact that poor residents had no way of evacuating. I also think Governor Blanco should have called for a mandatory evacuation sooner and that Mayor Nagin should have coordinated better with Amtrak.

The delay in ordering an evacuation of the city is echoed by the Select Bipartisan Committee report: "Despite adequate warning 56 hours before landfall, Governor Blanco and Mayor Nagin delayed ordering a mandatory evacuation in New Orleans until 19 hours before landfall."[23]

Elizabeth Fussell captures nicely the class differences that determined who evacuated and who remained in harm's way as the storm approached:

> The evacuation strategies of most upper and middle-income residents were quite straightforward: make a hotel reservation or arrange a visit with out-of-town friends and family, board the house windows if you can, pack the car, get some cash and leave town. These residents most often evacuated during the voluntary or mandatory evacuation period in the 24 to 48 hours before the storm was predicted to hit. For this group, the costs of leaving on Saturday were lower with respect to missing work or school since the storm was projected to arrive on Monday.[24]

It is generally agreed that approximately 100,000 of New Orleans's 460,000 residents remained in the city as it flooded, with waters reaching upwards of fifteen feet in some areas.[25] Cheryl Hayes of Pontchartrain Park put it plainly: "There are too many poor people in this town who could not escape the water, and nobody had a plan for that."[26] If San Franciscans of all kinds were thrown on the streets in 1906, those who found themselves awash in the fetid waters of the Industrial Canal and Lakes Borgne and Pontchartrain were primarily those without the material means of escaping the city.

Renee Martin, a clinical nursing assistant, was rescued on Monday, August 29, from her porch by a

> white male, about seventy-five years old with a brown dog who picked me up and . . . put me in the boat, and he picked up a girl, her husband,

**3.2.** A family of Hurricane Katrina victims walk past a covered body in front of New Orleans Convention Center, September 3, 2005. Photo by Eric Gay, AP Images

and her mama. . . . I remember him as the Man with the Dog. So the Man with the Dog took us to the Superdome area. . . . They had bodies in the water . . . big logs blocking the street, so we had to walk. It was scary because we had bodies and we had to walk through these bodies. . . . And we wasn't the only people. They had lots of people coming from different areas. . . . We were all walking from different areas.[27]

Prentiss Polk, a young man from the Ninth Ward, worked as a roofer before Katrina. When the Industrial Canal collapsed, sending a cascading wall of fusty brown water through his doomed neighborhood, Prentiss did what he could to help himself and others survive.

I stayed in that water for like three days. Helping people and bringing people food and water. First we built a raft. We went to an old tire shop, got some tires with air in them. Got some two-by-fours, and three sheets of plywood, and built it. We tried to save as many people as we could. They was in their houses, trying to stay in their houses. We did our thing, man. It got so bad, down in the Four, in the Fourth Ward, we had to take us a house that was up higher. And the people who was on the bridge by the Superdome and had no water. We went to Kentwood [water company], opened up their thing, and took all the Kentwood trucks. We brought them on the bridge, and gave everybody some water. We helped everybody. It was a storm.[28]

Shelly, a young African American woman, describes her experience on one of New Orleans's famed neutral grounds during the flooding:

A stranger rescued us from our porch and took us many blocks to the neutral ground. We were about 2 or 3 feet above the water. All day people were dropped off. Some people had suitcases full of stuff. Black people, white people and some Mexicans are on the high ground and glad to be there. We stayed all night.[29]

Violet Green was eighty-five years old in late August 2005. Living alone in Pontchartrain Park, she decided to ride out this hurricane like she rode out Betsy in 1965. But Katrina proved more potent than Betsy.

They had some young men in boats trying to help get people out of here, and we were in the window waving pillow slips or whatever we could find to let them know we were there. And after a while a young man came and got us and we had to get out of the window and get on top of the carport. So I am eighty-five and she is diabetic. Whew! The boat, it took us out to the Chef [Highway]. So we went to the shopping center and everybody was just in a daze or something. We just sat around and walked around and looked around. . . . So this young man said, "I'll tell you what, you older people, I'm going to take you all down to the undertaker and we're going to stay there." So we went to the undertaker's, the funeral home, and it was late, it was getting dark. No lights or nothing, so the young men went to the grocery store. They got candles for lights. Our group stayed together, and when daylight came they went to the grocery store for us and they got us groceries. We stayed at the undertakers for three or four days before a chopper came down low enough and he saw us. He asked us, "There are people staying in the funeral home?" We said, "Yes, live people, we are all alive."[30]

A woman recounts a story her aunt told about her cousin Denise, who had a trying time in her efforts to navigate a flooded city:

Denise said she thought she was in hell. They were there (The Convention Center) for 2 days, with no water, no food, no shelter. Denise, her mother (63 years old), her niece (21 years old), and 2-year-old grandniece. . . . When they arrived, there were already thousands of people there. They were told that buses were coming. Police drove by, windows rolled up, thumbs up signs. National Guard trucks rolled by, completely empty, soldiers with guns cocked and aimed at them. Nobody stopped to drop off water. A helicopter dropped a load of water, but all the bottles exploded on impact due to the height of the helicopter.

Denise said yes, there were young men with guns there. But they organized the crowd. They went to Canal Street and "looted," and brought back food and water for the old people and the babies, because nobody had eaten in days. When the police rolled down windows and yelled out "the buses are coming," the young men with guns organized the crowd in order: old people in front, women and children next, men in the back. Just so that when the buses came, there would be priorities of who got out first.[31]

A proper white middle-class lady who lived in the Algiers Point neighborhood of New Orleans, "Miss Grace," as she was called, had fallen on her stairs as she made preparations to flee the hurricane. Living alone and unable to move, she screamed for help. Two young men from Fischer Projects, a public housing complex a mile or so from her house, chanced to walk by and heard her screams. They called to her. Her door was locked.

I told them to break the window pane in the door and give me a hand as I was hurt. They broke the window, came in and helped me to my feet. I had hurt my knee. They got me to a chair. I asked one of them to get my son-in-law who lived a block away. One young man stayed with me while the other one walked to my son-in-law's house. A few minutes later my son-in-law walked in. He offered to pay the boys for their trouble. They took no money and left. I never saw them again.[32]

### A ROUSSEAUIAN WORLD

Reflected in these stories is life unhinged, mad, when all that once was in its more or less proper place is scattered about, as if mocking the very idea of order. Amid the chaos is a social world akin to Rousseau's life before civilization. Here, if only for a brief time, the ordinary barriers of geography and social kinds are replaced by a common recognition that everyone is deserving of respect as a fellow survivor who needs help and perhaps can help in return. Here is Peter Kropotkin's society of "mutual aid." "All artificial restraints of our civilization fell away," Emma Burke recalls, "with the earthquake's shocks. Every man was his brother's keeper. Everyone spoke to everyone else with a smile." For Ray Stannard Baker, it was a moment of "earthquake love."[33]

Anthony Letcher, from New Orleans's Lower Ninth Ward, deploying his own vernacular, describes what we might call "flood love":

> So man, we went in the stores and shit. . . . We went down to get food, and fed all the people that we got. . . . After I started helping people, man, I forgot all about money. That was insignificant. It was something bigger than that, and brother, it felt good in me, you heard me?[34]

One report from social scientists who visited the city three weeks after the levees broke quotes a "New Orleans law enforcement official . . . 'most people by and large really, really, really just helped one another and they didn't ask for anything back.'" The report continues, "The majority of citizens behaved positively and went out of their way to help one another."[35]

A romantic subtext informs these reminiscences, true. Perhaps there is a trace of exaggeration here and there. It is, however, hard to overlook the common thread that runs through these many and varied accounts of two chaotic times when novel forms of human togetherness emerged. In what is arguably a rhetorical stretch, Rebecca Solnit finds "paradise" in the wake of death and devastation. "If paradise now arises in hell, it's because in the suspension of the usual order . . . we are now free to live and act another way," to be, in short, our brothers' and sisters' keepers.[36]

Writing in 1961, Charles Fritz introduced the idea of the "therapeutic community" to conceptualize this communal moment in disaster. In this time betwixt and between the extraordinary and the routine, sympathetic identification with the other combines with informal communication to create an "unstructured" social field marked by spontaneous acts of helping. Several years later, Allen Barton revisits the idea of the therapeutic community, adding a new and more Durkheim-friendly concept, the "altruistic community."[37]

More than two decades after Barton, Eränen and Liebkind observe that a disaster "increases identification among victims, and previous class, race, ethnic, and social class barriers temporarily disappear." In his 2008 edition of *Response to Disaster*, Henry L. Fischer III writes, after "more than 40 years of research into the behavioral response to natural and technological disasters . . . [the] perceptions that individuals flee in panic . . . loot or behave in selfish ways [are] far more myth than real."

Not too deep within the conceptual and descriptive characteristics of this prosocial space of togetherness are discernible echoes of a premodern, more communal arrangement. It is here, in this emotionally charged time, that affinity with and empathy for the other undermine social and economic inequality. If only for a protracted moment, the spectacle of disaster trumps the capillaries of market power that produce and reproduce Tilly's "durable inequality."[38]

There is a close relationship between these expressions of genuine civility and selflessness across what are otherwise bounded social divisions and Max Weber's idea of the open society. The felt need to help and be helped by others is, Weber reasoned, a practical, self-interested response to an unstable and uncertain moment:

> If the participants expect that the admission of others will lead to an improvement of their situation, an improvement in degree, in kind, in the security or the value of the satisfaction, their interest will be in keeping the relationship open.[39]

The open, altruistic communities that quickly coalesce in the aftermath of disaster do serve the interests of survivors, but embedded in Weber's observation is one telltale reason they do not survive for long. It is captured in the conjunction *if*. If participants think that the presence of others, no matter how different in kind from them, "will lead to an improvement of their situation," social openness remains a possibility.

But an open society that minimizes or ignores difference, where one kind of person is no better than the other, is unsustainable in a market society. Here, inequality is more durable than communality. To restore a market society, human association must shift from selflessness to competition, a world wherein my relationship to you is bounded by my interest in bettering my competitive situation.[40] And therein lies the rub.

In these great derangements, we see both the collapse of two cities geographically arranged by class and social kinds and the emergence of two quite similar patterns of mutual assistance and selflessness. Ray Stannard Baker captures the idea at the heart of this chapter when he prefaces his account of the disaster that laid waste to San Francisco this way: "I merely wish to give enough of the story to bring out the spirit of those early days and paint in the background for a picture of what may be called the return from Utopia to modern business conditions."[41]

Baker's words foreshadow the next act in the drama of disaster recovery, "the return . . . to modern business conditions." The first move to rearrange what had been temporarily deranged is to begin re-sorting the varied kinds of people who were haphazardly tossed together in the maelstrom of catastrophe. In the following chapter, we look closely at how this restoring commences as the city, transformed into a collective *place*, a village of sorts, is inevitably reclaimed as a market *space*.[42]

# FASHIONING "THE LOOTER"
## REKINDLING RACIAL AND CLASS KINDS

*The market system was more allergic to*
*rioting than any other system we know.*

KARL POLANYI, *THE GREAT TRANSFORMATION:*
*THE POLITICAL AND ECONOMIC ORIGINS OF OUR TIME*

### ROUSSEAU OR HOBBES? A PLACE TO BEGIN

Ample evidence in the great derangements of San Francisco in 1906 and in New Orleans a century later supports the conclusion that a remarkable human quality was on display. Yet as survivors were making their way through the visceral destruction all about them, others were making up apocalyptic stories of sacking and plundering. Accompanying this Rousseau-like story of compassion and fellow feeling spontaneously appearing in the midst of utter confusion is a second counternarrative, reprising Hobbes's conviction that absent the authority of the state, there emerges what "we may properly call the state of nature . . . nothing else but a mere war of all against all; and in that war all men have equal right unto all things."[1]

This Hobbesian story is far less likely to be heard from the victims of disaster. It is a tale more often told by holders of political offices, city elites, members of the military, and the media. Reporting on the flooding of New Orleans for the *New York Times*, Maureen Dowd borrows a B-movie prose style, conjuring up "a snake pit of anarchy, death, looting, raping, marauding thugs, [and] suffering innocents."[2] In his own hyperbolic prose, Joseph R. Chenelly, with help from an army general, summons the imagery of a misbegotten war. His article in the *Army Times*, "Troops Begin Combat Operations in New Orleans to Fight Insurgents," published less than a week after the city flooded, begins this way:

> "This place is going to look like Little Somalia," Brig. Gen. Gary Jones, commander of the Louisiana National Guard's Joint Task Force, told *Army Times* Friday as hundreds of armed troops under his charge prepared to launch a massive citywide security mission from a staging area outside the Louisiana Superdome. "We're going to go out and take this city back. This will be a combat operation to get this city under control."[3]

Perhaps the general was responding to the surfeit of dark reports coming from high-ranking city officials. New Orleans police chief Eddie Compass reported: "We have individuals who are getting raped; we have individuals who are getting beaten." A few days later, Compass told Oprah Winfrey and her audience about "little babies . . . getting raped" in the Convention Center. On this same program, Mayor Ray Nagin adopts an eyewitness style, as if he were there: "They have people standing out there, have been in that frickin' Superdome for five days watching dead bodies, watching hooligans killing people, raping people."[4]

In the wake of these apocalyptic tales, it was assumed by some that martial law had been declared. "We have authority by martial law to shoot looters," Commander James Scott told his officers in the city's First District.[5] Wolf Blitzer on CNN reported on the arrival of the National Guard in New Orleans, offering his version of disaster rescue: "Eight convoys and troops are on the ground at last in a place being described as a lawless, deadly war zone."[6] Martial law, of course, was never declared. Nevertheless, the American Forces Information Service noted that the military deployed more men and equipment in response to Hurricane Katrina than it had in any previous disaster in US history.[7]

Dial back to April 19, 1906. A joint edition of the *Call-Chronicle-Examiner* announced definitively on its front page:

> At nine o'clock, under a special message from President Roosevelt, the city was placed under martial law. Hundreds of troops patrolled the streets and drove the crowds back. . . . During the afternoon three thieves met their death by rifle bullets while at work in the ruins.[8]

Anticipating the Hobbesian state-of-nature narrative that quickly emerged to describe the behaviors of those left in the waters of New

Orleans a hundred years later, police captain Thomas Duke told his own story of street life in 1906 San Francisco. His headquarters quickly began receiving "reports . . . that thieves were burglarizing wrecked stores and deserted homes, and it was learned that in the Mission District the body of a woman was found, the finger upon which she had worn several valuable rings having been amputated, evidently by some thief."[9] How anyone could know that the missing finger had been adorned with "several valuable rings" was not made clear in the captain's report.

In his July 1906 article for *Cosmopolitan*, Brigadier General Frederick Funston, commander of the Presidio Army Base, just outside San Francisco, described a meeting he had with Mayor Eugene Schmitz and the chief of police, Jeremiah Dinan, in which

> it was arranged that during the night the regular troops should patrol the wealthy residence district west of Van Ness Avenue, in order to prevent robbery or disorder by the vast throngs being driven thither by the progress of the fire. . . . San Francisco had its class of people, no doubt, who would have taken advantage of any opportunity to plunder the banks and rich jewelry and other stores of the city, but the presence of the square-jawed silent men with magazine rifles, fixed bayonets, and with belts full of cartridges restrained them.[10]

Contrary to the *Call-Chronicle-Examiner*'s claim, Theodore Roosevelt never placed San Francisco under martial law.[11]

## TWO OPPOSING NARRATIVES, ONE CONTESTED

Two contradictory narratives, one a story of primordial hostility in a protracted moment bereft of routine social and geographic constraint, the other pointing toward the theme of human goodness in a state of nature, invite some scrutiny. Does inconsiderate, hostile, perhaps even violent behavior occur during the emergency phase of disaster? We would be naive to think otherwise. It is, after all, a lingering moment ripe for opportunistic crime. But if we think of these two story lines as a continuum, with Hobbesian predation at one end and Rousseauian compassion at the other end, the overwhelming evidence suggests that most people, most of the time, are simply trying to survive the chaotic danger and help others along the way. In their studied assessment of behavior among those New Orleanians who fought to survive the moment, sociologists Rodríguez, Trainor, and Quarantelli might also be describing the conduct of San Franciscans a century earlier who too sought to help one another live another day: "The various social systems and the people in them rose to the demanding challenges of a catastrophe."[12]

The mounting stories of people, strangers, who joined one another in acts of togetherness and kindness to survive amid a disorganized disaster relief effort took their toll on the credibility of New Orleans's police chief and the city's mayor. Eddie Compass would resign in late September 2005 after admitting that he was simply reporting rumors of shootings, rapes, and pillage on *The Oprah Winfrey Show*. In what is most likely an intentional understatement, historian Douglas Brinkley notes in Spike Lee's documentary *When the Levees Broke: A Requiem in Four Acts*, "What Eddie [Compass] was trying to do was tell the truth. . . . His view was: 'I'll tell you everything you want to hear.' Unfortunately, he was spreading rumors."[13]

Not a month after Katrina swamped the city, Lisa Grow Sun notes, media, of all varieties, were busy retracting "much of their previous reporting, admitting that the reports of violence and crime were largely unsubstantiated."[14]

In his exhaustive study of the alleged "carnival of crime" that broke out in 1906 San Francisco, historian Henry Morse Stephens found it to be nothing more than a myth. "Documents in possession of the history committee show clearly the absence of crime in the months of April and May of 1906," he wrote. And in a specific reference to police captain Thomas Duke's story of amputated fingers, Stephens writes, "Of course, nothing of the kind occurred in San Francisco." Drawing on Stephens and others, Philip Fradkin writes in his definitive history of this disaster, "All later accounts by both officials and private citizens emphasized that looting was minor or nonexistent."[15]

Reporting on historian Kevin Starr's 2005 public lecture on the 1906 disaster at Stanford University, Krista Zala writes:

> Rumors and official accounts portrayed San Francisco inaccurately, Starr claimed, including tales of Asian-like "ghouls roaming streets" biting earlobes and fingers off the dead for their jewelry. In the "collective civic meltdown," unassimilated minorities were the first target, he said.[16]

Fradkin coined the expression *imagined crimes* to account for the myth-like stories that officials evoked to justify a military response to the disordering of routine urban life.[17]

These two disasters, justly so, inflamed the civic temper, but why, it is worth asking, did they also inflame the military temper?[18] The myth of disaster looting has been discussed at length in both popular and academic venues.[19] In spite of the general consensus that this behavior is more a fairy than a reality tale, it persists, inviting us to ask why. A tenacious myth that prevails in spite of evidence to the contrary survives to serve some purpose. Perhaps it has something to do with the primacy of property and the fear of losing it, forces that dwell deep in both the tissue of the market and, as Freud would suggest, the human character.[20]

Whatever the reason, the inevitable looting panic reminds us that society is more often concerned with combating what are assumed to be the natural forces within us than with those forces—economic, political, social—that threaten us from the outside; those forces deep within human nature constitute, we are told, a graver, more abiding danger. This alarm is sometimes referred to as "moral" or "elite" panic, purposely "engineered" terror deliberately fostered to justify the militarization of a disordered social scene.[21] This is a credible account of disaster and the looting scare.

How could a market-organized society not panic in the clutches of an urban disaster when some people are found foraging and finding—simply taking without paying—goods necessitated by their species' need to survive? In that moment when the city becomes a distorted landscape, inviting all to stay alive by whatever means necessary, what is typically understood as private property may well become public as people search for food, clothing, medicine, and other necessities of survival.

When catastrophe strikes a society organized around capital accumulation, the primacy of private property is likely to promote a fear of a particular kind of "other," one who pilfers and filches. Such behavior might well throw a primal scare into the heart of capital. The highly charged portrayals of looting found in public accusations, media accounts, and dramatic images are a striking reminder that catastrophe cannot commandeer the sanctity of private property. "Elite panic" resonates; it makes sound sense of this dramatic moment.

But there is also, conceivably, a deeper, more methodical force at play, one less emotion driven, but one likely to drive emotions. Perhaps the continual revival of the looting myth serves a market society's need to quickly re-create that arrangement of social kinds now in temporary disarray. Accumulating capital depends, in part, on difference—specifically, different kinds of people hierarchically placed both socially and spatially. In this seemingly anomic moment, compassion and survival nudge the market aside, confusing and blurring that routine urban configuration in which "forms of difference"—certain kinds of people in certain kinds of places—

behave in more or less prescribed ways. The word *urban* or *city* is a key link between the great derangement and the seemingly inevitable emergence of the looting myth.

## THE LOOTING PANIC AND THE MARKET CITY

The catastrophe most often associated with the kind of looting mythologized in political speech and media accounts and made concrete in the imposing presence of armed forces almost always occurs in cities. Go back a moment to October 8, 1871, and what is now known as the "Great Chicago Fire." As the city burned, it seemed to kindle the fear of looting madness. "An over-excited lawyer wrote his mother . . . 'the city is thronged with desperadoes who are plundering.'"[22] The son, as it happens, was needlessly worrying his mom.

Philip Sheridan, the decorated Civil War hero, rushed to the burning city with five companies of infantry. He would report days later that "no authenticated attempt at incendiarism has reached me, and the people of the city are calm, quiet, and well-disposed." Thomas B. Brown, the city's police commissioner, would later note that "during the fire . . . there were remarkably few cases of crime."[23] In spite of two accounts, one by an experienced general, the other by the city's police commissioner, describing a peaceful, well-behaved citizenry in the throes of mayhem, the scene Philip Fradkin describes in Chicago in 1871 foreshadows what would occur decades later in San Francisco and a century after that in New Orleans:

> The ultimate sanction was placed on the relatively harmless crime of looting. Allan Pinkerton ordered his private police force to kill suspected looters, even though people seeking food or personal belongings in the ruins could be, and were, easily mistaken for offenders. Whereas looting was envisioned as a class crime, little attention—and certainly not the extreme penalty of death—was paid to price gouging, an arguably greater crime in time of disaster.[24]

In rather stark contrast to their urban complements, smaller towns and counties struck by disaster are not likely to become alleged sites of lawlessness. While there might be the occasional reference to looting in these settings, it is the urban calamity that is most likely to trigger panic among the propertied classes. In 2011 a historic number of tornadoes struck several southern states, among them Alabama. A corporate business consulting firm reports on the work of Sergeant Jay Hawkins from the Alabama Lincoln County Sheriff's Department, who "found himself guarding one of the most heavily damaged neighborhoods. . . . His job was to ensure order and protect tornado victims from looting. While on guard, Sgt Hawkins had to arrest one individual for violating curfew."[25]

In response to this tornadic outbreak, Alabama's governor appointed business leaders, educators, physicians, and other professionals to what was named the Tornado Recovery Action Council. In its 117-page report, the noun *looter* does not appear. There is one, rather anodyne, reference to looting:

> One official said he went to Cordova the day after the disaster, and security was good. Then he went to another town in the same county on April 29, and there had been looting the night before.[26]

On May 3, 2016, a massive wildfire swept through Fort McMurray in Alberta, Canada, forcing the evacuation of tens of thousands of the town's seventy-eight thousand residents. More than twenty-four hundred buildings, mostly houses, went up in flames. The *Edmonton Sun* newspaper ran this headline on May 6: "Looting Not a Problem in Fort McMurray, Police Say."[27]

Slidell, Louisiana, a city with twenty-six thousand people in 2000, sits just across Lake Pontchartrain, thirty miles or so east of New Orleans. A little more than three weeks after Katrina's winds had whipped the lake's waters, creating a tsunami-like storm surge that swamped the city, Slidell police reported no more than five or six arrests for looting. In their field report on survivor behavior following the flooding of the city, Lauren Barsky and her colleagues note, "An overall theme that emerged when speaking to organizational actors was that there were more reports of looting in downtown New Orleans than areas outside the city."[28]

Georg Simmel would find nothing counterintuitive in the observation that looting occurs less frequently in smaller towns and rural areas struck by disaster. "The metropolis," he notes, "has always been the seat of money economy because the many-sidedness and concentration of commercial activity have given the medium of exchange an importance which it could not have acquired in the commercial aspects of rural life."[29]

If looting is not the front-and-center issue in non-urban disaster recovery, it is in part because these geographies are not densely packed arrangements in which an outsize number of diverse people are distributed by market forces into more or less ordered configurations. Viewed from this angle, the looting myth has no substantive role to play in reorganizing the rural communities disorganized by disaster.

From the vantage point of recovering inequality, the peculiar and persistent charge of looting is closely tied to the market city. In the wake of purported unhinged pandemonium, fashioning the looter becomes a key cultural gambit in restoring the primacy of class and race distinctions. If it wasn't the myth of looting that launches the repositioning of people and places in a morphing moment when things could be otherwise, I suspect another, related, variety of scare would emerge to do the same kind of work.

## SHOOT-TO-KILL ORDERS

On April 19, 1906, the day after the earth split open, the ruptured and burning city of San Francisco was all but officially under rule of martial law. According to news reports from California to New York, military rule had been enacted to aid the police force in protecting frightened citizens from rioters and looters. City officials anticipated the rise of an underclass that would ransack the hundreds of city blocks filled with houses and stores left in ruins by the quake.

Mayor Eugene Schmitz wasted little time in proclaiming that such vandalism would be met with lethal force. In his declaration Schmitz states emphatically:

PROCLAMATION BY THE MAYOR OF SAN FRANCISCO
The Federal Troops, the members of the Regular Police Force and all Special Police Officers have been authorized by me to KILL any and all persons found engaged in Looting or in the Commission of Any Other Crime.[30]

In late August 2005, days after one of the country's most destructive hurricanes left the state's largest city underwater, Louisiana governor Kathleen Blanco issued her own proclamation. In both imagery and tone, her message is markedly similar to Mayor Schmitz's dire warning:

PROCLAMATION BY THE GOVERNOR OF LOUISIANA
Three hundred of the Arkansas National Guard have landed in the city of New Orleans. These troops are fresh back from Iraq, well trained, experi-

enced, battle-tested and under my orders to restore order in the streets. They have M-16s and are locked and loaded. These troops know how to shoot and kill the hoodlums and they are more than willing to do so if necessary and I expect they will.[31]

If Governor Kathleen Babineaux Blanco was aware of the spirit of co-operation and mutual support that emerged in response to the flooding of New Orleans, she chose to focus her attention on another, alleged, kind of behavior. The governor echoed the sentiments of Mayor Schmitz a century earlier when she told news reporters that she was "furious" about the alleged looting. "What angers me the most is disasters tend to bring out the best in everybody, and that's what we expected to see. Instead," she concluded, "it brought out the worst."[32]

The media sided with the governor, choosing to see the spectacle of "looting" as a far more interesting story than random acts of kindness. The persistent attention of newspapers and their kindred mediums on the "looter" and the drama of looting in lieu of reporting on the more prosaic acts of caring and mutual aid that spring from the swift collapse of normal urban routines and protocols is illustrated in two newspaper accounts, one written at the beginning of the twentieth century, the other a hundred years later.

The *Los Angeles Times*, reporting on the almost complete destruction of San Francisco in 1906, deployed a medieval prose style to describe "looting by fiends incarnate that made a hell broth of the center of the ruined district. Sixteen looters were shot out of hand on April 19, while robbing the dead."[33] In his reconstruction of events after the earthquake, reporter Q. A. Bronson described "looters wantonly shot in their tracks by Federal troops, miscreants hanged in public squares, and ghouls found cutting off the fingers and ears of corpses for rings and earrings attached."[34]

A century later, the *New York Times* would adopt a more matter-of-fact tone to describe the purported problem of looting. Although New Orleans was

> shut down for business, the Rite Aid at Oak and South Carrollton was wide open on Wednesday. . . . The young and the old walked in empty-handed and walked out with armfuls of candy, sunglasses, notebooks, soda and whatever else they could need or find. No one tried to stop them. Across New Orleans, the rule of law, like the city's levees, could not hold out after Hurricane Katrina. . . . One woman outside a Sav-a-Center on Tchoupitoulas Street was loading food, soda, water, bread, peanut butter and canned food into the trunk of a gray Oldsmobile.[35]

The idea that these "looters" might well have been taking what they needed, in a protracted moment of chaos, to get by one more day was not part of the *Times'* narrative.

Framing survival behavior as looting allowed those with a stake in describing mayhem and disorder to make survivors' conduct independent of their motives, so their needs, their will to survive, could be ignored. What the *New York Times* reported, in an unconvincing euphemism, as "crimes of opportunity" were—far more often than not—desperate acts of survival.[36] If mass bedlam created a moment of social openness that belied the routine race and class topography of both cities, the charge of looting would rekindle those categorical distinctions. It is worth asking, what is this "looting" and who is this "looter" who stirs up such a fright that the first order of business in responding to an urban disaster is the militarization of the city?

## KIND MAKING: "LOOTING" AND "THE LOOTER"

The word *looting* originated in the early nineteenth century as an anglicized version of the Hindi word *lūṭ*, from Sanskrit *luṇṭh*, or "to rob."[37] "Looters" are allied with "plunderers" and "bandits."[38] To understand what it means to commandeer goods *illegally*—to seize something "often by force or violence"—as *Merriam-Webster's* defines *looting*, is also to grasp just who gets to determine when a specific act of taking someone else's property is a criminal act.[39] Perhaps the act in question is someone taking someone else's property to help him or her stay alive or help others in their efforts to survive. Who, in other words, gets to create "the looter"? The question of just who gets to name a given act "looting" and the actor "the looter" is the type of query that many smart people have struggled with for some time.

Nietzsche found names and naming a foundational challenge to that part of him that held on to the idea that there is something essential, inborn, in each of us. "This has given me the greatest trouble and still does," he writes, "to realize that what things are called is incomparably more important than what they are. . . . Creating new names . . . is enough to create new 'things.'" Thomas Hobbes, who did not share Nietzsche's penchant for the innate, asks a rhetorical question: "How can any man imagine that the names of things were imposed by their natures?"[40]

A social kind, Hacking reminds us, is not a flesh-and-blood person. Rather, it takes its shape and form from the work of "interested parties" who possess the power to create "value-laden kinds."[41] "Making up people" is always situational; each kind "has its own history."[42] Aided by these names, it is possible to sort people into those who are normal and those who are abnormal, those who are law abiding and those who are breaking the law, and so on. Kind making, in short, is a dividing practice.

## MAKING UP "THE LOOTER"

Hearing that General Funston ordered his soldiers to march to San Francisco, Mayor Schmitz told his chief of police:

> The United States troops are on their way down here from the Presidio. As soon as they arrive, send fifty men into the banking district, put ten men on every block on Market Street and a guard for the City Hall. Give these men instructions . . . to shoot to kill everyone found looting. We have no time to waste on thieves.

The mayor's first concern was for the banking and market districts, the heart of the business center of the city. Schmitz would later order troops to guard the city's wealthiest neighborhoods, areas like Nob Hill and Van Ness Avenue, from those who lived south of Market and the Barbary Coast, poor and working-class neighborhoods.[43]

In addition to the military and six hundred policemen, armed and ready to respond to the deranged social and geographic landscape of the stricken city, paramilitary groups emerged to protect property and restore order. A citizens' committee with no legal status deputized a thousand citizens, providing them with official-looking badges. The "Citizens' Special Police" was made up of people who either knew someone considered "reputable" or was himself among that social kind deemed well-thought-of in San Francisco's respectable society.[44]

For some San Franciscans, the presence of armed troops, policemen, and paramilitary groups provided some comfort. Mary Austin remembers: "The will of the people was toward authority, and everywhere the tread of soldiery brought a relieved sense of things orderly and secure."[45] Perhaps for Mary and her genteel community, there was some relief in seeing "soldiery," but for those less fortunate these representatives of law and order posed a risk greater than either the earthquake or the fires. Henry Fichtner, a nurse, was helping his "elderly landlady escape the fire" when he came upon this scene:

> I saw one soldier . . . beat with the butt of his gun a woman—apparently a servant girl—who wanted to get a bundle of clothing that she had left on

the sideway. . . . This soldier was worse than a brute, and beat the woman fearfully.[46]

In another deadly encounter, a member of the special police, a "retired National Guard captain killed a man carrying a chicken—the captain incorrectly thought it was stolen."[47]

We have no way of knowing what or whom the "retired National Guard captain" thought he was looking at when he shot this man. But the chances are good that he did not see a Stanford University professor who had made his way to the stricken city. Consider the professor's story:

In the afternoon I had chanced to meet General Funston and he had kindly given me a military pass. The city was not under martial law, although there were rumors to that effect, but the pass proved useful for with it I was allowed to pass through fire lines.

I went back to the club to have a last look at the place where I had spent so many happy hours. Many paintings and drawings still remained on the walls, though a couple of truck-loads had been hauled out to Golden Gate Park for safety. With my pocket-knife I cut several choice ones from their frames, rolled them up and carried them away. Among them were two priceless cartoons by Thomas Nast which he had made for the club, and an apron from a Lambs' Washing of the Lambs of New York, signed and illustrated by all the leading artists and actors of the day.[48]

With his pass in hand, the professor behaved in a manner that surely would have brought an untimely end to a person of another kind who entered the club and "cut several choice" paintings, "rolled them up and carried them away."

Moshe Cohen, a news photographer, found himself on O'Farrell Street, where he witnessed a man exiting a store who was likely of a different sort from the professor:

His arms were full and so were his pockets. . . . [T]he soldiers dropped him with a shot clean through the back. . . . How did they know that he wasn't entitled to the stuff? He could have worked at the place. . . . But none of those soldiers even bothered to find out.[49]

Numerous accounts of the disparate treatment of the city's residents along racial-ethnic and class lines provide ample evidence that the militarization of the city increased fear, rather than security, for some and began the process of repositioning the social and geographic distinctions so visibly disordered in the maw of disaster. "In reality," Fradkin notes, it was not martial law or civil law that reigned on the streets of San Francisco. It was, rather, "the law of the moment."[50] In these moments, decisions to shoot and kill were made on a case-by-case basis, predicated on the "law" enforcer's assumptions about just what social kind was rescuing valuable artwork, or grabbing a bundle of clothing, or a chicken, or cartons of something or other from an abandoned store.

With this idea of social kind in mind, what sense, then, can we make of proper Victorian people taking what is clearly not theirs from the ruins of the San Francisco Palace Hotel? Or the "'high railroad officials,' 'society people,' 'capitalists,' and 'reputable businessmen' . . . caught pouring over the ruins of Chinatown in search of gold"?[51] "Chinatown suffered severely," writes Charles Morris, not a year after the disaster, "the merchants of that locality possessing large stock of valuable goods, many of which were looted by seeming respectable sightseers after the ruins had cooled off, bronze, porcelain and other valuable goods being taken from the ruins."[52] One Helen Pardee, the wife of California governor George C. Pardee, it is noted, "acquired two statuettes in this manner."[53] Were the appropriately attired Victorians "respectable sightseers" or "looters"?

We do know that neither Helen nor anyone else was shot or arrested—as Fradkin kindly puts it—for "poring over the ruins of" either the Palace Hotel or Chinatown. Two "reputable businessmen" were arrested and charged with looting. Neither was found guilty. The court concluded, "They were merely *sightseeing*."[54] We might conclude that whether this "elite looting," for want of a better term, met *Merriam-Webster's* definition of appropriating a good "illegally," those charged with sorting looters from nonlooters concluded it did not. A "sightseer" too is a particular kind of person, curious, adventuresome, but one who is not likely to be accused of stealing.

## ELITE LOOTING?

Sorting "looters" from "sightseers," "reputable businessmen," and "society people" was not an onerous task.[55] It simply required a quick appraisal of the class and race identity of the person carrying a chicken or the person searching for undamaged goods in the ruins of the Palace Hotel or Chinatown. Although "society people" began looting Chinatown the day the fires waned and continued for weeks, at most they were warned to stop.[56]

Nor was it difficult to distinguish between "scrounging" and "looting" or "benign looting" and "illegal looting." The official formula for matching

**4.1.** Proper Victorians "sightseeing" or "looting" the ruins of Chinatown.
US National Archives

the vocabulary of social kinds to the varied people who were making their way through the ruins of San Francisco was, in the end, a straightforward accomplishment. "From available anecdotal evidence in newspaper stories and personal accounts," Fradkin concludes, "it appears that the shoot-to-kill order was carried out aggressively when the targets were poor people or ethnic minorities. One exception was the mistaken shooting of a member of the ruling citizens' committee. More words were devoted to this one incident than to all the others."[57]

Not surprisingly, the behavior of the military did not, at least officially, meet the conditions necessary to warrant the label looting. While some personal accounts explicitly refer to soldiers who were seen appropriating goods as "looters," suggesting that they were doing so illegally, the US War Department described this behavior using quite different nomenclature. Detailing the events of the day on April 19, the official military report refers to the troops "gathering" food from private warehouses, remaining bakeries, and factories not yet destroyed by the fires, purportedly to distribute to the homeless. Other accounts recall how hungry "cadets *scrounged* candy bars and cookies from shuttered grocery stores" and the military sanctioning "what might be termed *benign looting*" of stores about to be dynamited.[58]

There were also cases of "necessary medical looting" by "parties with official badges, Red Cross armbands, uniformed officers, and official-looking faces and dress."[59] One eyewitness recalled the actions of an "ex–Salvation Army woman":

> When we arrived at a drug-store . . . she jumped out, and, finding the door locked, seized a chair and raising it above her head smashed the glass doors in and helped herself to hot-water bags, bandages, and anything which would be useful in an emergency hospital.[60]

Neither a solider nor "an ex–Salvation Army woman" matched the characteristics of that social kind "the looter."

In summarizing the ruling-class response to the San Francisco earthquake and fires on the one hundredth anniversary of the disaster, Kevin Starr, professor of history at the University of Southern California, concludes—with a touch of exaggeration—that in their intemperate actions, "the oligarchy of San Francisco" exposed an "inner evil subconscious frightened of its underclass" and determined to restore the "high tide of its identity."[61]

## A CENTURY LATER

Let's fast-forward to the mayhem of a disaster at the dawn of the twenty-first century. What do we make of a simple distinction between one who "buys" and one who "gets," or, the more inflammatory, one who "finds" and one who "loots"?

Eerily similar to San Francisco, the first order of state business in response to the flooding of New Orleans was to protect property. In the first several days of the disaster, emergency responders, including the National Guard and regular army troops, were ordered "to concentrate on arresting looters and deterring crime."[62] Corporeal works of mercy, feeding the hungry and burying the dead, could wait.

In addition to the official military presence in the city, and mirroring the paramilitary mobilization in San Francisco a century earlier, approximately 150 mercenaries from the notorious Blackwater USA arrived in the city. It is telling that Blackwater USA was patrolling the streets of the city before the arrival of the Red Cross. Under contract with the Department of Homeland Security, their official duties were securing neighborhoods and confronting criminals. Andrew Bynum writes, "Arriving in unmarked cars, combat attire, and fully equipped with fully automatic weapons, the troops fanned out amidst purported and expected chaos, seeking to restore order and security to the city at large."[63]

Fourteen or so days after the city flooded, Jeremy Scahill notes, "The number of private security companies registered in Louisiana jumped from one-hundred and eighty-five to two-hundred and thirty-five. Some, like Blackwater, are under federal contract." Others were hired by New Orleans's elite to guard their private estates. Chris Kyle—the man celebrated in the movie *American Sniper* for his exploits in Iraq—"bragged about traveling into New Orleans in the days after Hurricane Katrina with a fellow sniper and shooting at least 30 looters from the roof of the Superdome." There is no evidence anything of the sort ever occurred.[64]

The lifesaving operations undertaken were more or less left up to those who could and were willing to help others. Jeffrey Jackson describes "the self-styled 'Robin-Hood Looters' . . . who rescued stranded victims and searched for food and supplies among the abandoned homes, giving it to those in need."[65] But self-styling, creating your own social kind, was the exception to the rule. It was others doing the naming. Take Sara Roberts, who made it her mission to lend a needed hand.

Sara lived some distance from New Orleans. Once she reached the city, she did what she could. Reflecting on her experiences ten years later, she remembers seeing two men almost floating out of a Walgreens drugstore, their heads just visible above the foul brown water. The drugstore sat next to a high-rise apartment complex where dozens of elderly men and women were trapped by the high water. "And I was just so frustrated and so angry," Sara recalls, "that these people had looted and had broken in with all this tragedy around. . . . I later found those guys had broken into the Walgreens to *buy*, I mean to *get* medical supplies for those elderly people."[66] Sara unwittingly captures the unsteady vernacular in play to make sense of just what people were doing to help themselves and one another to live another day.

If Sara Roberts expresses a moment of thoughtfulness as she exchanges the word *buy* for *get*, what sense should we make of media coverage that parses what appear to be the identical efforts to survive the flooded city of New Orleans into a young man who is "looting" and a young couple who are "finding"?

In what is now an iconic image, two photos and text fragments from two separate publications show a young black man wading or floating his way to, we assume, a safe location. Aside this photo the Associated Press attached this text: "A young man walks through chest deep flood water after *looting* a grocery store."

**4.2.** Making up "the looters." Photo by Dave Martin, AP Images

The international Agence France-Presse writes a markedly different description aside a photo of two young white people who are also attempting to make their way to higher ground: "Two residents wade through chest deep water after *finding* bread and soda from a local grocery store."[67]

Why would images of black and white people engaged in seemingly analogous acts mark one act criminal and the other legal? Why is one an act of "looting" and the other an act of "finding"? Akin to the floating signifier, *looting*, it appears, becomes a word in search of a referent, granting those with the means to deploy it—politicians, soldiers, police officers, journalists—the power to make up their own kinds of people. I myself experienced this sorting into kinds.

Days after the floodwaters had subsided, I was in the city with several colleagues, walking the streets with cameras and notebooks. While I was taking a photo of a house that had literally floated off its cinder-block foundation, collapsing next to the precast cement steps that once welcomed family and visitors alike, a military vehicle drove by. When I turned to look at the Humvee-like truck, a solider waved at me. I waved back. Later, as I walked down the street, I passed this young man in his truck. He asked me if I was a "news reporter." I said no and explained that I worked at the University of North Carolina at Greensboro. "I have an aunt who lives in Asheboro" (a town near Greensboro), he replied. We both agreed that all about us was a horrific mess, and with that we went our separate ways. From this

**4.3.** Making up "the finders." Photo by Chris Graythen, AFP

**4.4.** While taking this photo I encountered a soldier in a military vehicle and from his vantage point, I might have been a "news reporter"; I was clearly not—as he saw me—"a looter." Photo by author, September 2005

soldier's vantage point, I might have been a "news reporter"; I was clearly not—as he saw me—"a looter."

"Looters," "finders," "buyers," "getters," "news reporters" are among the seemingly countless and always evolving panoply of names we deploy to identify this or that kind of person and act toward them on the basis of the names we assign them. Hacking found kind making both necessary and risky. It is highly likely, he warns, that the "objective identification of instances of the kind of person in question misses what is important about it, and deludes us into thinking that a straight and simple road is to hand."[68]

This simplistic style of reasoning was on full display in one of the more egregious efforts to keep the chaotic urban disarray that was New Orleans from spilling into adjacent geographies. Fearing a tide of displaced people making their way from the predominantly black Lower Ninth Ward to safer environs, citizens in neighboring, predominantly white, St. Bernard Parish piled cars, vans, and trucks atop one another to create both a symbolic and a physical boundary between themselves and "Lower Nine" residents.

In a more aggressive and potentially lethal incident, the police force in Gretna, a town across the Mississippi River, just south of the city, feared the contagion of what appeared to be nothing short of mass chaos. Seeing predominantly poor black evacuees' attempts to enter their properly arranged suburban enclave as a threat to order, the police fired shots over their heads, forcing them back across the Highway 90 bridge to the flooded city.

"According to paramedics" who witnessed this scene, at one point the Gretna police crossed "the bridge into New Orleans, attacking and disbursing flood evacuees awaiting evacuation in a makeshift camp on the median of the Pontchartrain Expressway—seizing" what they assumed to be "their 'looted' food and water."[69] Three years before the terrorist attack on September 11, 2001, William Rehnquist, chief justice of the US Supreme Court, quoted Cicero's potent words: "Inter arma silent leges" (In time of war the law is silent).[70] And so it was on the streets of New Orleans in 2005.

Framing the hunt for food and water as looting was a common practice in this protracted moment of confusion. In *New York Times* reporter Kate Zernike's article "The Hunt for Life's Necessities," the scene is certainly tense, anxiety producing, and frustrating for people waiting to obtain food, water, and gas. Zernike describes unarmed, desperate people waiting in long, slow-moving lines. Some could not wait and tried to get to the front of the lines. Others simply rushed into stores and rushed out with "cases of water, soda and cigarettes." These others were, according to Zernike, ex-

**4.5.** Boundary between St. Bernard and Orleans parishes.
Photo by author, September 2005

ceptions to the rule.[71] But how are we to interpret these acts? Is this wanton stealing? Or are these acts of desperation, heaves of the will to live another day? Italian law has a fundamentally different answer to this question.

Italian legal doctrine includes a curious phrase, "Ad impossibilia nemo tenetur" (No one is expected to do the impossible). This doctrine was recently invoked to conclude that a homeless man in Rome who stole €4.07, or about $4.70, worth of cheese was not guilty of the crime of theft. A former member of the Italian Supreme Court noted, "If you can't eat because you have absolutely no money, and cannot sustain yourself without taking something you don't own . . . Italian criminal law justifies this theft."[72] This is a reminder that some market societies—particularly those with histories that far predate the market—might, now and then, put the interests of human survival ahead of the interests of capital. Back to our story.

## "LOOTING" AND RECLAIMING THE MARKET SOCIETY

Consider the question "Can't you see what's before you?" For those of us accustomed to thinking deeply—if not always clearly—about things, this sort of question begs a thoughtful discussion. When I look out at the world, what is apparent? What is obvious? This apparent world is not something that exists outside reality—far from it. It is the world as it appears to anyone who seeks to survive in it, and to achieve that survival arranges it in this way or that way according to her own purposes.[73]

Making up "the looter" in both San Francisco and New Orleans points to the inherent clash between two apparent worlds. One world is inhabited by those unfortunates who find themselves seized by the mayhem. For them, every ordinary fact of life seems to have gone astray. In arranging this world in order to endure and make it out alive, they might well be thinking something like the following: "If I'm to survive this crazy danger, I may need a good deal of human togetherness, plus food, water, bandages, medications, and more that if I cannot buy, I must take."[74] Here, in this mutable, unpredictable milieu, chance encounters with wholly different kinds of people may become the occasions for forging uncustomary social ties, warm circles, that extend to each an extra hand or two in their struggle to live another day. Life in an urban disaster does not promote that chilly, civil indifference that Simmel calls the "blasé attitude."[75]

But to those with an investment in Simmel's disciplined mien of unconcern who embody the "complete money economy," wherein capital is the shared language and "money takes the place of all the manifoldness of things," it is obvious that this emergent life of mutual aid cannot continue.[76] What is apparent to them is what is obviously missing from this jumbled, seemingly formless scene. Looking about them, they do not see punctuality, exactness, and the sacred respect for private property; they do not see, they can't identify, those personal attitudes, practices, styles of life, both public and private, that eschew the instinctive and irrational, all essential pieces of a society organized around the regulated exchange of goods and services in the pursuit of profit.

Simply put, this antinomian moment cannot continue. The warm human circle must be broken. Making up "the looter" is a rather matter-of-fact way to begin the process of returning from that unhinged phase of camaraderie—that innocent immersion in human togetherness—that ignores social divides, leaving each feeling deeply for the other, to return to, recalling Ray Stannard Baker, "modern business conditions."[77] If disaster becomes an occasion for violence, it is safe to say that it is more the barbarous efforts of those dedicated to a return to market life than the alleged criminality of the ordinary citizen.

If these two great derangements created spaces wherein categorical differences were suspended and a corporeal communality prevailed, fashioning "the looter" with an Asian, working-class, or black face was the first step in re-sorting the populations of both cities. This re-sorting would continue in the administration of disaster relief that deployed its own versions of us versus them in the somewhat tortured vocabularies of worthiness.

# REBOOTING INEQUALITY, THE ROAD TO RECOVERY

# DISASTER RELIEF
## PARSING THE VERNACULARS OF WORTHINESS

*Inequalities are nested inside the discourse of civil society.*

JEFFREY ALEXANDER, "THE MEANINGFUL CONSTRUCTION
OF INEQUALITY AND THE STRUGGLE AGAINST IT: A 'STRONG
PROGRAM' APPROACH TO HOW SOCIAL BOUNDARIES CHANGE"

If disaster acts to disorder the market hierarchy that organizes urban life, "the looter" is the scapegoat, the victim sacrificed to launch the rescue of order. Crime, after all, not mutual aid—Durkheim knew—is essential to the normal arrangement of things. In this chapter we look in some detail at what occurs both during and long after the looting panic subsides: the bureaucratic, methodical work of distributing disaster relief.

The onset of recovery efforts following the destruction of a major urban center is often preceded by a prophetic declaration of renewal and rebirth, typically uttered by someone of considerable public stature. Recalling the spirit of cooperation and the warm human circles that emerged in the great derangement, this person of note publicly celebrates both the tenacity of the human spirit and the new chance, wrought by utter ruin, to make things better for all; so it was in both San Francisco and New Orleans.

In his strident panegyric on San Francisco and its people, the wealthy and well-connected James Phelan pledged days after the last fires were put out:

San Francisco has always enjoyed the love and affection of her own people, and they are more closely wedded to her now in affliction. Suffering has always been a source of patriotism. . . . Even after devastating wars, at home and abroad, it is a matter of common observation that the energies of the people are stimulated, and great prosperity ensues. . . . Better work, unhampered by tradition, shall mark the new era in San Francisco's life.

Individuals may suffer, but the community is bound together by new and endearing ties. . . . San Francisco is a natural and necessary city, the affection of the people for it is unshaken, and their courage is equal to their love—a factor in its rebuilding that cannot be overestimated.[1]

Phelan's romantic tribute to human resilience, the promise of "great prosperity," and the "endearing ties" among survivors would fast become an exercise in the reordering of class and race differences temporarily disordered by the earthquake and fires.

President George W. Bush, in his turn, sounded his own paean to New Orleans and its people. Standing in Jackson Square, with the St. Louis Cathedral in the background, he told survivors and the nation at large:

> Let us restore all that we have cherished from yesterday, and let us rise above the legacy of inequality. . . . When the streets are rebuilt, there should be many new businesses, including minority-owned businesses, along those streets. When the houses are rebuilt, more families should own, not rent, those houses. . . . And all who question the future of the Crescent City need to know: There is no way to imagine America without New Orleans, and this great city will rise again.[2]

Look closely at the president's words; you'll notice a telling confusion. His opening gambit, "Let us restore all that we have cherished from yesterday, and let us rise above the legacy of inequality," confounds the wish to "restore all" of the past and at the same time lift the city above its "legacy of inequality." Perhaps this confusion helps account, in part, for why the promise of a new urban equality, replete with more "minority-owned businesses" and more families who own rather than rent their houses, could not shoulder the burden of federal, state, and private-sector recovery efforts that would parse out relief based on the algorithm of market inequality. Disaster recovery in New Orleans, like that occurring a century earlier in San Francisco, required the restoration of social inequality temporarily suspended in the wake of destruction.

Though he lacks the historical gravitas of a Phelan or a Bush, economist Jack Hirshleifer is more prescient than either in his understanding of recovery from disaster in a market-oriented society. He writes, plainly: "Historical experience suggests that recovery will hinge on the ability of government to maintain or restore property rights together with a market system that will support the economic division of labor."[3]

The administration of disaster relief following the earthquake and fire in 1906 San Francisco and the flooding of New Orleans in 2005 adheres in some fashion or another to Hirshleifer's prescription for successful disaster recovery. While the two relief efforts were administered in quite different ways, as we will see, both relied on what we might call a formula of *market worthiness* to determine who received what and why. This formula is on display in the following two vignettes.

## THE CASE OF MR. SANTOS, SAN FRANCISCO, OCTOBER 1906

Mr. Santos was a cabinet maker. His one year old child was sick. His wife suffered from "pelvis troubles." The Associated Charities of San Francisco [ACSF] sent him "to work as a laborer at the United Railroads, earning $1.50 for a nine-hour day, then to the California Canneries, to earn $1.50 for a ten-hour day." Mr. Santos himself "was ill and unable to work steadily." He did not earn enough "to pay the rent on a tenement considered in 'unspeakable condition.' . . . Mr. Santos kept coming down with illnesses," his caseworker noted, "he should not work but he will have to. . . ." The caseworker recommended "continuation of emergency aid until the 'man is able to work for his $1.50 a day.'"[4]

## THE CASE OF MS. SIMPSON, NEW ORLEANS, SEPTEMBER 2005

The week after the hurricane struck, Ms. Simpson used a computer to apply to FEMA for housing assistance. A few weeks later she received a packet of information in the mail which contained references to documents that were supposed to be included in the packet, but were not. The package contained a copy of her application, which had numerous errors. Weeks later she was told she must establish proof of her pre-disaster residency. But she had lost all documents which could verify her place of residence. She asked FEMA to send an inspector to her prior residence where some of her belongings were still stored. FEMA refused. In November she received a call from FEMA and was told once again to submit proof of residency, proof she did not possess. Ms. Simpson has been essentially homeless, drifting night by night to different persons' homes without belongings or funds to afford housing or other necessities.[5]

What ties together these two rather different accounts of the trials and tribulations of applying for disaster relief is a common plot. In each story, class and its kindred category race—Mr. Santos immigrated from Mexico, and Ms. Simpson is African American—crucially shape both relief claimants' abilities to successfully portray themselves as deserving victims and secure an adequate measure of assistance. Seen through the eyes of the victims of disaster, theirs is a tragedy of circumstance. Viewed from the actions of those who administer disaster relief, if there is a tragedy, it has more to do with character than circumstance. Mr. Santos must find a way "to work for his $1.50 a day." Ms. Simpson should, but does not, possess the proper "documents which could verify her place of residence."[6] The difference between circumstance and character in sorting out the complexities of disaster relief has a long history.

## RUIN AND THE BLAMELESS VICTIM IN A MARKET SOCIETY: A BRIEF EXCURSUS

In the summer of 1790, the second session of the First US Congress considered two petitions for damage relief submitted by private individuals. The legislators voted to grant both petitioners' requests. It might reasonably be said that on June 14, 1790, the role of the federal government in disaster relief commenced with "An Act for the Relief of Thomas Jenkins and Company."

> *Be it enacted, &c.,* That the duties, amounting to one hundred and sixty-seven dollars and fifty cents, be remitted on a parcel of hemp, duck, ticklenburg, and molasses, the property of Thomas Jenkins and Company, merchants, of the city of Hudson, in the State of New York, which were lost by fire in the brig Minerva, on her passage from New York to the city of Hudson, her port of delivery.[7]

Not two months later, on August 4, 1790, Congress passed "An Act for the Relief of John Stewart and John Davidson."

> *Be it enacted, &c.,* That so much of the duties accruing on eighteen hundred bushels of salt, imported in the ship Mercury, into the port of Annapolis, in the state of Maryland, some time in the month of April last, on account of Messieurs John Stewart and John Davidson, as relates to thirteen hundred and twenty-five bushels thereof, which were casually destroyed by a flood on the night of the same day on which the said salt was landed and stored, shall be, and the same are hereby remitted.[8]

The first two successful petitions for federal disaster relief were granted to businessmen who had lost commodities in a fire and a flood, respectively, and each could document his specific losses. They were, in Vincanne Adams's potent words, "market visible."[9]

The tie between federal disaster aid and market visibility expanded four years later. In 1794 Congress initiated a new pattern of disaster relief by appropriating moneys for a specific class of persons, in this case all US citizens who could document damaged or destroyed property during the Revolutionary War. In 1796, during a severe drought, Congress granted a decrease in distillery duties for those who experienced the "destruction of fruit." Between 1802 and 1947, three years before Congress passed its first Disaster Relief Act, it granted relief to 128 petitioners.[10]

From providing relief to victims of an arsenal explosion in the District of Columbia to assisting people struck by yellow fever and appropriating funds to offset the loss of valuable crop seed eaten by hordes of grasshoppers, a common narrative thread ties together the disparate claims for relief beginning in the late eighteenth century and continuing down to the present day. The story can be summed up this way: the victims of disaster are unwitting innocents, prey to chance events and circumstances that inflict losses to their market—and perhaps physical—well-being. Having satisfied this criterion of a disaster victim, the government can legitimately provide a measure of relief in the form of dollars and cents. Blameless suffering in a fate-filled world, in short, begs state compassion, provided the suffering might result in a loss of class standing.[11]

The phrase "blameless suffering" is an admittedly raw description of presumably all who, first, are victims of untoward events or random accidents and, second, suffer some loss of property, but it is arguably fitting in this context. Unlike the sightless Lady Justice, promising fairness to all, regardless of rank and kind, the state administers disaster relief through a finely honed lens. A continuum, beginning with who is blameless and deserving, at one end, and who is something else altogether, at the other end, is used to determine what sorts of persons receive what kind and amount of benefit, if they receive anything at all.

The taxonomic gaze of the state was on display in April 1874 when the Mississippi flooded the southern delta. Wm. J. McCulloh, Esq., a former US surveyor general for Louisiana, estimated that "the area submerged by crevasses, and overflow by high and back water, to be in *Louisiana* about 8,065,000 acres, or 12,600 square miles."[12] Low-lying New Orleans suffered severe flood damage.

In his plea to Congress to legislate disaster funding for his state, Louisiana's Fifth District Republican representative Frank Morey plainly states: "This distress is confined to no class of people. The colored laborer and the tenderly nurtured southern lady are alike suffering." Though Representative Morey made this legislative body aware that the flooding affected the poor and the propertied classes alike, the petition Congress authorized states unequivocally that those who owned little or no property, the "ordinary poor" of Louisiana, would receive no relief. Substantial assistance, however, was provided for those whose "homes have been swept from under them [and are now] without means to obtain a single meal."[13]

To be eligible for assistance, in other words, a person must have suffered a measure of downward mobility by an act of God or fate. In sum, though this catastrophic event struck a blow to the well-being of most everyone alike in this massive flood, from the very beginning those who administered relief deployed a species of casuistic reasoning to discriminate between categories of people more or less deserving of aid.

The moral reasoning informing the federal implementation of disaster relief was neither an isolated nor a discrete practice unique to the government's response to catastrophe. On the contrary, it was embedded in the deep grammar of nineteenth-century American life. It is echoed, for example, in several questions found in the 1867 *Aetna Guide to Fire Insurance Handbook*. To wit:

"What is the general character borne by the applicant?" "Are his habits good?" "Is he an old resident, or a stranger and an itinerant?" "Is he peaceable or quarrelsome, popular or disliked?" "Is he pecuniarily an embarrassment?"[14]

The late-nineteenth-century insurance industry was organized around more than actuarial predictions. Aside the numerical calculations trusted to forecast losses, there was a prescribed moral calculation, summed up in the *Aetna Guide*. In Aetna's deploying a moral continuum quite similar to that used in administering disaster relief, people were sorted into risk categories of high, medium, and low, based, in part, on their respective moral profiles.[15] Pecuniary embarrassments suffered the consequences.

More than faintly discernible in both the *Aetna Guide* and the proclivity of Congress to grant disaster assistance exclusively to the propertied classes are the virtues Max Weber identified as essential to the making of modern capitalism. Weber's ideal man in a market society has a spotless moral character: he is "sober, conscientious, and unusually industrious"; he clings to "work as to a life purpose willed by God."

It is no accident that the quintessential American, Benjamin Franklin, modeled Weber's ideal market-centered man. Franklin himself identified with a kindred fellow found in the book of Proverbs: "Seest thou a man diligent in his business? He shall stand before kings" (22:29).[16] Such a gentleman is worthy, laudable, someone deserving of assistance in those freakish moments when fate intervenes to displace and destroy.

Literary fiction also fashioned its versions of the ideal man in a market society. With their defining moniker the "Gilded Age," Mark Twain and Charles Dudley Warner captured the confluence of class, capital, corruption, and moral worth that defined late-nineteenth-century America.[17] Twain and Warner's humorous story of life lived in parvenu affluence found its corollary in contemporary hope-filled stories of rags to riches.

In *Ragged Dick*, Horatio Alger Jr. created a modern champion. Alger's hero is a young, penniless boy whose fortunes change dramatically when a stroke of luck brings him face-to-face with a businessman who starts him on a journey toward what we would call today upper-middle-class respectability. The book's cover sports an image of a young man who accents the stereotypical Victorian physiognomy of the moneyed class, slightly upturned nose, sharp, bold features, hair cut just so.[18] *Ragged Dick* is a coming-of-age tale, a modern-world bildungsroman that promises success to those white men who work hard, practice self-reliance, and evidence a rock-solid moral character, exemplars of the "American Dream."

By 1906 a mashup of administrative, business, and cultural texts formed a potent national ethos, one centered on the primacy of the individual as the agent of his or her own destiny. From the reckoning of moral worth informing federal decisions around disaster relief to the virtuous character calculations of insurance companies and to the honorably upright and hardworking, hardscrabble hero shaped by a popular genre of fiction, a potent assumption that it was one's personal qualities that made him or her this or that kind of person took deep root. These texts worked in tandem with a persistent Protestant message, fueled by the Second and Third Great Awakenings, that encouraged an expressive Christianity coupled with a disciplined life of sobriety, family, and hard work.[19]

The archetypal symbol of the sober, decent man who labors as if it was life's purpose would challenge the "justice for all" promise of America's famous pledge.[20] The romantic conviction that the universal criterion of citizenship was the sole basis for determining who was entitled to the benefits of life in the compassionate state could not survive the blunt tool of a case-based reasoning that sorted people into social kinds. In spite of the Fourteenth Amendment, in early-twentieth-century America and again a century later citizenship was no guarantee that a person would receive his or her fair share of disaster relief.

While federal disaster relief provisions and aid distributions had commenced in the late eighteenth century, a formal, codified state response was not put into place until 1950, with the passage of the Disaster Relief Act.[21] Before passage of the act, towns, cities, and regions facing the overwhelming task of aiding victims and rebuilding had to cobble together material and financial assistance from a broad spectrum of nonfederal resources, including other towns and cities, states and nations, charitable citizens, and the occasional philanthropist to fix all that was broken. Moreover, the actual administration of relief was organized and managed at the local level. Aid was collected, combined, and dispersed by local committees. Relief was administered in a more or less face-to-face manner. Personal accounts correlated with observations by caseworkers were used to determine eligibility. And so it was in San Francisco on that fateful day in April.

## SAN FRANCISCO 1906:
## WHO IS ABLE-BODIED? WHO IS WORTHY?

If there is any reason to append the word *lucky* to the city of San Francisco on that horrific day in April 1906, it might be that Congress just happened to be in session. At the turn of the twentieth century, the legislature, not the chief executive, determined whether disaster relief would be granted. If Congress was adjourned, absent a call for a special session, relief would have to wait. Congress approved $2.5 million in funding to aid the stricken city, roughly the equivalent of $62 million in 2016 dollars.[22] This money was appropriated to support the military in its recovery work. More money would follow.

Andrew Carnegie contributed $100,000, by all accounts out of a philanthropic spirit of compassion.[23] Two other wealthy men donated substantial sums, but more than a charitable spirit was behind their acts of largesse. William Randolph Hearst approached the disaster that befell the city as an opportunity to enhance his public image and the reputation of his newspaper the *San Francisco Examiner*.[24] In one arguably egregious act, he funded a makeshift maternity hospital for displaced women. A woman was given $100 for the birth of a child, a little more than $2,500 in 2016 dollars, while her husband was assisted in finding employment.[25] The *Examiner* did not report on the birth of the first four babies, all girls. But upon the birth

**5.1.** San Francisco, 1906, after the last fires were extinguished. US National Archives

of the first baby boy, the headline read: "W. R. Hearst Eby Is Name Given to Little Lad."[26]

If Hearst was motivated to provide disaster relief as a vehicle for burnishing his public reputation as a civic-minded capitalist, John D. Rockefeller's contribution to the relief effort sprang from a somewhat different motive. San Francisco's catastrophe was Rockefeller's opportunity to salvage a bit of his reputation as the owner, in the words of the *Literary Digest*, of "this black thing from hell, this standard oil."[27] Reviled for his predatory business practices, John D. sought a measure of redemption, contributing upwards of $200,000 to assist the stricken city, the equivalent of roughly $5.5 million in 2016 purchasing power.[28] One hundred thousand dollars was handed out by Rockefeller's employees on the streets of San Francisco. For Rockefeller's generosity, Hearst's paper printed in bold headlines:

ROCKEFELLER SENDS AID

New York, April 19—John D. Rockefeller today authorized his agents in San Francisco to expend $100,000 for the relief of the homeless and destitute of that city.[29]

A guilty conscience is often a powerful motivator.

The wounded city received somewhere between $9 and $9.5 million from cities, states, countries such as Canada and England, and private individuals.[30] To put this in a contemporary perspective, that $9 to $9.5 million is worth between $180 and $190 million today.[31] Two questions quickly arose: Who would administer this considerable sum of relief funding? And how, specifically, would it be administered?

## "WE PAY THEM TO DISCRIMINATE"

San Francisco's mayor, Eugene Schmitz, quickly assembled a committee of businessmen, civic leaders, newspaper reporters, and politicians to organize the administration of the funds. Schmitz, however, was already under scrutiny in a federal graft investigation; he seemed an unlikely choice to lead the relief effort.[32] James Phelan, a banker and respected businessman whom we heard from earlier, saw an opportunity to reenter the public realm after losing a mayoral race to Schmitz; he convinced the mayor to appoint him head of the committee. Phelan and his Committee of 50, a misnomer as there were more than one hundred members, represented progressive, pro-business interests.[33]

William F. Humphrey, president of the Tidewater Oil Company and head of San Francisco's prestigious Olympic Club, recalled a market version of the warm human circle that emerges in the immediate wake of destruction. Humphrey thought he was witness to a "wonderful fraternalism" materializing among San Francisco's business class: "Old rivalries were forgotten; old jealousies disappeared, and even bitter enmities of long standing were wiped out. Everyone was in the same boat, so we forgot all else and pulled as a team."[34] The immediate need to rescue the market drove this newfound fraternalism. The overriding authority of the Committee of 50 ensured that San Francisco's recovery would likely mirror the city's pre-disaster social hierarchies.[35]

As San Francisco's elite worked to organize themselves and fires raged about the city, President Theodore Roosevelt sent a public message, urging people around the country to wire money to the Red Cross. Roosevelt's initiative "established the policy, ever since followed by succeeding presidents, of giving to the [Red Cross] Society the moral support and guarantee of the highest official of our Government."[36] While Roosevelt's plea made its way across the nation, Professor Edward T. Devine was making his way from New York to the stricken city. An expert in social welfare, founder of the journal *Charities and the Commons*, and professor of social economy at Columbia University, Devine was appointed by Roosevelt to lead the Red Cross response to the catastrophe.

James Phelan and his Committee of 50 and Edward T. Devine and the Red Cross would soon collaborate, creating a single administrative unit. They settled on the somewhat awkward moniker the SF Relief and RC Funds. That the actions of the SFRRCF were informed by a style of reasoning that sought to sort disaster survivors into categories based on their perceived worth as citizens of a market society is succinctly captured in Professor Devine's terse description of the relief workers' task: "We pay them to discriminate."[37]

That stark statement reflected the intent of the SFRRCF's mission: to catalog survivors according to their perceived moral worth and reward those who were deemed worthy. Such a sorting and rewarding process would, it was thought, ensure that funds were not wasted on the immoral and unreliable. In the spirit of moral reform, perhaps some Red Cross relief workers hoped that at least a few among the dissolute would take notice of how disaster aid was distributed and change the course of their lives, but this was not the primary goal of the organization's relief effort.

For James Phelan and his Committee of 50, Devine's casuist reasoning made good business sense. Disaster recovery, from their vantage point, was synonymous with a return to pre-disaster industry and commerce. The quicker business practices were revived, the quicker all San Franciscans would recover, so they reasoned.[38] For Phelan and his committee, the immediate dilemma was to secure the work of laborers, at a cheap wage, to rebuild the physical infrastructure of the city. Food appeared to be one incentive.

Phelan proposed the draconian idea of distributing food exclusively to women and children, forcing men "to seek work, of which there is much of rough character in cleaning up the city and preparing for reconstruction."[39] "Fortunately," Marian Moser Jones writes, "Phelan's proposition failed to gain traction and many able-bodied men remained on food relief." The class politics of food is further illustrated on a broader policy level with the decision by the Red Cross, just days after the last fire was extinguished, to sell food rather than give it away. The aim was to encourage personal discipline among survivors and, it was hoped, encourage both men and women to return to work posthaste. Wage earners, in the words of the Red Cross, would help ensure a "swift return to normal capitalistic practices."[40]

To help identify a sober, stable pool of labor, a nomenclature was created, based on an unalloyed faith in the democratic ideal of the individual, the citizen, who used his or her freedom to fashion a secure place in a market-oriented society. Despite a progressive emphasis on environmental versus biological causes of human misery, it was the yardstick of morality that served to measure the good citizen.[41] Labor was sorted into a classification that included the "dangerous classes," the "unworthy" or "undeserving poor," and the "worthy poor." The poor deemed "worthy" worked in factories, in construction, and in semiskilled trades like tailoring, earning somewhere between $240 and $435 annually.[42]

Armed with a taxonomy derived from a democratic belief in the primacy of the citizen and the utility of the moral measure, the first task for relief workers in San Francisco was to match all those individuals and families who were not middle and upper class with the social kinds "working poor," "unworthy poor," "dangerous classes," and a fourth group, "the Chinese."[43] More visible than the poor and working class, and already branded as looters or potential looters, "the Chinese" were easier to resegregate. In the end, however, as we will see in the next chapter, this group ultimately frustrated San Francisco's business class, which sought to appropriate their neighborhoods and move them to a less desirable location on the outskirts of the city.

Social agencies responsible for relief quickly concocted an impromptu "worthiness" scale to determine who would receive aid, what kind, and how much.[44] In fact, several worthiness measures were deployed at various times to make these determinations, among them the simple distinctions between "able-bodied" and "disabled" and "moral" and "immoral."[45] Indicators of immorality included "laziness," "vicious habits," "drunkenness," and "unemployment."[46] A third measure of worthiness allowed that most disaster survivors were at least nominally dependent and sorted them into three categories:

1. Dependency because of abnormal conditions.
2. Dependency because disaster had converted semi-dependency into complete dependency.
3. Dependency because character and circumstance, irrespective of abnormal conditions, induced dependency.[47]

Category 1, those people whose dependency was created by the earthquake and fire, were generally understood as the middle and upper classes.

Category 2, those people who lived marginally before the disaster, consti-tuted the working poor. And category 3 corresponded with the group gener-ally called the "unworthy poor."[48] In the absence of detailed documentation on the status of the working and nonworking classes, identifying where a person was located along the worthiness continuum required observation.

## THE VISITOR'S GAZE

The nomenclature of disparity, sorting the city back into market-directed social kinds, was referred to as "rehabilitation," a term rooted in late-nineteenth-century social reform movements. Determining a person's or family's eligibility for rehabilitation assistance, to match them with a cate-gory of worthiness, required a visual inspection. The *San Francisco Relief Survey* report to the Russell Sage Foundation notes, "The Committee . . . took the sensible ground that as far as possible there should be investiga-tion of each applicant."[49]

Applicants for relief, in other words, were subject to what we might call the visitor's gaze. These visitors, "a large untried force," varied in eth-nicity and biography, but all were middle to upper middle class, represent-ing the respectable, the model of worthy. One group assigned to a specific neighborhood included a physician who had previous experience "working among poorer people," "a trained nurse," and seven Stanford University stu-dents, among others.

Visitors were asked to describe the "physical condition and previous oc-cupation of the breadwinner" and to sum up the person's or family's "losses and its present resources." What, the visitor would ask, is a person's or family's "former or present relation to its church, its lodge, its employers?" Did the individual or family have "a plan for recovery?" What was the visi-tor's "estimate of this plan?"[50]

Not infrequently, visitors would call on a person or family once or more a week for a period of time.

> A visitor called on each family in her charge at least once a week. On a stated day each week she sent a report . . . which stated whether the help . . . should be continued one week longer, with an estimate of how long relief would be necessary.[51]

The emphasis was on surveillance.

A visitor's report was made on a "record card." This "graphic presentation . . . gave a picture" of where the individual or family was located on the worthiness scale.[52] A visual inspection recorded on a card determined whether relief was offered and, if so, what kind. A note in the Red Cross report neatly summarizes the indifferent manner in which such determinations were made:

> An old mother and son had lost furniture and personal effects estimated as worth $400. They applied for rehabilitation and a sewing machine. . . . As the son was unmarried, able-bodied and under forty years of age, the grant was refused on the ground that he should support his mother.[53]

Labor was needed to recover the city's manufacturing base. Roughly three hundred thousand people evacuated San Francisco to escape the fires.[54] There was, as a result, a severe shortage of workingmen that could well impede the timely rebuilding of the city's commercial sector. If disaster relief was perceived as an impediment to securing that labor, one means of getting a man to work was to deny him and his family financial assistance. By October, five months after the earthquake and fires, "the policy had been adopted of making no further grants to able-bodied single people or to heads of families capable of supporting those dependent upon them."[55] The keen interest among San Francisco's propertied class was a timely return to "modern business conditions."[56]

Drawing from the public records of social service agencies providing relief to victims, Marie Bolton describes the class-based travails of one workingman. Mr. Vincenti, a laborer with eight children, found work shortly after the fires were put out. A freak accident crushed his hand, and Vincenti found himself unemployed. The Associated Charities of San Francisco stepped in to help the Vincenti family. But help was contingent on Vincenti finding new work. He did, but at a far lower wage. With Vincenti working, the family was now eligible for relief, but acquiring services required a constant stream of visits to social service offices to ask for the simplest of needs. At one point, the Associated Charities of San Francisco refused to provide his children with shoes and clothing, claiming that Vincenti could find a better-paying job.

By way of contrast, Bolton notes:

> [When the] ACSF dealt with . . . stable upwardly mobile families, its response was completely different. The Agency defined these families as "worthy" and made them grants or loans designed to help them attain long-term stability and prosperity."[57]

To help achieve relief for worthy families beset by the miseries of the earthquake and fires, James Phelan and the ACSF initiated a "confidential case" assessment, a strategy that deliberately avoided the visitor's gaze.

## CONFIDENTIAL CASES AND CLASS BIAS

In a Finance Committee meeting held on May 6, Edward T. Devine made clear that in his opinion, when determining the amount and kind of disaster assistance, "Exceptional consideration should be given to professional men and women, and to persons who have been engaged in clerical positions."[58] The phrase *exceptional consideration* was translated into policy with the emergence of the "confidential case." By treating a request for disaster assistance as confidential, the ACSF could deploy a strategy that purposely sidestepped most of the onerous steps to qualify for aid.

To be considered a confidential case, not surprisingly, an applicant for relief must be a respected member of San Francisco's market-oriented society. "Confidential case procedure," Davis notes, "circumvented regulations by eliminating the required Associate Charities investigation."[59] For those identified as confidential, the required home visit and visual assessment of the applicant and his or her material setting were replaced by a revealing practice that went by the name "peer reviewed." A single relief official, a fellow member of middle- to upper-middle-class peerage, would simply approve the applicant for "hundreds of dollars in aid."

Confidential case records were kept in separate locations, apart from the more routine relief files. Perhaps aware of the potentially damaging evidence that might emerge should a fellow peer's financial dealings be made public, Phelan personally "submitted numerous confidential case applications to shield grant recipients from investigation." When all was said and done, those applicants whose cases were handled by Phelan were far more likely to receive substantially larger relief checks than those applicants who were forced to submit to the visitor's gaze.[60] While the algorithm of inequality was guiding the distribution of relief funds, it was also in play in the location and distribution of temporary housing for those who would be needed to help rebuild the city and work in the reopened industries.

## "DEMIXING" AND THE POLITICAL ECONOMY
## OF HOUSING SEGREGATION

If San Francisco was to recover its economic niche as a port, trade, and manufacturing center, it would require a socially stable and cooperative workforce. Far from disposable, labor was critical to rebuilding the city. By May 13, 1906, city relief organizations established more than one hundred separate housing camps with over eight thousand "refugee houses," wooden structures capable of accommodating several families.[61] One prominent goal of the housing movement was "demixing" San Francisco's citizens. An awkward term, *demixing* conveyed the need to resegregate the city per class and race distinctions.[62]

Together these dozens of camps reflected middle-class concerns with the recovery of proper civil conduct, spatial segregation, and, ultimately, economic viability. A quick distinction was made between unofficial and official camps. Unofficial camps were inhabited by people who either had been forced out of the city's authorized areas or knew beforehand that they would not be welcomed in these more "proper areas." A quick correspondence emerged between the unofficial camps and the unworthy poor and the official camps and the worthy poor.[63] While not an exact equivalence, the correlation between unofficial-unworthy, on the one hand, and official-worthy, on the other, was striking.[64]

The unofficial camps were considered both unsanitary and immoral, two terms intimately tied together in the Progressive Era. The official camps, on the other hand, were regulated, and something close to a martial order emerged, bringing in the words of one middle-class reformer "a certain calm and order to the working people."[65] Calm and order were enforced by both the military and the readiness of the relief agencies to withhold resources to those who did not comply with the rules of the camps.

Demixing, it appears, applied to more than temporary housing. A striking anecdote signaling the recovery of that civic skein of inequality rent in the wake of catastrophe is found in the *San Francisco Relief Survey*. Describing the "community kitchens" that sprang up throughout the stricken city, the report draws a distinction between "refugees" and those with some discretionary cash: "The disaster kitchens [were opened] to serve hot meals both to refugees and to persons able to pay for their food." The distinction between "refugees" and the cash-solvent was further drawn in this description: persons able to pay were afforded "the privilege of sitting at separate tables and of ordering a better quality of food than that furnished at the free tables."[66]

By 1908 most middle- and upper-class families were living as they had before the earthquake and fire.[67] That disaster relief and its cognate, inequality, were achieved was unwittingly described by a J. B. Deacon in his report to the Russell Sage Foundation, *Disasters and the American Red Cross in Disaster Relief*:

> Some critics have claimed that a more equitable distribution of the funds would have been to give the poorest class as much as to the more fortunate refugees, but a careful examination of the facts shows that the policy adopted was more feasible as well as more expedient. *Our task was to assist families to recover and to regain their accustomed social and economic status.*[68]

The city was rebuilt not in the spirit of mutual well-being but rather, as Ray Stannard Baker put it, "by an intense struggle of each man for immediate profit, little mercy for the weak, less thought of the ultimate public good."[69] In his wicked prose, Baker captures the modus operandi of disaster relief in a market society. His words would ring true a century later.

The decades between 1906 and 2005 witnessed seismic changes both in the role of the federal government in the lives of individual citizens and in the evolution of capital. Among the most profound and long-lasting rearrangement of the government in its relationship to the lives of individuals was the emergence of what Dauber calls the "sympathetic state."[70] The reach of government into the personal lives of citizens who needed certain kinds of assistance to make their lives livable had a lasting effect on the American character, one that continues into the twenty-first century. It also expanded considerably the bureaucratic reach of the government into the private sphere.

## PAVED WITH GOOD INTENTIONS, CONSTRUCTING THE FEDERAL MAZEWAY

The year 1906 was a historic period for federal activism. In addition to the proactive response of Theodore Roosevelt and Congress to the destruction of San Francisco, the federal government, Roosevelt in particular, was moved to action by the publication of Upton Sinclair's *The Jungle*. A fictional account of lives lived in Chicago's exploitative, hazardous, and dangerously filthy meatpacking yards, Sinclair's story provoked the president and Congress to action.[71] In the same year that Washington was assisting San Francisco, Congress passed the Federal Meat Inspection Act. The FMIA, in turn, mandated the creation of the US Department of Agriculture. Theodore Roosevelt's activism foreshadowed his fifth cousin's historic administration, highlighting the potential role of the state in overseeing the well-being and safety of its citizens.

At the turn of the twentieth century, however, progressive government was far more a personality- than a legislative-driven phenomenon. Roosevelt's compassionate response to the catastrophe that leveled San Francisco and his successful efforts to pass safe-food legislation were undertaken on his personal initiative. Without a codified federal response to disaster or a wider swath of laws designed to protect the public, the personal beliefs and values of presidents and the momentary composition of Congresses played an outsize role in shaping the state's response to public problems.

It wasn't until Franklin D. Roosevelt assumed the presidency and succeeded in persuading Congress to pass what would become the foundational legislation of the New Deal that an activist state was put on sound legal footing. This more compassionate state would concern itself with the well-being of citizens in unprecedented ways. No fewer than twenty-four laws were enacted, among them the Federal Emergency Relief Administration, the Indian Reorganization Act, and the Social Security Act. As a practical matter, this seismic change in the role of the federal government in meeting the needs of diverse populations required a massive and diffuse bureaucracy; importantly, it also came to rely increasingly on documentation. Paperwork—certificates, titles, licenses, registrations—became the rationale for including or excluding a person from the rights and privileges of citizenship.[72]

FDR would die in office. His vice president Harry Truman would codify the state's concern for victims of disaster by ensuring the passage of the Federal Disaster Relief Act (Public Law 81-875) in 1950. Public Law 81-875 authorized the president to provide federal assistance when a governor requested help and the president declared the event a major disaster. Between 1950 and 2005, Congress passed no fewer than six separate pieces of disaster legislation, among them the creation of the Federal Emergency Management Agency in 1979 and the Office of Homeland Security in 2002.[73]

In response to the terrorist attacks in 2001, Congress made the decision in 2002 to nest FEMA within the comprehensive OHS, creating a complex and hard-to-navigate bureaucracy. If the administration of disaster relief was a local accomplishment in 1906 San Francisco, by 2005 an extralocal and disaggregated organizational combine was in charge of assisting the victims of Hurricane Katrina. Agencies, caseworkers, advocates, courts, private contractors—some accessible only by phone, mail, or computer—would all play key parts in allocating relief. As the geographic and bureaucratic maze of disaster aid evolved through the decades of the twentieth century, so did the means by which people claimed that they were the innocent victims of overwhelming forces that destroyed all or some of their property.

## NEW ORLEANS, AUGUST 2005: "TO QUALIFY FOR ASSISTANCE YOU MUST HAVE A COPY OF . . ."

On August 27, 2005, Governor Kathleen Blanco asked President George W. Bush to "declare an emergency for the State of Louisiana due to Hurricane Katrina for the time period beginning August 26, 2005, and continuing."[74] Hours later, Bush designated Louisiana as a state of emergency. Following his declaration, the president assumed FEMA would take the lead in responding to the crisis. He was on *Air Force One*, headed west for a vacation.

A day later, on August 28, the Louisiana National Guard asked FEMA to provide seven hundred buses to evacuate New Orleans. In response, FEMA sent one hundred buses. On August 29, FEMA director Michael Brown briefed the president by phone on the severity of the storm: "This is, to put it mildly, the big one, I think." At that same briefing, Max Mayfield, the director of the National Hurricane Center, tried to put this storm in context for the country's chief executive: "This is a category 5 hurricane, very similar to Hurricane Andrew in the maximum intensity, but there's a big big difference. This hurricane is much larger than Andrew ever was. . . . [T]here's obviously a very very grave concern."[75] By eleven on the morning of the twenty-ninth, the Lower Ninth Ward was under six to eight feet of water. This was just the beginning.

## THE POWER OF THE DOCUMENT

If an oral account of loss coupled with a visual assessment of personal character was the principal means of determining a person's eligibility for disaster relief following the earthquake and firestorms in 1906, by the beginning of the twenty-first century a victim of Hurricane Katrina would be awarded or denied relief based on his or her ability to present in person—or more likely forward to an anonymous office somewhere far removed from

**5.2.** A barge breaches the levee flooding the Lower Ninth Ward.
Jocelyn Augustino/FEMA

home—"proper documentation." FEMA's "Reimbursement Procedure" relied on utility bills, marriage licenses, birth certificates, proof of insurance,
and similar life records. FEMA states flatly that these documents must be
"able to stand the test of the audit. . . . [F]ailure to properly document" was
grounds for judging a request for assistance "ineligible."[76]

Faced with unparalleled regional destruction, FEMA quickly "hired
30,000 new case-level decision makers," many of whom had no prior experience applying FEMA eligibility requirements to claims for assistance.[77]
In an Orwellian play on words, these "case-level decision makers" only infrequently met face-to-face with those seeking help, that is, their cases. All
too often, between the victims attempting to establish their claims to relief
and the persons judging their cases valid or invalid were computer screens,
phone lines, and the US Postal Service.

Qualifying for disaster assistance, being considered eligible—read:
morally worthy—required that someone, somewhere, determined that the
documentary evidence submitted characterized the applicant as deserving. But what if a person's life was lived outside the boundaries of "proper
documentation"? Or what if a person's life was properly documented, but
she had lost, or did not have access to, her records of authenticity? In either
case, these people would not be able to rely on personal accounts to docu-

ment the what, why, and wherefore of their lives. Proper or official documents are purposely depersonalized. Eligibility was not coupled to personal stories, accounts, and visits by caseworkers. It was, rather, single-mindedly tied to forms, receipts, titles, or, perhaps, simply a phone number.

Take, for example, the case of Billy Smith. His home in Orleans Parish was destroyed by Katrina's floodwaters. He rented a room with six other men; everyone shared one phone line. On September 2, 2005, Billy Smith applied to FEMA by phone, requesting temporary housing assistance. FEMA informed him that he was ineligible for this benefit because someone else had applied for housing assistance using the same phone number. Smith attempted to explain his living situation to the person on the other end of the line. A week later, he called FEMA to check on the status of his application. During that conversation he was accused of making multiple applications.[78]

If the signifier "worthy poor" identified a person whose personal story and assessed moral fiber met the requirements for disaster relief in 1906, by 2005 the signifier "eligible" identified someone who could produce what anonymous employees deemed a credible phone number, legal title to a house, a utility bill, a driver's license, and so on through the varied ways we lay claim to a properly documented life. Though they differ in vernaculars and implementation, these two means of administering disaster relief unmask the ways society assesses the moral worth of the individual at two quite different moments in time. The ancestral vernacular of "eligible" or "ineligible" is "worthy" or "unworthy."

The Red Cross made quite clear in early-twentieth-century America that its task in San Francisco "was to assist families to recover and to regain their accustomed social and economic status." To accomplish this, disaster aid was deliberately distributed proportionally based on a person's place in a socioeconomic category. By the twenty-first century, a subtler, but no less effective, discourse was in play to accomplish the same objective.

### AVOIDING THE ENTITLEMENT HAZARD

"The storm didn't discriminate," the president intoned in his first visit to the city, "and neither will the recovery effort."[79] The president's promise to avoid separating and categorizing Katrina's victims, however, would bump up against the interests of a market society whose stakeholders sought to avoid what they deemed a problem more injurious than discrimination—to wit, the risk of what we might call "the entitlement hazard." In his run for the presidency in 2008, Mitt Romney captured the moral claim behind the entitlement hazard in his alliterative-like distinction between two social kinds: "makers" and "takers." The takers "are dependent upon government, who believe that they are victims, who believe the government has a responsibility to care for them, who believe that they are entitled to health care, to food, to housing, to you-name-it."[80]

From the late 1970s on, the grammar of "entitlement" has taken on an insidious mien. Ronald Reagan was the first conservative to bend the meaning of the word away from the right to a living wage, housing, education, and so on through the chain of human rights toward the idea of the "welfare queen," living off society's largesse.[81] By the time of George W. Bush's presidency, the entitlement hazard, the idea that some people were prone to misrepresent themselves to secure public benefits they did not deserve, was firmly embedded in the political landscape.[82]

FEMA director Joe M. Allbaugh, who preceded Michael Brown, anticipated its key role in responding to the victims of Katrina. In his testimony to Congress in 2002, Allbaugh announced his chief priority as director of FEMA: reduce the federal government's role in disaster mitigation and prevention. These activities, he explained, involve local decision making:

> It is not the role of the federal government to tell a community what it needs to do to protect its citizens. . . . Many are concerned that federal disaster assistance may have evolved into . . . an oversized entitlement program.[83]

Allbaugh's worry that disaster relief was evolving into the bad practice of allocating benefits to those who were not entitled to them resonated with the general public. The *New York Times* reported that many people were outraged at the behavior of Katrina survivors, who allegedly "were spending disaster relief, paid by taxpayers, on tattoos, $800 handbags and trips to topless bars."[84] This fable, like the fable of mass looting in the great derangement phase of the disaster, is part of the mythology of Miss Katrina. We witness the insistent logic of the entitlement hazard in two particularly egregious rules put into practice while 80 percent of the Crescent City lay beneath fusty, filthy water. Each rule, as we will see, worked to avoid this chimerical risk by sorting victims into two social kinds: "eligible" and "ineligible."[85]

When the city flooded, 28 percent of the population, one in four New Orleanians, lived below the poverty line. More than 80 percent of them were black. With a mean household income of $35,317, New Orleans "ranked 96th out of the 100 largest metropolitan areas" in percentage poor, a grim measure of human well-being. Renters exceeded home owners, and many home owners housed extended family and nonfamily boarders in acts of goodwill or to help meet expenses.[86] Here is Beatrice's story:

> Beatrice B. McWaters has not received any Temporary Housing Assistance from FEMA even though she applied 2 months ago. Ms. McWaters was a resident of Orleans Parish when Hurricane Katrina struck. She and her brother lived in a home that her mother owned, and paid her approximately $1,000 per month in rent. Her mother is 93 years old, and her brother is 61 years old and disabled. Her pre-disaster home is now uninhabitable. On approximately September 2, 2005, Ms. McWaters went to the Kelly USA shelter in San Antonio, Texas to apply for FEMA benefits. On October 10, Ms. McWaters was told by a FEMA worker (via telephone) that she, her brother, and her mother had all claimed to be owners of the same residence and that there was the appearance of fraud. Ms. McWaters tried to clear up the misunderstanding over the phone with the FEMA worker without success. . . . On October 26, Ms. McWaters received a call from FEMA and was told that she, her mother, and her brother all had been suspended or eliminated from the FEMA system.

Beatrice McWaters, her mother now in her ninth decade, and her disabled brother were designated ineligible for FEMA disaster aid under the agency's "shared-household rule." Based on this clause, "FEMA will include all members of a pre-disaster household in a single registration and will provide assistance for one temporary housing residence."[87]

Encoded in the shared-household rule is the market society's fear of the entitlement hazard. Assigning relief assistance to one designated street address would prevent people from the same address applying for benefits individually. The street address becomes, officially, a metonym for the nuclear family. Relying on this reductionist reasoning precludes consideration of the personal stories of people who find themselves living with extended family, a friend, an estranged partner, or the other morphing ways in which those whose resources or circumstances preclude home ownership have found places to live. When disaster struck, the state reasoned that a single family resided at a single address. Here, surely, is a necessary condition that must be met before someone is deemed "eligible."

## THE LONG ROAD HOME AND HEIR PROPERTY

Shortly after the floodwaters subsided, Governor Blanco and the legislature created the Louisiana Recovery Authority. The LRA would work in collaboration with FEMA and other federal and state agencies to organize the restoration and rebuilding work that lay ahead. The Road Home Program was nested within the LRA. The key idea behind this initiative was to distribute federal dollars to home owners who sought to sell or rebuild their houses.

Under Road Home, eligible home owners could receive up to $150,000 to help cover the costs of rebuilding their damaged houses. The grants were set up to give home owners several options. They could stay in the city and rebuild. They could sell their houses to the state and find a new residence somewhere in Louisiana. Or they could sell their houses to the state and move to one of forty-nine other states. People who took the third option were penalized 40 percent of their total awards. What proved particularly hard for many New Orleans residents was the stipulation that if a home was not properly insured at the time of the disaster, the home owner was docked 30 percent of his or her total grant.[88]

Following the neoliberal trend to privatize public services, the state contracted with ICF International to administer what amounted to a local program. ICF had no previous experience with this type of public money dispersal. Moreover, alarmed by the threat of the entitlement hazard, ICF resisted posting the rules for accessing Road Home funds on its website, "for fear they would become a road map to fraud."[89] One ICF representative—echoing former FEMA director Joe Allbaugh—opined that Road Home was viewed by those who lost their houses and possessions as an "entitlement program."[90] To avoid the phantom of the entitlement hazard, ICF International would give each application due vigilance. One particular warning sign was the prevalence of heir property owners seeking Road Home assistance.

Though an exact number is hard to come by, it is safe to say that tens of thousands of people living in homes around New Orleans in late August 2005 claimed ownership of their houses through a common line of descent, from father to daughter, mother to son, uncle to nephew, and so on. Most transitions were written on paper and tucked away somewhere, perhaps agreed upon orally, or maybe they were simply assumed. Notarized wills were rarely drawn up.

This transfer of property was a viable cultural practice, a kin norm that kept the residence within the primary or extended family. The property was passed down the familial line, to the heirs, who became heir property owners. Over time, the original legal title to the house might be misplaced or lost. In many if not most cases, a formal succession, granting legal title of the house to the descendant or descendants, was never filed. This arrangement was—as is the case in most villages over the centuries—a part of commonsense understanding, and it worked reasonably well until Hurricane Katrina made landfall.[91]

Richard Kluckow puts it this way: "In the months that followed Hurricane Katrina . . . huge numbers of homeowners lacked the clear title required to take advantage of the available recovery options."[92] ICF International, a corporate stakeholder in the neoliberal recovery effort, was little prepared for the complexity of the heir property owners' claim for Road Home funds. It was ready, however, to challenge any claim that appeared to risk granting those deemed ineligible the funding to rebuild their damaged houses.

Consider the story of Mr. Levi, whose "brother and niece," as Kluckow explains, "were living in the family home when the storm struck and levees breached":

> My mother and father had left that property to us. After they died, it automatically came into our name, but we had to do a succession on it and stuff like that. . . . We had started [the succession] right before Katrina, and then Katrina had came. We never finished it. We just started the process, and then Katrina had came, and all the paperwork was destroyed. So we had started immediately right after Hurricane Katrina doing that, and we got that done. My brother, like I said, he was the only owner occupying the property, and so he gave me power of attorney to process the claim on the house. . . . We simply filed it with what I had. They still asked me for an electric bill, and I kept telling him we don't have no electric bill in his name.

Kluckow sets the context for this Lewis Carroll–like scene:

> There was a range of suitable documents to include in the application to demonstrate occupancy at the time of the storm. Chief amongst these was an electric bill or another kind of dated, personally addressed bill. As Mr. Levi's brother had poor credit, the bills were all in the name of his niece who was also living with him, but wasn't a co-owner. This posed a

problem as a possessing heir needed to prove occupancy in order to be eligible for federal recovery assistance.

Mr. Levi continues:

> When I appealed it, it had my affidavit in there, and his original FEMA application had his name, address, Social Security number on there, and his ID card, and his last arrest record showing that he was living there. They was formal documents, but it wasn't the documents that they were requiring.[93]

Here we see how the fog of paperwork mirrors the confusing ways in which lives are combined into living arrangements that make some sense at the time but may well become impediments to qualifying for that all-important identity: eligible for disaster assistance. Also visible in Mr. Levi's case is how the problem of "formal documents" that do not line up with corporate or state expectations triggers the prevailing fear of the entitlement hazard. When the levees failed, the market assumed home owners had clear titles to their houses and the requisite documents to prove it. This is how a market society works.

The shared-household rule and the heir property restrictions are both reminders of what is likely to happen in a historical era—like ours—when society is run as an adjunct to an economy based on private property, capital accumulation, and the unequal distribution of wages and wealth. The intrinsic logic of document confusion combined with the determination to avoid the unlikely risk of someone receiving a benefit he or she does not deserve are two of the many ways in which the intrinsic logic of the market—and not a human concern for the well-being of the other—was in control of the recovery efforts. Let's look briefly at one more example of how this market logic was in play.

### LOCATION, LOCATION, LOCATION

Alana is a college graduate. She lives in a historically black neighborhood, Pontchartrain Park. Her troubles were not connected to the shared-household or heir property rules. She found herself disadvantaged by the perceived value of her neighborhood. Alana summed up her experience with ICF and the Road Home Program this way: "In the end we got some

Road Home money but nothing to write home about."[94] Her experience with this privately contracted, publicly funded initiative was all too common. Alana's story represents yet another way people were sorted into distinct kinds, in this case based on the location of their houses in this or that neighborhood.

This method of dividing used a somewhat different formula than that used in the shared-household and the heir property rules. Rather than creating kinds of people to determine the allocation of relief funds, the ICF distinguished between kinds of neighborhoods. The calculus used to make this areal distinction was based on a rationale for determining the amount of grant awarded that had a direct impact on middle- to lower-middle- and lower-income neighborhoods. The market logic of the rationale was transparent. A grant would not reflect the actual cost of repairing a damaged house. Rather, it would be based on either the value of the damaged house before it was flooded or the estimated cost of repairing the damage, whichever figure was lower.[95]

The market value of a house generally reflects both the cost of the construction and, importantly, the class makeup of the neighborhood. So in a low-income neighborhood, the pre-flood value of a house whose construction costs are similar to a house in a middle-income neighborhood is more likely to be lower than the estimated cost of repairing that house. The immediate problem for the home owner in this neighborhood is that the cost of Formica countertops, solid wood or veneer flooring, and roofing shingles will be identical to the costs incurred by those home owners who live in more affluent areas of the city.

"Sheetrock," Gary Rivlin writes, "cost the same whether you lived west of City Park" in the upscale Lakeview neighborhoods or in the lower-middle- to middle-class neighborhoods of Gentilly. "So, too," he continues, "did an electrician and a roofer. Yet Road Home decreed that the same three-bedroom, two-bath arts-and-crafts home was worth $100,000 less in Gentilly than in Lakeview."[96] In short, the higher the status of the neighborhood, the more money residents are likely to receive to rebuild their damaged houses, though the cost of rebuilding is essentially the same in both the lower- and the higher-income neighborhoods.

### "HELLIFIED FIGHTING": A BRIEF CONCLUSION

The household-exclusion, the heir property, and the Road Home appraisal rules remind us that disasters in market societies are moments in time in which we can witness—if we care to look—how society assesses the social (read: retail) worth of the individual. Reflected in the administration of disaster relief are market-informed strategies of exclusion and inclusion. The point is, from a business perspective, to rearrange what has been deranged.

Susan Sterett presciently observes: "FEMA rules hold that individuals receiving help cannot use disaster assistance to reorganize their lives." At best they can get themselves back to where they were before the calamity knocked them to the ground. Vanessa Gueringer, a resident of the Lower Ninth Ward, laments, "The big takeaway is the Road Home is still a very long road for those African-American families who lived here for generations and who could not return home." Her voice intensifies: "We came back, and it's been about punishment ever since. Everything you see rebuilt down here is from some hellified fighting."[97]

A studied account of the relief benefits available to victims of Katrina concludes, "*Substantively*," these benefits "are designed for higher-income households who have assets to fall back on after the disaster."[98] The same could be said about the logic of relief distribution in San Francisco a century earlier. The complex work done in the name of aid and assistance in both cities ensured that those social and geographic divisions that structured urban life before catastrophe were successfully reclaimed. Andrea Rees Davies concludes her incisive study of relief and recovery following the San Francisco earthquake and fires with words that would be apropos to the recovery of New Orleans a hundred years later: "In the drive to restore the city's losses, the new San Francisco reconstructed the social divisions it claimed to eschew."[99]

Social kinds, measures of worthiness, and the market collude again in San Francisco's Chinatown in the aftermath of the earthquake and fires and New Orleans's public housing following in Katrina's wake. In chapter 6 we witness the concerted efforts of urban elites to confiscate the spaces of two politically vulnerable populations. The varying outcomes of these two attempts are potent reminders of our own, American, version of durable inequality and the importance of the historical moment in making sense of calamity.

# SPATIAL ACCUMULATION
# BY DISPOSSESSION
## TWO ATTEMPTS TO ROB THE MARGINAL

*Mah deah, there is much more money to be made in
the destruction of civilization than in building it up.*

MARGARET MITCHELL, *GONE WITH THE WIND*

In chapter 5 we took a close-up look at the practices, policies, and vocabularies that fashioned the work of disaster relief in two catastrophes separated by a century. This chapter shifts from the administration of relief guided by the invisible hand of the market to the visible ways market interests drove urban elites and their political allies to capitalize on the mayhem of the moment to take what did not belong to them.

Destruction, notes David Harvey, "is often required to make the new urban geography out of the wreckage of the old." Harvey was writing in 2010, but his words recall the brutal history of the early-seventeenth-century enclosure movement. A legal maneuver to consolidate farm holdings by privatizing once common grazing land, enclosure was among the key dynamics in the making of a market society. An official document prepared for the use of the English Lords of the Realm notes with a tone of high authority: "The poor man shall be satisfied in his end: Habitation; the gentleman not hindered in his desire: Improvement."[1]

By enclosing once open land, the lords and nobles remade small farmers into a landless working class. This emergent proletariat would provide the labor to power the rise of industrialism in cities like Manchester and Liverpool. "Enclosures," Polanyi notes, "have appropriately been called a revolution of the rich against the poor. The lords and nobles . . . were literally . . . tearing down the houses which the poor had long regarded as theirs and their heirs." E. P. Thompson echoes Polanyi: "Enclosure (when all the sophistications are allowed for) was a plain enough case of class robbery."[2]

In this chapter we examine two modern versions of the historical enclosure movement.

The histories of San Francisco's Chinatown following the 1906 earthquake and fire and of New Orleans's public housing following Hurricane Katrina in 2005 reveal how powerful class interests collude with the fog of disaster to lay claim to the urban spaces of the poor and marginal. In these two catastrophic moments, we witness the concerted efforts of urban elites to confiscate the spaces of two politically vulnerable populations: the Chinese in 1906 and low-income African Americans in 2005. The widely varying outcomes of these two attempts reveal a good deal about the intersection of calamity, class, race, and citizenship in American history.

Writing almost sixty years ago, Austrian economist Joseph Schumpeter unwittingly brought disaster and the market together in a provocative analogy: capitalism, he observed, is like a "gale of creative destruction."[3] Did Schumpeter have an inkling of how intertwined disaster and capitalism would prove to be in the twentieth and into the twenty-first centuries? Probably not, but what is certain is that the material destruction wrought by catastrophe is more often than not a source of what David Harvey, channeling Marx, calls "accumulation by dispossession."[4] While it cannot be said that we have quite commodified disaster as we have, say, sperm and egg cells, the potential market benefits of material devastation are always part of the equation of disaster recovery.[5]

The correlation between material destruction and capital accumulation is particularly strong in cities. In *The Culture of Calamity*, Kevin Rozario cites the work of several critical geographers to make the case that "modern capitalism thrives on the constant reshaping of urban space, to the point, we presume, where calamities can be good for business."[6] In the following story, two urban disasters created opportunities for political and business elites to appropriate urban spaces occupied by people pushed just beyond the far edges of accepted society. But the two attempts at what we might call, following Harvey, spatial accumulation by dispossession had two contradictory outcomes. In one case, a seemingly powerless racial minority prevailed, preventing a commanding combination of political and business elites from acquiring control of the contested urban space they called home. In the other case, an overwhelming commercial and political alliance succeeded in displacing thousands of poor people of color from their urban homesteads, freeing the land for capital development.

In this story, I recount these two opposing outcomes, examining in some detail those varying political and economic factors that coalesced in one case to prevent the forced exclusion of one vulnerable population from its urban space and those factors a century later that worked in tandem to remove thousands of people from their homes and neighborhoods. A studied look at these two cases underscores the interrelated significance of class, race, and citizenship and their relationships to an always shifting market-oriented state. It is also an opportunity—in the case of New Orleans—to look briefly beyond the idea of recovering inequality to something we might call amplified inequality, the successful effort to capitalize on the mayhem of catastrophe to seize the property of those on the margins of society.

## TWO GALES OF CREATIVE DESTRUCTION

### SAN FRANCISCO, APRIL 1906

Publishing days after the April 18 earthquake and firestorms, the *Washington Star* concludes with a brutal frankness: "About the only gratifying feature of the San Francisco horror is the fact that Chinatown has been destroyed. That pestilential community is no more."[7] In this newspaper's xenophobic message is one irrefutable fact: Chinatown—all of it—was destroyed. Between the quake and the fires, this patch of the city was ground zero. Nothing was left.

Pierre Beringer found a silver lining in San Francisco's totalizing urban devastation. Writing for the *Oakland Monthly*, he adopts a blunt tone:

**6.1.** Chinatown, April 20, 1906. Courtesy Library of Congress

Fire has reclaimed to civilization and cleanliness the Chinese ghetto, and no Chinatown will be permitted in the borders of the city. It seems as though a divine wisdom directed the range of the seismic horror and the range of the fire god. Wisely, the worst was cleared away with the best.[8]

Amid the complete and utter ruin of Chinatown lay an opportunity to reclaim this valuable real estate for development by San Francisco's business and political elite. The *Argonaut*, a weekly newspaper, concluded two weeks after the disaster that the Chinese must be moved permanently and "one of the best parts of the city" recovered for the use of native San Franciscans.[9] The *San Francisco Call* was, if anything, blunter in its appraisal:

Strike while the iron is hot. Preserve this fine hill for the architecture and occupancy of the clean and moderate Caucasian. We now hold the situation in the hollow of our hand. We have but to say the word and fine edifices will in the future grace that commanding slope, filched from us by the insidious, gradual occupation of the Mongol.[10]

Even the noted *New York Times* could not avoid editorializing on this opportunity to expel the Chinese from San Francisco's Chinatown:

The Old Franciscan Chinatown was a much greater blemish and absurdity than that of New York. For it occupied the slope of the hill at the base of which is the chief commercial quarter, and the top of which is the chief residential quarter. No Franciscan of those parts could pass from his business to his home or back again without passing through it. What is more, his womankind could not "go shopping" without traversing it.[11]

Acutely aware of the mounting sentiment to prevent the rebuilding of the Chinese quarter, a Chinese-owned newspaper lamented, "It is predictable that the old Chinatown cannot be restored."[12] Working feverishly behind the newspaper coverage was a powerful political initiative to appropriate the six square blocks of Chinatown for white-owned businesses and residences.

On April 27, nine days after the disaster, the mayor appointed the "Subcommittee for Permanent Location of Chinatown."[13] The subcommittee was composed of experts in architecture, sanitation, medicine, and other specialties that were thought to be of importance in finding and building a new location for the displaced Chinese. Backed by the press and a good deal of popular opinion, committee members had little doubt that they would accomplish their goal. Abraham Ruef, the chair of the subcommittee, offered this somewhat patronizing take on his work: Chinatown would not be rebuilt, and the former residents would be moved for their "own protection and safety and happiness to live together as they had in the past."[14]

From this vantage point, there seemed little the Chinese could do to reclaim their destroyed properties. Under federal law, most were permanent aliens, not US citizens. Moreover, all but a few were renters with no legal title to property. Adding appreciably to their predicament, the material losses sustained by the Chinese were orders of magnitude greater than the losses of other groups and neighborhoods.[15] These three factors combined with a virulent and tenacious racism made the prospects of winning a struggle to rebuild their lives in Chinatown appear out of reach. The cards, in short, were stacked against them. Many in the white community, as writer Jerome A. Hart recalled at the time, "congratulated themselves that Chinatown was gone."[16] Their celebration, however, would prove premature.

## NEW ORLEANS, AUGUST 2005

The massive material destruction of New Orleans a century later was similarly viewed by several powerful public and private interests as an opportunity to appropriate valuable urban land and reshape the demographic profile of the city. Recalling the words of Pierre Beringer, who linked "divine wisdom" to opportunity in the burning of Chinatown, Representative Richard Baker of Baton Rouge was quoted shortly after the storm: "We finally cleaned up public housing in New Orleans. We couldn't do it. But God did."[17]

Several months later, New Orleans's city council president, Oliver Thomas, himself Creole, opined during a housing committee meeting:

> We don't need soap opera watchers right now. We're going to target the people who are going to work. . . . [A]t some point there has to be a whole new level of motivation, and people have got to stop blaming the government for something they ought to do.[18]

Not two weeks after the city flooded, *New York Times* columnist David Brooks wrote:

> Katrina . . . separated tens of thousands of poor people from the rundown, isolated neighborhoods in which they were trapped. It disrupted

**6.2.** The Lafitte housing complex, scheduled for demolition, was ranked among the best public housing of its era. It was demolished in 2008.
Photo by Fred R. Conrad, NYT/Redux, 2005

the patterns that have led one generation to follow another into poverty. . . . If we just put up new buildings and allow the same people to move back into their old neighborhoods, then urban New Orleans will become just as rundown and dysfunctional as before.[19]

Alphonso Jackson, the African American secretary of Housing and Urban Development (HUD), deploys a more granular approach than Brooks, distinguishing between "only the best" and the rest:

Some of the people [who lived in public housing] shouldn't return. . . . Only the best residents should return: those who paid rent on time, those who held a job and those who worked.[20]

Ten months after the storm, in June 2006, HUD quietly announced that no former residents would be allowed to return to any of the four housing complexes. HUD ordered the properties fenced and guarded. This order was given in spite of the fact that three of the four complexes were immediately habitable. The reason quite simply was that HUD intended to tear each of them down.[21]

This decision might well seem less than reasonable. Eighty percent of the housing stock in New Orleans was damaged by Katrina's water and winds. Fifty-six percent of the city's rental units were flooded.[22] New Orleans was in an acute housing crisis. Nevertheless, the decision was made to raze the complexes.[23]

Examined together, these two calamities and all that ensued tell an intricate story about the predatory logic of market economies in pursuit of land value. In doing so, they also light up historical shifts in the relationship of skin color and social class. Finally, each city and its historical period help us see the strengths and weaknesses of citizenship in the always morphing logic of state, international, and now global politics.

## CHINATOWN, PERMANENT ALIEN STATUS, AND CATASTROPHE

San Francisco was incorporated in 1848, and a year later the first Chinese arrived in this new outpost of western America.[24] Cheap labor was needed to mine gold and later build the railways. Thousands of Chinese heeded the call and immigrated to California, most passing through the port of San Francisco on their journey. Some immigrants saw opportunities in the growing metropolitan area of San Francisco and stayed to open retail shops and businesses.

In what would prove to be an ironic twist on the privileges of citizenship, the early immigrants from China to America were, as Erica Pan describes, "not enthusiastic about becoming US citizens. . . . They had come to make money, not to obtain citizenship."[25] These early pioneers were "sons of China" and had no intention of risking their status as Chinese nationals for American citizenship.

The initial reluctance of the Chinese to accept US citizenship provoked more than an occasional vitriolic response from white Americans. In his autobiography recalling the last decades of the nineteenth century, Pardee Lowe spoke for many whites when he wrote, "We hated the Negroes because they are citizens. We hated the yellow dogs because they will not be."[26] The stance of the Chinese immigrants toward naturalization began to change over the years, however, with many seeking US citizenship. But few received it. And with the passage of the Chinese Exclusion Act in 1882, Chinese immigrants were legally designated "permanent aliens," excluding them from applying for US citizenship status.[27] Their legal status as "permanent aliens," somewhat counterintuitively, would prove to be of considerable worth in the months following the 1906 earthquake and fire.

By 1855 a section of San Francisco was popularly known as "Chinatown." This ethnic enclave continued to expand as anti-Chinese violence drove immigrant miners in the eastern part of the state back to the coast and the relatively safe confines of this emerging ethnic settlement. Moreover, within San Francisco itself, working-class whites, supported by the anti-Chinese rhetoric of many of the city's elites, intimidated and threatened immigrants living among them, pushing those Chinese dispersed around San Francisco toward the Chinese quarter.

> By 1877, Chinatown was six blocks in length, running north and south on Dupont Street from California to Broadway, and two blocks wide from east to west on Sacramento, Clay, Commercial, Washington, Jackson, Pacific, and Broadway streets, and from Kearny to Stockton, crossing Dupont.[28]

Chinatown was composed of the full spectrum of economic classes, from poor to rich, working class to successful merchant, all manner of immigrant found in this six-block swath of the city. The virulent nativism among whites did not discriminate between poor and working-class Chinese and their more affluent and economically successful countrymen. All Chinese, from poor to wealthy, were subject to discrimination, intimidation, and violence.[29]

The forced ghettoization of the Chinese created a city within a city. Moreover, life in Chinatown assumed a fraternal ambience. Chinese of all social strata could trace their geographic origins in China to primarily four districts in the same province. The lineage ties within Chinatown were used to form associations that acted as resources for the residents. Complementing these familial associations were the *hui kuans*, consisting of organizations representing the four geographic districts in mainland China. "Every Chinese immigrant," Pan writes, "was a member of one association or another."[30] Credit, loans, shelter, and assistance of all kinds were provided by these benevolent associations. The racism that pushed almost all Chinese into Chinatown unwittingly created a diverse class base that would prove itself a valuable resource in the ensuing struggle to return after the last fires were put out.

## EARLY EFFORTS AT ENCLOSURE

The destruction of San Francisco in 1906 was not the only time Chinatown had been threatened by elites aiming to appropriate their urban homestead. In 1878 China officially recognized the Chinese American community, establishing its first consulate in San Francisco. A building was purchased in Chinatown to house the consulate and his staff.[31] It did not take long for some observers to note the seeming paradox of a despised minority group occupying prime urban real estate. By the mid-nineteenth century, the *Daily Alta California* was recommending the removal of the Chinese from Chinatown to some other less desirable location:

> Dupont Street is one of the most desirable in the city . . . and it seems a pity that so fine a street should be occupied with so much filth and nastiness. . . . [The] Chinese community . . . ought to inhabit a portion of the city by themselves . . . further removed from the heart of the city.[32]

Arguably, the most egregious effort to displace the Chinese occurred in 1900, when an outbreak of bubonic plague was suspiciously traced to Chinatown. The plague was quickly identified as a "rice-eaters disease" by local whites; the Chinese were quarantined, and calls for the complete destruction of Chinatown ensued.[33] A member of the California Board of Health advocated burning the confined area to the ground. "I think it would prove the cheapest course in the end," he surmised.[34] It is worth noting that while the state and city acted quickly to close off the area and confine the Chinese, white business owners operating in Chinatown were allowed to open their shops and travel to and from the quarantined area. Moreover, political and business leaders throughout the state minimized the risks of the outbreak when addressing white audiences.[35]

But the Chinese and Chinatown weathered the plague of 1900. They would also survive the City Beautiful movement, organized by San Francisco's business elites in 1905. Inspired by architect Daniel Burnham's design for the 1893 Chicago World's Fair, provocatively called the "Great White City," James Phelan, perhaps the richest man in San Francisco, hired Burnham to draw up plans for San Francisco's version of this gleaming, pure metropolis.[36]

The double entendre of the "Great White City" could not have been lost on early-twentieth-century Americans, whose concern with skin color was deeply embedded in cultural and social life.[37] To achieve the San Francisco version of the Great White City, clearly Chinatown would have to be razed and the Chinese moved from the center to the periphery of this emerging metropolis.

## THE WHIMS OF "THE EARTH DRAGON" AND HISTORY

It was during this latest struggle to appropriate Chinatown from the Chinese and transform this urban space into a place more amenable to a white San Francisco that disaster struck. On April 17, 1906, Daniel Burnham presented his plan to Phelan and the city's political leaders.[38] Less than twenty-four hours later, 5:12 on the morning of April 18, the first temblor was felt. What city planners were having trouble accomplishing, the earthquake and fire did in a matter of hours.

Between the earthquake and the army's efforts to stop the advance of several fires by starting conflagrations, Chinatown was destroyed. Reporting on the blaze, the *Oakland Tribune* wrote, "The fire had full sway and Chinatown, for the removal of which many a scheme has been devised, is but a memory."[39] The Chinese watched helplessly as their houses and businesses were destroyed by the combined forces of geology and human error. More than a few attributed the devastation to the capricious whims of "the Earth Dragon."[40]

Catastrophes do not occur in historical vacuums; rather, they take shape and form in part through the social, political, and economic forces in play at the moment of impact. There is an intersection, in other words, between material destruction and historical circumstance. It just so happens that at the moment in time when Mother Nature collaborated with human error to level San Francisco and obliterate Chinatown, Chinese nationals living in the United States and their counterparts in homeland China were collectively opposing American anti-Chinese discriminatory policies and practices.[41] Although Theodore Roosevelt never championed racial and ethnic equality, he recognized by 1905 that fair treatment of the Chinese was emerging as a paramount issue for his administration and its relationship with the Qing court in China.[42]

Chinese immigrants to the United States had been sending money back home for decades. While the Qing government was slow to recognize the contribution these immigrants were making to the Chinese economy, by 1905 the Qing's empress dowager was pressuring the Roosevelt administration to prevent the renewal of the 1894 Sino-American Treaty. This treaty legalized the exclusion of Chinese immigrants to the United States and denied naturalization to immigrants already on American soil.[43] Responding to the call for representation from Chinese nationals who wanted to bring their relatives to the United States and secure American citizenship, the Qing government demanded the repeal of the Sino-American Treaty.

Opposition from both the population of permanent Chinese aliens living in the United States and the Chinese state escalated into a massive boycott of American goods in 1905. On strictly economic terms, it is not clear if the boycott succeeded or failed. American businessmen trading in China at the time, however, had no doubt about the negative effects of the boycott and testified to their losses in Senate hearings on the matter.[44] Moreover, US students, educators, and missionaries living in China in the early years of the twentieth century reported massive support for the boycott and a growing disillusionment with America and its citizens.[45] By the turn of the twentieth century, global trade was fast becoming a mainstay of the US economy, and China was the leading Asian trade party with Western nations.

With these intertwined forces in play, it is perhaps not surprising that the Roosevelt administration saw in the earthquake and fire an opportunity to offer a gesture of goodwill to Chinese citizens living in America. Such a display would also send a message to the Chinese government that America valued an amicable relationship with its Asian trading partner. On April 23, 1906, five days after the disaster, Roosevelt wrote to his secretary of war, William Howard Taft:

> According to the newspaper reports the suffering and destruction are peculiarly great among the Chinese. I need hardly say that the Red Cross work must be done wholly without regard to persons and just as much for the Chinese as for any others.[46]

But the Chinese government was not about to rely solely on the benevolence of the Roosevelt administration toward its citizens in the United States. Days after the disaster, the empress dowager wired fifty thousand US dollars to assist the displaced Chinese immigrants—dollars, it should be noted, that had been sent to China by Chinese immigrants laboring in the United States.[47] Moreover, "speaking from deep within the Forbidden City," the empress "demanded that her people be housed where they had long wished to be housed."[48] To put some muscle in her order, she dispatched an official party to America to lobby on behalf of the Chinese nationals living in San Francisco. In *Denial of Disaster*, Gladys Hansen and Emmet Condon write that the "arrival of a delegation from the Chinese Legation to the

United States changed the tone and tenor of the 'relocation rhetoric.'"[49] The *San Francisco Chronicle* quotes a Chinese delegate who reminded the United States that China itself was a property owner:

> America is a free country and every man has a right to occupy the land which he owns provided that he makes no nuisance. The Chinese government owns the lot on which the Chinese Consulate of San Francisco formerly stood, and this site on Stockton Street will be used again.[50]

The Chinese delegate evokes the strong value placed on property rights in America. Denied the right to purchase US property by various versions of the Chinese Exclusion Act, however, few residents of Chinatown owned their residences and places of business. This would seem to place them in a difficult legal position in their struggle to reclaim Chinatown. But here again, their status as permanent aliens would unexpectedly serve them well in their zoning battles with the city's power elite.

Forced into a ghetto-like setting by anti-Chinese sentiment, Chinese nationals were willing to pay exorbitant rents to white landlords to secure residences and businesses in the relatively safe confines of Chinatown. In what we can only conclude is an instance of capital outflanking race, these same white landlords, fearing the loss of their rent-gouging revenues, came to the aid of the Chinese in their struggle to reclaim their homestead.

Erica Pan writes, "The participation of the white property owners in the motion for the return of Chinatown changed the conflict between the white and the oriental into that of white against white."[51] The efforts of San Francisco's political and economic elite to appropriate the valuable urban real estate that was Chinatown would become even more complicated as cities up and down the West Coast offered the displaced Chinese a place to call home.

It was never the intention of the moneyed interests in San Francisco to rid the city of the Chinese; rather, they wanted to relocate them to a far less desirable location on the outskirts of town. By 1906 there were between a thousand and fifteen hundred shops and businesses in San Francisco's Chinatown. Tourism was a growing business, with tourists spending more than $300,000 annually in this six-block district of the city.[52] It is worth noting that using the consumer price inflation index as a measure, $300,000 in 1906 was the equivalent of $7.7 million in 2017.[53] In addition to tourism, San Francisco had become the central port for the distribution of Chinese goods throughout the country. Import duties paid by the Chinese added substantially to the revenue of the city. By 1906 Chinese trade through the port of San Francisco was providing one-third of the city's annual budget.[54]

Perceiving the Chinese as an urban economic engine, several West Coast cities, from Los Angeles to Vancouver, Canada, petitioned San Francisco's Chinese population with offers to relocate. As early as May 1, two weeks after the disaster, the *San Francisco Chronicle* quotes a prominent San Francisco businessman who reminded his influential business and political colleagues: "If the situation were not wisely handled the bulk of San Francisco's Oriental trade might be diverted to other Pacific Coast ports. Seattle," he continued, "is making a strong bid for this trade and would like to welcome the Chinese to this city." Chuen Hung, a Chinese merchant, reminded the citizens of San Francisco, "We are not overlooking the fact that Portland, Tacoma or Seattle . . . desire the investment of many millions of money."[55]

The economic success of the Chinese in San Francisco was inextricably tied to their homeland, the source of their market goods, and their unique culture. What motivated the early Chinese labor and merchant classes was their felt obligation to send US dollars to China. And many reasoned that they would return one day to their homeland. In a particularly poignant passage, an anonymous author who identifies herself only as a "Southern colored woman" captures this close nationalist identification of the Chinese immigrant and his homeland. Writing in 1904, she exclaims, "Happy Chinaman! You can go back to your village and enjoy your money. This is my village, my home, yet I am an outcast."[56]

### AMPLIFIED REBOUND

Immediately following the complete and utter destruction of Chinatown, San Francisco's city elite saw a clear path to removing once and for all these permanent aliens from this valuable piece of US real estate. They went about their work to rid the old Chinatown of Chinese immigrants with a certain taken-for-granted hubris. What, after all, would prevent them from accomplishing their objective? But on July 8, approximately twelve weeks after the greatest urban disaster in US history, the Subcommittee for Permanent Location of Chinatown admitted defeat and petitioned the mayor to dissolve the group. "Let the Chinese locate where they please," a resigned James Phelan announced. "If they prove obnoxious to whites they can gradually be driven to a certain section by strict enforcement of anti-gambling and other city laws."[57]

A little less than two years after the disaster, the *New York Times* ran a story titled "San Francisco's New Chinatown." The article reports the return of more than fifteen thousand Chinese to Chinatown. The article notes the Chinese were constructing "new buildings, as picturesque as those destroyed by the fire and earthquake, but more convenient and sanitary."[58] Far from removing Chinatown and its Chinese, the new Chinatown would prove to be more colorful, earthquake proof, and sanitary than its older pre-disaster version. In what is arguably the greatest irony, by all accounts Chinatown experienced a more robust and successful recovery than many of the other damaged neighborhoods in the city.[59] Some disaster scholars are fond of calling this variation of recovery "amplified rebound."[60] A new Chinatown, more ornate, comfortable, and secure than the old one, reminds us that disasters are always embedded in history, intersecting with social, cultural, and political forces that may, at times, conspire to fashion the unexpected.

Keep this case in mind as we leap one hundred years ahead to a precarious sliver of land betwixt a mighty river and a massive lake. Here a quite different disaster, again one part natural and two parts human made, engulfed another of America's iconic cities. On August 29, 2005, New Orleans's levees proved no match for the tidal surge of a Category 3 hurricane.

## PUBLIC HOUSING, NEW ORLEANS, AND THE PERILS OF CITIZENSHIP

In the spirit of the New Deal ideas of the time, President Franklin Delano Roosevelt signed the Wagner-Steagall Housing Act into law on September 1, 1937. The housing act launched America's first federally funded public housing initiative to improve the living conditions of low-income families. Under this act, the United States would disperse subsidies to local public housing agencies, which would administer the funds to assist families in need.[61] New Orleans was among the first cities to build large-scale public housing. Undesirable neighborhoods were demolished and replaced with low-cost housing for those who were temporarily struggling through hard times.[62] In 1938 a New Orleans newspaper announced plans to build the first public housing complex in the city:

> The buildings will be built around a court with play space for children and yard space for each living unit. . . . This arrangement not only provides light and ventilation but eliminates traffic hazards for children. The

negro project will include a community building with provision for a nursery school where mothers may leave their small children while they are working.[63]

Although the Wagner-Steagall Housing Act was written with America's poor in mind, by the end of the third decade of the twentieth century, poor and black were kindred identities in New Orleans, as signaled by the term *negro project*.

Over the decades, as the social democratic philosophy of the New Deal retreated in the face of an escalating individualism, the kind that Tocqueville warned us against, we have moved from a society where "love your neighbor as yourself" had some tangible meaning to those in need to a society that ascribes to the contrary idea that "God helps those who help themselves."[64] A robust culture of sovereign individualism and financial opportunism helped to ensure that the plight of the poor living in America's public housing assumed a character and quality Dickens would have recognized. Hard times tended to last for many in New Orleans, and the projects became a place for "the poorest of the poor."[65] But the federally subsidized projects nevertheless provided housing security to those who needed it most.

As the decade of the 1980s wore on and Reagan's trickle-down economics gained traction, public housing in the United States was underfunded and the Department of Housing and Urban Development, the federal agency responsible for its administration, was understaffed. In the spirit of public-private partnership, an initiative that highlights the neoliberal ethos of the latter part of the twentieth century, Congress created what it called, with the inadvertent hint of irony befitting Jonathan Swift, HOPE VI.[66] The intent of HOPE VI was to create joint ventures between public housing authorities, residents, and the private sector to acquire the necessary capital to invest in the infrastructure of the housing units. In the words of a HUD document, HOPE VI sought "partnerships that marry public goals, private-sector energy and funding, and the dormant hopes of community residents."[67] The public-private partnership that launched HOPE VI intended to reconfigure the urban landscape to ensure the highest possible financial rate of return. It was understood by the parties involved that this initiative would reduce the subsidized housing stock for the increasing numbers of people who need it.

New Orleans's St. Thomas housing project was the first to be transformed under the HOPE VI program. In the mid-1990s the project was placed in the hands of a private contractor, who razed the more than sixteen hundred apartments that composed St. Thomas and constructed middle-income apartments, planned a high-income tower, and left sixty units for low-income families. The new development, called "River Gardens," provided housing for less than one-fourth of the former low-income minority residents.[68] For low-income families and others concerned about housing in New Orleans, River Gardens became a symbol of what one critic called the "whitewashing of New Orleans."[69]

By 2005 four major HUD-managed public housing complexes—C. J. Peete, B. W. Cooper, Lafitte, and St. Bernard—provided shelter for upwards of twenty thousand working-class to poor African Americans. Eighty-eight percent of families living in public housing are single-parent households. The single parent is, with very few exceptions, a woman of color.[70] It was against this shifting political and economic terrain of public housing that "Miss Katrina's" winds and water proved too much for New Orleans's famed levees.

## "GET OUT OF TOWN!"

On August 28, 2005, the mayor of New Orleans ordered the first mandatory evacuation in the history of the city. "Anyone who's thinking of staying—rethink it," he commanded. "Get out of town!"[71] At the time of the mayor's unprecedented order, the Housing Authority of New Orleans (HANO), which operated under the authority of the federal Housing and Urban Development agency, managed 7,369 public housing units. Approximately 5,000 of these units were occupied at the time of the disaster.[72] In response to the mayor's directive, all public housing residents were evacuated from the city.[73] As New Orleans filled with water, an estimated twenty thousand people were suddenly displaced, exiled from housing they had fashioned over many years into homes.

As the water retreated, however, it divulged an arguably upbeat fact—to wit, only one of the public housing complexes, B. W. Cooper, sustained significant damage. The other three complexes required minimal repair. If Chinatown was ground zero for the San Francisco earthquake and fire, New Orleans's major housing projects stood post-flood as testaments to their hard-wearing construction and their elevated geographic locations in low-lying New Orleans. As the waters receded, hundreds of apartments sat empty, awaiting the return of the residents. A Massachusetts Institute of Technology architecture professor, John Fernandez, examined all four of the complexes. He concluded that each of them, even B. W. Cooper, could be rehabilitated.[74] Built in the early 1940s, the complexes were in need of some refurbishing and updating. The costs of making this housing stock a more desirable place for its long-term residents to live, however, were far less than tearing them down and building anew.

The Lafitte housing complex, for example, would require approximately $20 million in renovation. Demolishing it and rebuilding would cost in excess of $100 million. Likewise, even B. W. Cooper, the project sustaining the most damage, could be rehabilitated and updated for about $135 million. It would take more than $220 million to tear it down and rebuild fewer units.[75] But saving money and returning people to their accustomed housing were not what the city business and political elite had in mind.

With New Orleans's poor scattered about the fifty states, accumulating the valuable land that the four public housing complexes occupied made a good deal of sense to some very powerful interests. Bill Quigley and Sara H. Godchaux write:

> Once Katrina hit, there was an express decision by political and business leaders in the city, as well as HANO and HUD, to use this as an opportunity to demolish public housing in New Orleans. Public housing residents who wanted to return were locked out of their apartments and forced to live elsewhere.[76]

Seven months after HUD announced that no residents could return to public housing, New Orleans's city council voted unanimously on December 20, 2007, to demolish the four housing complexes. At a public meeting shortly after the vote, the city's Creole mayor, and former president of a telecommunications company, Ray Nagin, applauded the council's decision:

> The decisions made today were ones of compassion, courage, and commitment to this city. This is an incredible day. You heard lots of pain today. The City Council in its wisdom has come up with a solution that will allow us to move forward.[77]

While it is unclear what moving "forward" meant for Mayor Nagin, one thing is certain: the "us" he refers to did not include the displaced residents of public housing.

New Orleans's public housing would not be demolished without a fight, or at least a scuffle. Many former residents who were able to make their way back to the city protested the decision to raze these four historic complexes. Public demonstrations, sit-ins, marches, and other forms of social protest escalated.

Displaced residents also created a survivors' village adjacent to the fenced-off St. Bernard project. They lived in makeshift tents, akin to wandering migrants in impoverished countries.[78] Sharon Jasper, a low-income former resident of public housing, made this promise: "If you try to bulldoze our homes there's going to be a fight. There's going to be a war in New Orleans."[79] At least two grassroots organizations emerged to fight eviction and displacement: Hands Off Iberville and May Day New Orleans.

Tepid support for those evicted issued from some powerful sectors of government. The Speaker of the House, Nancy Pelosi, and the Senate majority leader, Harry Reid, sent a letter to President George W. Bush in December 2007, requesting a brief moratorium on the decision to demolish the four public housing units:

> We are writing to request an immediate 60-day moratorium on the demolition of New Orleans' public housing developments. . . . Given the poor condition of New Orleans rental housing stock, [and] the rising levels of homelessness in the City . . . these housing resources should not be demolished without a viable full replacement plan in place.

The letter ends by reminding Bush that "HANO has also not provided meaningful opportunity for residents to collect their belongings."[80] There is no record of the president responding to this letter.

More vigorous support for their cause came from several high-profile national and international nongovernmental organizations (INGOs) that also represented the evicted residents. Among them were the Concerned Citizens of Harlem, the National Association for the Advancement of Colored People, Amnesty International, the International Action Center, the National Economic and Social Rights Initiative, the International Alliance of Inhabitants, and the National Economic and Social Rights Initiative.

Several INGOs, including Amnesty International and the International Alliance of Inhabitants, alerted embattled residents through web pages and personal contacts that international law was on their side. In 1998 the

UN Office of the High Commissioner for Human Rights issued Article 21, "Guiding Principles on Internal Displacement." The principles were written in response to the increasing number of people throughout the world who lost their homes due to a growing number of dislocating forces:

> Internally displaced persons are persons or groups of persons who have been forced or obliged to flee or to leave their homes or places of habitual residence, in particular as a result of or in order to avoid the effects of armed conflict, situations of generalized violence, violations of human rights or natural or human-made disasters, and who have not crossed an internationally recognized State border. Internally displaced persons shall enjoy . . . the same rights and freedoms under international and domestic law as do other persons in their country. . . . Every human being shall have the right to be protected against being arbitrarily displaced from his or her . . . habitual residence.[81]

In addition to Article 21, at least four other UN articles on human rights were invoked in various legal proceedings to halt the demolition of the four public housing complexes:

Article 6: International Covenant on Civil and Political Rights
Article 11: International Covenants on Economic, Social and Cultural Rights
Article 25: Universal Declaration of Human Rights
Article 27: Convention on the Rights of the Child[82]

On July 28, 2006, roughly one year after the flood, the UN Human Rights Committee issued a stinging public report, condemning the US government's role in human rights abuses in New Orleans. The report laid specific stress on the burdens of displaced persons of color who could not find adequate housing in the disaster-affected city. On February 28, 2008, two UN human rights experts took up the cause of the city's displaced low-income African Americans, issuing a joint statement in Geneva criticizing HUD's plan:

> The authorities claim that the demolition of public housing is not intentionally discriminatory, but at the end of the day African-American residents will be denied their internationally recognized human rights to safe and affordable housing.[83]

Not a month later, on March 7, the UN Committee on the Elimination of Racial Discrimination issued its *Special Procedures Bulletin* with the header "United Nations Experts Call on US Government to Protect the Rights of African-Americans Affected by Hurricane Katrina in New Orleans, Louisiana."[84] The United States is a charter member of the United Nations and one of five permanent members of the UN Security Council. Framing the right to safe, habitable housing as a human right transcends US federal and state law, raising the specter of the United States violating international law. All for naught.

## FAR FROM AN AMPLIFIED REBOUND

The four public housing projects that were home to roughly twenty thousand people have been demolished. Private developers built new mixed-income housing on two of the sites, with additional plans in place to begin building on the remaining two sites. In January 2009 the financial giant Goldman Sachs announced plans to make a major investment in the construction of apartments on the site of the now demolished C. J. Peete complex. The firm would underwrite the construction of 460 rental units.

Lloyd C. Blankfein, Goldman Sachs's chief executive officer, was quoted as saying, "We recognize the potential new capital can play in overlooked . . . sections of urban America." Alicia Glen, managing director and head of Goldman Sachs's Urban Investment Group, added, "We are honored to be a part of this joint effort between the public and private sectors to invest capital that will also create jobs and catalyze the revitalization of this community." On May 11, 2011, Goldman Sachs took out a full-page ad in the *New York Times*, touting its investment in "rebuilding an entire community in New Orleans." "Harmony Oaks," a mixed-use development, now stands where C. J. Peete once stood.[85] Mirroring the housing reconfiguration launched with HOPE VI, of the 460 rental units making up Harmony Oaks, 186 qualify for public housing–assistance vouchers.

Among the four developers awarded contracts to demolish the existing housing and build a mix of residential, apartment, and business properties was "Columbia Residential," a company formerly owned in part by HUD secretary Alphonso Jackson.[86] On March 31, 2008, Jackson resigned his post. His resignation stemmed in part from his conflict of interest surrounding the public-private partnership to demolish New Orleans's public housing and replace it with "mixed-use" development.

Ten years after the flooding of the city, Amnesty International wrote:

**6.3.** View of what was part of B. W. Cooper housing complex from Earhart Boulevard. It was demolished in 2008. Photo by Infrogmation of New Orleans, Wikimedia Commons

In 2015, the Housing Authority of New Orleans reports having 1925 total public housing apartments available for low income people, over 3000 less than what existed prior to the storm, meaning that thousands of former public housing families and residents in New Orleans were not provided a home to which to come back.[87]

The conclusion is inescapable: despite the authority of international law, the representation of many high-profile national and international nongovernmental organizations, direct intervention by the United Nations, an appeal by the Speaker of the House and the Senate majority leader, and a battery of lawsuits, the destruction of the four major public housing complexes in New Orleans occurred more or less on schedule.[88] If the Chinese and Chinatown experienced an amplified rebound, a century later the working poor in New Orleans who called public housing home were burdened with what we might call amplified inequality.

### THE HOUSING QUESTION: ENGELS REDUX

In his pamphlet *The Housing Question*, written in 1872, Friedrich Engels observed that with "the growth of modern cities," it is inevitable that the value of "centrally situated" land would increase "artificially and colossally," so much so, in fact, that "the buildings erected on these areas depress this value instead of increasing it."[89] Destroying these urban enclaves and un-raveling their long-standing social ties have occurred under the name of "renewal" at least since the days of Baron Haussmann and the remaking of Paris in the 1850s.

It takes no stretch of the imagination to see how disasters of the kind that struck San Francisco in 1906 and New Orleans in 2005 fashioned, to recall E. P. Thompson, opportunities for "class robbery." Each calamity created—in its own fashion—the chance to accumulate valued urban real estate for those with a market interest in the properties. What Engels did not consider in his foretelling analysis are the complicating factors of race and class, the variable role of the nation-state, and the fickle history of citizenship in anticipating the success or failure of attempts at spatial accumulation by dispossession.

## THE CHANGING PROTOCOL OF RACE AND CLASS

Instructions for making sense of the relationship between race and class in early-twentieth-century America might be summed up simply as follows: "The color of one's skin trumps the color of money." In 1906 San Francisco, skin color was a more potent signifier than relative wealth. To be Chinese in America at this point in time was to be seen first and foremost as a member of an alien race, no matter how much money a person or family possessed.

What this meant demographically and socially is a key to understanding how Chinese nationals succeeded in fending off the predatory actions of ar-guably the most powerful men in San Francisco. By virtue of the apartheid-like culture of race relations in early-twentieth-century San Francisco, poor as well as working-, middle-, and upper-class Chinese lived within the geo-graphic boundaries of Chinatown. Subject to denigration and possible physical violence when they ventured beyond their enclave, few if any Chi-nese lived anywhere else in town. A culture of fraternalism and mutual aid emerged. The forced ghettoization of the Chinese population made this co-hort a far more formidable foe than they might have been if they dispersed, unorganized, about the city. The wealthy merchant class spoke for all rich and poor Chinese when it threatened to move its operations to Seattle or Vancouver if efforts continued to usurp their urban space.

It was this indiscriminate racism that "placed" the early-twentieth-century black population of New Orleans into segregated neighborhoods. Here, the poor and those few who managed to crawl into the middle class lived together in separation from whites and wealthy Creoles. By the twenty-first century, however, the old rapport between race and class had changed.

Reflecting the gains made in the 1960s civil rights movement, African Americans no longer constituted what is popularly called "the black community." Strictly speaking, this community does not—and most probably never did—exist, if by community is meant collective identification and heartfelt ties among all black people living in the United States. A modicum of success among some sectors of the African American population in the past two to three decades created class cleavages that marked significant differences between lower, middle, and upper strata. More than fifty years ago, E. Franklin Frazier warned those listening of the effects of a "black bourgeoisie" on the life chances of African Americans. Affirming Frazier's concern, William Julius Wilson wrote more than thirty years ago that the once potent significance of skin color in American society has moderated over time, "so much so that now the life chances of individual blacks have more to do with their economic class position than with their day to day encounters with whites."[90]

In his redolent turn of phrase, Adolph Reed Jr. notes that it is now possible "to deal black people in and poor people out."[91] A strong black middle- and upper-middle class in particular effectively separated itself from low-income blacks and not infrequently criticizes this group for failing to take advantage of opportunities to succeed. The poor and working-class families of the housing projects, in other words, did not have the support of those African Americans who laid claim to middle- and upper-middle-class status. Perhaps they had their sympathy, but certainly not their active, vocal support. Eugene Robinson labeled America's black poor "abandoned," living in forgotten neighborhoods, making their way without the support of middle-class African Americans.[92]

It is worth noting that a middle-class redevelopment group formed in the flooded subdivision of Pontchartrain Park, the first planned African American housing tract in the United States. Started through the efforts of actor Wendell Pierce, who grew up in the subdivision, the Pontchartrain Park Neighborhood Association lobbied with considerable success to rehabilitate and revitalize the neighborhood.[93] Plans included adding green zones and refurbishing and updating a golf course and swimming pool, among other aesthetic and life-enhancing measures. Notably, this influential association has been noticeably silent on the issue of public housing. Indeed, many among New Orleans' successful black middle- and upper-middle classes see the demise of public housing as a step forward for the city.

An indiscriminate racism pushed the Chinese together, making them a far more potent collective voice. A century later, a more nuanced and class-based racism is in play; it effectively separates African Americans by material circumstances, leaving those with comparatively little to fend for themselves or rely on the good intentions of nongovernmental organizations and a panoply of international laws.

## THE CAPRICIOUS VALUE OF CITIZENSHIP

Citizenship is to the nation as class is to the market. "Nationality," Wai Chee Dimock writes, "ought to be synonymous with a guaranteed safety." To be a citizen in one's own country is or ought to wrap that person in certain inalienable protections. To tinker with a Bob Dylan verse, "Burned out from exhaustion, buried in the hail," we want to hear from those charged with ensuring our welfare, "Come in, we'll give you shelter from the storm."[94]

If citizenship matters to individuals and communities, it is because the rights that come with this status are guaranteed by the state. A stateless citizen is an oxymoron. It would seem reasonable to most anyone looking at the struggle of the Chinese to reclaim their urban American space following the earthquake and fire that they faced an uphill and promethean struggle. As permanent aliens, citizens of a vast, largely unknown nation who spoke an impenetrable language and dressed in a most un-American manner, surely they would fail in the face of a powerful coalition of financial and political elites. But with more than a touch of irony, it was precisely their legal status as Chinese nationals at a historical moment when US and Chinese relationships were of paramount concern to the Roosevelt administration that opened a potent space for the Chinese state to represent its citizens on US soil.

A century later, in another disaster in another city, a similar struggle over housing justice versus prime real estate played out quite differently. The New Orleans residents who occupied the housing complexes were not permanent aliens at all; they were and are citizens of the United States. With their housing units for the most part intact, with a severe shortage of habitable housing following the flood, and, finally, with the inalienable rights that purportedly come with being US citizens, how could the citizen-residents of public housing fail to thwart the political and economic interests that would deprive them of their homes?

At its most rudimentary, spatial accumulation by dispossession succeeded in displacing public housing residents and demolishing their homes precisely because they were American citizens, albeit citizens without representation. Absent a political state to speak on their behalf, their legal citizenship status in the United States was inconsequential. Not even the United Nations could save them.

Chinatown and public housing are two variations of urban infrastructure. In the next, and final, chapter, we continue the theme of infrastructure by examining how the recovery of inequality lights up the quite different ways the two cities themselves fared in the years following their respective catastrophes.

# ONE CITY NECESSARY,
# ONE CITY EXPENDABLE

*When its urban interests are at stake,*
*"Capitalism . . . outflanks catastrophe."*

LAWRENCE J. VALE AND THOMAS J. CAMPANELLA,
"CONCLUSION: AXIOMS OF RESILIENCE"

In the last several chapters, we paid close attention to the ways people and populations of both cities navigated the historic destruction of San Francisco in 1906 and New Orleans in 2005. We saw how each city worked out its own version of recovering inequality, creating those social kinds and categories that justified in their various definitions the parade of initiatives and activities that went by the names "disaster assistance" and "relief."

In this final discussion, a departure of sorts, I want to take a brief look at the recovery of the cities themselves. The contrasting trajectories of San Francisco and New Orleans years after their catastrophic losses expose the differences in how the region and the nation appraised the social and market value of each city at that moment in time when disaster struck.

What we find in an admittedly cursory look at this complex topic would surprise neither Engels nor Marx. It is no accident that each man sought the roots of capital in places like Paris, London, Berlin, Bonn, Cologne, and Manchester, in industrializing cities. Engels took an up-close look at Manchester in the throes of early industrialism, and the Marx family was all too conscious of its often pitiful efforts to purchase life's basic needs in the sordid tenements of a London whose landscape was changing rapidly. Life in each city confirmed what their books and ruminations taught them: capital is always consolidating geographies, building and investing here rather than there and, like loaded dice, favoring those opportunities that promised gain.[1]

Cities, literally and figuratively, are place markers in the political, social, and market identities of states, regions, and the nation at large. The reach of western cities, their power to shape the geosocial and economic landscape, has waxed and waned with the vicissitudes of history, particularly with restless capital's flux and flow. The city, writes Sharon Zukin, "exaggerates the money economy by refracting its social power through many different markets—primarily, for housing, land and labour, but also for capital itself."[2]

If cities are our most successful attempts to fashion market-centered worlds, it is reasonable to assume that the morphing forces of the market will be on vivid display as urban centers struggle to recover from disaster. In some ways, just as people are sorted in the wake of disaster into those who are deserving of relief—read: market worthy—and those who are not, so too are cities.

We begin with the two quite different responses of two Republican presidents to the flooding of New Orleans in 2005 and to the earthquake and fires in San Francisco a century earlier. Look closely and we can discern in their respective behaviors the perceived national significance of these two cities at two very different points in time.

### GEORGE AND THEODORE

At eight in the morning on August 29, 2005, New Orleans mayor Ray C. Nagin reported levee breaches in New Orleans. "We will have significant flooding, it is just a matter of how much," he declared.[3] As news out of New Orleans and the Gulf Coast got worse by the hour, Bush was on vacation in Arizona, celebrating Senator John McCain's birthday.[4]

Later that morning, Bush traveled to a resort to promote his Medicare drug benefit. By eight that evening, the president was in California, attending a San Diego Padres baseball game with Donald Rumsfeld. While Bush was enjoying the game, Louisiana governor Kathleen Blanco called him directly for assistance: "Mr. President, we need your help. We need everything you've got." Bush went to bed the night of the twenty-ninth without responding to Blanco's request.[5]

The next day, the thirtieth of August, Bush addressed the problems in Iraq at a California naval base. Around two that afternoon, a picture was taken of him playing guitar with country singer Mark Willis looking on. That evening Bush returned to Crawford, Texas, for the last day of his vacation. He had yet to contact Governor Blanco.[6]

His vacation over, the president took his first tour of the flooded city on September 12, two weeks after the levees failed. Perhaps it was a coincidence that on this day Michael Brown, FEMA's director, resigned amid a torrent of criticism over the way his agency was responding to the disaster.

If we go back in time to April 18, 1906, and the city of San Francisco, we come upon a qualitatively different response from the chief executive of the United States to an unprecedented urban catastrophe. Approximately four hours after the earthquake struck the California coast, President Theodore Roosevelt—not waiting to be contacted by a California official—wired the state's governor, George Pardee, and San Francisco's mayor, Eugene Schmitz:

> Hear Rumors of great disaster through an earthquake at San Francisco, but know nothing of the real facts. Call upon me for any assistance I can render. Theodore Roosevelt.

Sometime later that day, Roosevelt sent a second message to Mayor Schmitz:

> It was difficult at first to credit the news of the calamity that had befallen San Francisco. I feel the greatest concern and sympathy for you and the people not only of San Francisco, but of California, in this terrible disaster. You will let me know if there is anything that the National Government can do. Theodore Roosevelt

He then sent the following, quite similar, wire to Governor Pardee:

> I share with all our people the horror felt at the catastrophe that has befallen San Francisco, and the most earnest sympathy with your citizens. If there is anything the Federal Government can do to aid you it will be done. Theodore Roosevelt[7]

Roosevelt did not stop there. He quickly requested an appropriation from Congress and asked the newly reorganized American Red Cross to take a lead role in responding to the disaster.

Review these two responses and it is clear one president was deeply concerned and proactive about the fate of one city, while the other president, by all accounts, was uninterested in the destruction of the other city. We should also remember that at the turn of the twentieth century, the federal government had no legislated role to play in responding to disaster. A hundred years later, it is the president, at the behest of the governor, who declares an official disaster and sets in motion the federal relief efforts. In addition, the technologies of communication in the 1900s were prehistoric compared to the instant, on-demand high-tech devices common today. Perhaps a part of these two bluntly disparate chief executive responses is explained by the personality differences between Theodore Roosevelt and George W. Bush. They were markedly dissimilar men.

But there is something more complex than human temperament and character in play here. Roosevelt knew in 1906 what most everyone in public life knew: San Francisco was *necessary* to both the nation's market viability and its military security. Roosevelt approved of the emerging power of labor in San Francisco and the growth of the banking and industrial sectors of the city, and he was particularly aware of the importance of the San Francisco Bay and port to the trade ties between the United States and Asia. He also recognized the city as a strategic bulwark against the growing military might of Japan.[8] By 2005, on the other hand, New Orleans played no real role in either national security or the market's overall well-being.

In that televised Katrina fund-raiser when Kanye West tossed off his now historic line, "George Bush doesn't care about black people," he may have unwittingly expressed what political scientist, and former New Orleanian, Adolph Reed Jr. concluded after reflecting on New Orleans and Katrina—to wit, "race is a language through which American capitalism's class contradictions are commonly expressed."[9] Beneath skin color, in other words, are the machinations of capital.

The simple, but compelling, idea is that compared to San Francisco at the turn of the twentieth century, New Orleans at the dawn of the twenty-first century was, from a market standpoint, *expendable*. The polarized responses of these two presidents to these two disasters signify the dramatic differences in the perceived worth of the Paris of the Pacific in the early 1900s and the Paris of the South in the first years of the third millennium.

## REMAKING THE PARIS OF THE PACIFIC, A.K.A. THE JEWEL CITY

By the end of the nineteenth century, San Francisco was the eighth-largest city in the United States and boasted a population that included more than 20 percent of the West Coast from its northern to its southern tip. In addition to its sizable population, at the moment the earth cracked open in mid-April 1906 San Francisco was also the center of finance in the western United States, with an overwhelming concentration of depository and correspondence banks, insurance and underwriting companies, stock exchanges, and brokerage houses.[10] In the years following the catastrophe, the city would polish its reputation as the "Wall Street of the West," an appellation bestowed upon it by the admittedly biased *San Francisco Call and Post* in its 1926 special section "The Magic City of Western Finance."[11]

The city also housed a substantial industrial base. An urban geographer sums it up this way:

> Local machine shops turned out tools and equipment for sawmills, sugar mills, printers and factories of every kind. . . . Union Iron Works became a major shipbuilder, and many lumber schooners, ferries and fishing boats were built at the bay's edge. Ships and merchants were supplied with barrels, boxes, cordage and sails. Carriages, buckboards and cablecars were assembled in San Francisco by Pioneer Carriage Works and many small workshops. The biggest oil exploration and refining company of the time, Pacific Coast Oil . . . built the state's largest refinery; from there they exported kerosene and lubricants to China, Hawaii and Mexico. Rolling mills . . . and foundries were commonplace.[12]

By the early 1900s, San Francisco was reputed to have the best-organized and best-paid workingmen in the country. Hayden Perry offers one plausible explanation for this state of affairs: "The bosses were willing to raise wages. They had little choice since there was no pool of surplus labor west of Chicago." Though their collective bargaining power would wane as time passed, through the early years of the twentieth century the San Francisco laborer and his union were a formidable combination, "exercising more influence than organized labor in any other major American metropolitan area."[13]

The local working class was essential for the rapid revival of industry and commerce in San Francisco. While industrialists everywhere were quick to point out their version of the character flaws of the workingman, particularly his voracious appetite for higher wages, early-twentieth-century America depended on the laborer. "Thousands of men found work on civic and private reconstruction projects. They worked around the clock. . . . The jobs seemed endless for able-bodied men as salvage work created space for new construction. . . . Skilled laborers found themselves in high demand."[14] Infrastructure recovery proceeded at a rapid rate.

Following the ruin of the city, however, people with a stake in its future were not of the same mind regarding how to rebuild. The Progressives lobbied to use more fireproof building materials and require city permits to certify that the structures rebuilt met the proposed codes. Those with commercial interests lobbied Mayor Schmitz to simply use what was at hand and rebuild as quickly as possible.

Their allies, such as the "Down Town Property Owners' Association," implored the California Senate to recover "San Francisco's commercial supremacy." As Davies succinctly puts it, "The debate ended before it started as business interests were too strong to be swayed by the good intentions of Progressives."[15] Rebuilding would race forward with little or no regard for safe construction practices. By 1910, four years after the destruction of approximately 80 percent of the city, San Francisco was rebuilt, if not necessarily up to proper code.[16] Shoddy reconstruction aside, San Francisco's business class was eager to advertise the city's recovery to the United States and the world. It was time for a coming-out party.

### THE PANAMA-PACIFIC INTERNATIONAL EXPOSITION

An idea floated a couple of years before the disaster was revived: San Francisco should host an international exposition. The revival of this proposal was linked to the completion of the Panama Canal, through which ships regularly traveled to and from the city, thus inspiring the moniker the Panama-Pacific Exhibition. With a nod to hyperbole, Gavin McNab, a local magnate, made this plea, linking the speedy rebuilding of San Francisco to the remarkable feat of digging and engineering that built the Panama Canal:

> The greatest physical work of any nation is the cutting of the Panama Canal; but the greatest physical achievement of any City in History has been the rehabilitation of San Francisco. In three years we have swept away the vestiges of a calamity greater than befell Rome under Nero. . . . We now ask recognition for our services to American fame and name in rebuilding this City with our own hands.[17]

It is fair to say that McNab's hands did not soil themselves in the work of rebuilding. But the city's many industries were, for the most part, back in full employ, commercial interests were once again pursuing profit, and the rehabbed skyline of the Paris of the Pacific beckoned recognition.

But San Francisco was not the only city vying to be the site of the exhibition. With a touch of irony, early-twentieth-century New Orleans competed vigorously for the honor. After all, its port also served the ships to and from the Panama Canal on the Gulf of Mexico side of the Atlantic.

**7.1.** "The Jewel City" suggests that San Francisco had already achieved a remarkable recovery by 1915. Pacific Novelty Co.

The Paris of the South sent several prominent citizens to Washington in March 1910 to persuade President Taft to honor the city with the exhibition. Taft demurred, telling the group that Congress would have to decide the matter.[18] Congress awarded San Francisco the privilege of hosting the 1915 exhibition.

San Francisco set aside more than six hundred acres to construct its exhibition spectacle. The building site employed hundreds of workingmen and -women who, by 1913, were suffering job and pay losses on the heels of a major national economic downturn. Strikingly similar to the worthy-unworthy sorting that was deployed in the city's disaster relief efforts, those who sought a job working to build the exhibition infrastructure were subject to a "forty-eight-hour registration period [that] sorted 'the honest workers from the idlers.'"[19]

In 1915, nine years after the almost total destruction of the city, San Francisco trumpeted its return to the world as the host of the Panama-Pacific International Exhibition. Helen Keller, Thomas Edison, Buffalo Bill Cody, and Theodore Roosevelt were among the many luminaries who sang the city's praises and walked among the twenty-one international pavilions, each symbolizing both the country's and the city's progress. Approximately nineteen million people visited the exhibition and what would come to be called the "Jewel City."[20]

## REMAKING THE PARIS OF THE SOUTH, A.K.A. THE "CITY THAT CARE FORGOT"

Almost two-thirds of San Francisco was destroyed. Yet the city emerged from its devastation a towering tribute to industrial progress, commercial banking, and military significance. A century later, technological advances in river-port work along with the market's transition from a labor to a finance economy had eviscerated the industrial base of New Orleans. By 2005, as we will see, the once robust New Orleans port had become more or less a minor part of both the city's economic and its cultural identity. The post-disaster fortunes of New Orleans affirm with a vengeance Anthony Oliver-Smith's discerning observation that a catastrophe is "likely to accelerate changes that were underway before the disaster."[21]

The sobriquet the "City That Care Forgot" goes back to at least 1938, when it is mentioned in a Federal Writers' Project guide to New Orleans.[22] It is the title of a song by New Orleans legend Dr. John. It is found on the occasional park bench. It is, admittedly, an ambiguous nickname, allowing for a variety of implied meanings.

One afternoon in late 2009, I was sitting in the Crown and Anchor, a pub in Algiers Point, a neighborhood just across the Mississippi River from Canal Street. A man I had met years ago while living on "the Point," Dan Villiers, walked in and took a seat next to me. We talked as if a decade or so had not passed since the last time we set eyes on one another. The infamous hurricane and the flooding of the city were on both our minds.

Aided by a wry smile, Dan intoned, "Yes, you know us, the 'City Care Forgot,' a timely expression, I think. Yes, New Orleans, the City FEMA Forgot, the City Bush Forgot, the City Hope Forgot, the Forgotten City." I remarked that it sounded to me like he had repeated this line on more than one occasion. "It's my mantra," he replied simply. Quite unaware, Villiers had captured in his clever turn of phrase the stark difference between the post-disaster fortunes of San Francisco and those of New Orleans a century later.

In one vital sense, of course, New Orleans is not the "Forgotten City." It is still a southern Creole, Cajun, cultural mecca. New Orleans's food, music, Mardi Gras, festivals, and more beckon tourists from near and far. In 2014 the city welcomed approximately nine and a half million visitors who spent close to seven billion dollars in one year alone. As a tourist destination, the Crescent City retains a prominent place in the popular imagination.[23] But taking a longer view of Villiers's use of the adjective *forgotten* and his nickname for the city does clarify some important ways in which the modern version of New Orleans distorts its past. To recall an observation made in chapter 2, in 1900 San Francisco was the eighth-largest city in the United States, whereas New Orleans was the twelfth most populous city. By 2005, when the levees failed, New Orleans ranked fiftieth in total population among the top-fifty cities in the country.[24]

While the Paris of the South was always a place where folks *laissez les bons temps rouler*, it was also once a bustling port, with both industries and an array of businesses. Based on its substantial growth from the late nineteenth to the early twentieth centuries, in 1915 the New Orleans

> Dock Board undertook the construction of huge riverfront warehouses to encourage cotton shippers to use the city as a market of deposit. . . . With the approval and assistance of the Cotton Exchange, the Board constructed the first units of its Public Cotton Warehouse and Wharf Terminal in 1915. . . . By 1919, the 4.85 miles of water front under direct control were capable of berthing eighty-four vessels lying alongside the docks.

A local writer, Julia Truitt Bishop, waxed upbeat in 1915, calling the New Orleans port "one of the best and busiest and most economical . . . in the entire country."[25]

New Orleans's port was the principal harbor for America's cotton until 1964, when the Cotton Exchange closed its doors. Capital is never stationary. The loss of the exchange and the increased mechanizing of loading and unloading ships reduced by significant figures the numbers of working blacks and whites who made their living off the docks. The city found itself competing with smaller ports like Mobile and Gulfport. "Great ports," Richard Campanella points out, "no longer needed great port cities."[26] The port of New Orleans is still busy; you simply can't see it unless you know what you are looking for. It is disconnected from the society and culture of the city. Justin Nystrom explains why:

> Automation has transformed global shipping in the last four decades and divorced port activity from the daily lives of the city's inhabitants, a separation that fundamentally altered the social, economic, and cultural land-

**7.2.** The Canal Street levee on the Mississippi River in New Orleans, 1900.
Photochrom by William Henry Jackson, Everett Collection Inc./Alamy Stock Photo

scape of New Orleans. Life on the docks governed the city's tempo for its first two-and-a-half centuries, yet by the next generation, few people will have firsthand memory of the culture of labor and commerce that once thrived along the water's edge.[27]

A decade or so before the port was downsized, white middle-class families by the droves decamped from the city, fleeing the 1954 Supreme Court order to desegregate the schools.[28] The exodus of port and dock employment coupled with the out-migration of the white middle class reshaped the city into a majority black and underemployed population. But still more would be taken from the city.

The worldwide oil crash in the 1980s wreaked further havoc with New Orleans's economy, reducing its management role in the global petroleum industry. Adding to an already failing economy, "the meteoric rise of Houston and the broader Texas Gulf Coast port and refinery complex had already put a dent into what was for much of the nineteenth century and early twentieth century the most bustling port in the South."[29] The erosion of marine-based employment continues.

In 2010 Northrop Grumman, a major defense contractor, announced it was closing its Avondale shipyard, located just outside of Orleans Parish. The company closed the facility in 2013. An attempt to create a petroleum pipeline terminal at the site did not materialize. Approximately five thousand employees found themselves out of work. Beci Brenton, a spokeswoman for Northrop, notes, "Avondale's workforce has been trimmed to about 300 people, down from nearly 1,500 in October 2013 and 5,000 a few years ago."[30]

But long before the shipyard closed, the city was shedding the remnants of its industrial and commerce past, and a new aestheticized version was beginning to take shape and form. Former office buildings were converted to hotels for a growing hospitality industry.[31] Joe Vetter describes the scene:

> In the late 1960s Bourbon Street, Royal Street and the area around Jackson Square in the French Quarter were closed to vehicle traffic. Decatur Street, which had previously been a home to very rough seamen's bars, was "cleaned up." The Jax brewery, which was located across the street from Jackson Square, was closed and converted into an upscale tourist shopping center.[32]

By the time the city flooded, New Orleans lacked a vibrant working class that could be mobilized to begin the Sisyphean task of rebuilding.

If 1906 San Francisco had at the ready able-bodied residents—the worthy poor—to remake the city, labor, particularly skilled labor, was in short supply in New Orleans when the levees failed. Many of those who could have helped had voluntarily—or involuntarily, in the case of the public housing residents—evacuated. The extent of the devastation and the poorly managed relief efforts precluded a prompt return. While there was an immediate need for labor to rebuild the city, local labor proved hard to come by.

Some of this need was met by the hundreds of volunteers who poured into the city to help. Latino workers also came to New Orleans in search of work, many of whom toiled in good faith only to find themselves victims of wage theft.[33] Similar to San Francisco, much of the rebuilding proceeded without adhering to city construction ordinances. The recovery trajectory of New Orleans continued and in some ways amplified the already declining fortunes of the city. Enter what amounts to a leisure industry–led effort to revive the city.

## "THE TOURISM SOLUTION"

Not surprisingly, tourism was quickly hyped as the most opportune path to refashioning New Orleans. Kevin Fox Gotham and Miriam Greenberg aptly christened this "the tourism solution." As the floodwaters subsided,

> New Orleans tourism officials and their staff explicitly positioned themselves as the saviors and master planers of a "new" New Orleans. . . . "The future of New Orleans has never been brighter thanks to the renaissance of the tourism industry," according to the NOMCVB (New Orleans Metropolitan Convention and Visitors Bureau).[34]

While tourism generates local and regional revenue, and a tourist city may well be a destination for foreign travelers, the link between tourists and either industrial or financial capital is weak at best. Tourism capital cannot compete with its counterparts in finance and industry. Businesses are not as likely to invest in cities that do not have a history of economic stability.[35] As New Orleans became increasingly synonymous with tourism, its place in the market scheme of things became more a footnote than a formidable chapter in the story of the US economy.

By 2011 the leisure and hospitality industry employed roughly seventy-eight thousand people in the Greater New Orleans area. Tourism employs more people than work in oil, gas, and shipping combined.[36] Service-sector businesses are fragile, often requiring state and federal government incentives to start up and train employees. It is also worth noting that many of the chronically underemployed or underpaid service employees also need assistance from government programs whose budgets are frequently trimmed to satisfy the neoliberal austerity principle.

It is safe to assume that a democratic city in a bright-red state like Louisiana is not likely to get much in the way of state compassion in this area, and the federal government was already spending historic amounts to help the Gulf Coast and New Orleans rebuild. If tourism "cannot save cities in the throes of decline," as Melanie Smith suggests, it is not likely to salvage an already waning city two-thirds of which is suddenly submerged in the most massive urban flood in US history. But perhaps not surprisingly, it tried.[37]

The New Orleans tourism industry wasted little time in monetizing the disaster, creating its own version of pop-up tourism. "We had Katrina tours pop up," notes Jennifer Day-Sully of the New Orleans Convention and Visitors Bureau. "So the visitors who were coming, even if they were coming to see the destruction, were helping the recovery." Isabelle Cossart, who owns one of the tour companies in the city, "Tours by Isabelle," boldly claims that "employees of her company who lost their homes and belongings were able to make a living again only because she began offering 'Post-Katrina Tours' to curious visitors."[38]

I took one of these tours in 2008, though not the one offered by Isabelle. To slake our thirst as we drove through flood-ravaged neighborhoods on a blisteringly hot day in an air-conditioned van, we tourists were offered one of New Orleans's own signature cocktails that goes by the name, somewhat disconcertingly, "hurricane," a drink with rum, fruit juice, and grenadine.

"Hurricanes" aside, the simple fact is that the tourism industry cannot create a vibrant middle class. Nor can it help those who were most damaged by the disaster. "The great irony of New Orleans' reconstruction," Roberto E. Barrios writes, "is that the disaster . . . has become an ongoing part of everyday life."[39]

One bright spot in the city's recovery trajectory is the investment the federal government made in health care delivery. A 2007 federal grant totaling $100 million helped create several local primary care clinics that serve the uninsured. The recent opening of the University Medical Center, which replaced the heralded Charity Hospital, is also contributing to the creation of more jobs that pay a livable wage.[40] But if the federal government giveth, the state government taketh away. In 2009 Governor Bobby Jindal eliminated funding for New Orleans's adolescent mental health facility. Gary Rivlin puts this budget cut in perspective:

> The city had endured a terrible trauma yet lost dozens of psychiatric beds along with hundreds of mental health professionals. Five years after Katrina, the suicide rate in New Orleans was still at least twice as high as it was before the storm.[41]

In their 2013 article in *Business Insider* "11 American Cities That Are Shells of Their Former Selves," Pamela Engel and Rob Wile place New Orleans at the top of their list of cities in dramatic decline. At its peak in 1960, the city's population stood at 627,525. By 2015 the New Orleans

Data Center reported a total population of just under 390,000, a decline of slightly more than 40 percent of its 1960 total. Writing in 2014 for the *New Orleans Times-Picayune*, Robert McClendon offers an unsparing assessment:

> New Orleans ranks second worst in the country for income inequality, according to Bloomberg, which maintains a ranking of the most unequal cities in the country. The report puts inequality in New Orleans roughly on par with that in Zambia, according to statistics kept by the Central Intelligence Agency.

A year later, in 2015, the tenth anniversary of Katrina, New Orleans ranked "second in income inequality among 300 US Cities."[42] And so it goes . . .

Nine years after its earthquake and firestorms, San Francisco hosted the 1915 Panama-Pacific International Exposition. The city was the center of a ten-month spectacle announcing its return from unimaginable destruction. At the center of the exposition was the "Tower of Jewels," more than one hundred thousand pieces of cut glass, "Novagems" rising 435 feet in the air.

In 2015, ten years after the waters breached the levees and flooded the city, President Barack Obama traveled to New Orleans to speak at a rebuilt community center in the city's Lower Ninth Ward, a neighborhood that still bore the unmistakable reminder of the crushing flood. He praised those in attendance as examples of "what's possible when, in the face of tragedy and hardship, good people come together to lend a hand, and to build a better future."[43]

The president's words belie the evidence surrounding him. Ten years after Katrina laid waste to 80 percent of the city, New Orleans boasts no Tower of Jewels announcing its return. Rather, just down the street from the community center the president chose as his venue, the abandoned shells of houses speak quietly of a city not deemed worthy of recovery.


## ON BEING "FORGOTTEN": A CODA

To characterize New Orleans as "forgotten" might seem a stretch if we look at the extraordinary amount of federal money that poured into the flooded city. After all, the federal government spent $120.5 billion on the city's recovery. Roughly $75 billion of that sum, however, as Allison Plyer of the New Orleans Data Center explains, "went to emergency relief, not rebuilding," while "private insurance claims covered less than $30 billion of the losses."[44]

**7.3.** Two houses in the Lower Ninth Ward, December 2016. Photos by author

People, at least some people, were helped. But the infrastructure of the city, its basic physical and structural facilities, New Orleans's very foundation, was not of prime concern. When Dan Villiers invokes the epithet *forgotten*, he is calling attention to twenty-first-century America in the crucible of a morphing market society and a wounded New Deal.

I wonder what Villiers would make of Bryn Mickle's opinion column written for the *Flint Journal News Leader*: "Flint, Michigan: Welcome to America's Forgotten City." Published in March 2016, Mickle describes the cruel twist of events that turned the "once proud birthplace of General Motors and the United Auto Workers Union," home to colleges, museums, and a symphony, into a city where four in ten live at or below the poverty line and no one has safe drinking water.[45]

The story of the Flint water crisis connects in some fashion to the story of New Orleans. Both add some credence to the idea animating this chapter—to wit, in a market society, capital will find a way to rescue a city deemed market worthy. Consider, for example, the Great Chicago Fire of 1871. While a harrowing tale of destruction, the Great Chicago Fire could not change the trajectory of a city with a robust and growing economy.

In his 1933 book on the historic development of land value in Chicago, Homer Hoyt observes, "Many of Chicago's commercial rivals hoped that (the fire) would permanently halt the industrial and commercial progress of the city. . . . The railroad band of iron and steel and the trade connections of Chicago, however, were too thoroughly established to permit that happening."[46] The contrasting paths of Chicago, San Francisco, New Orleans, and Flint in the years following their own unique tragedies remind us that market-driven recoveries will likely vary with the morphing forces of capital.

# BY WAY OF CLOSING

*There are classes of problems that free
markets simply do not deal with well.*

ECONOMIST THOMAS C. SCHELLING, QUOTED IN
PETER G. GOSSELIN, "ON THEIR OWN IN BATTERED
NEW ORLEANS," *LOS ANGELES TIMES*

A long trek through history with several side trips along the way, whirling facts, concepts aplenty—much has been discussed in these past chapters. The juxtaposition of materials, some of which are not routinely associated with one another, begs the reader's patience. Few will find themselves completely satisfied with all that makes up this collage. Nor am I.

Yet there is a discernible point of view—I trust—that connects these many fragments. No one way of looking at things, William James knew, "can ever take in the whole scene."[1] Look at something this way, and you are not likely to see it that way. In this tale of two American disasters, we took a hard look at a potent, if unsettling, idea: when it comes to disaster recovery in societies organized around the pursuit of capital, there is, simply put, no alternative to market logic.[2] It is this way of looking that connects the many pieces and fragments of this inquiry, and it is this way of looking that I have sought to pass on.

Early-twentieth-century America differed markedly from America in the first decade of the twenty-first century. A vibrant Progressive movement responded to the challenges of a rapidly emerging industrial economy. The architects of social Darwinism, Herbert Spencer and William Graham Sumner, were soundly criticized by muckraking journalists such as Jacob Riis, activists—think Jane Addams—and a variety of intellectuals, including sociologist Lester Frank Ward, who argued persuasively for the social origins of inequality. Predatory businessmen like John D. Rockefeller were targets of sharply critical social commentary. The working class found its voice in unions. A sympathetic state was in the making.

By 2005, however, capital had made significant strides in freeing itself from labor, and a more polished, less biocentered version of social Darwinism was back in play. Working families increasingly bear the risks of predacious financial schemes, unions are eviscerated, and free-market solutions are relied on to create a neoliberal version of American exceptionalism. By the 1980s President Reagan could claim that "the size of the federal budget is not an appropriate barometer of social conscience or charitable concern." The private sector, volunteers, and NGOs—President George H. W. Bush's "Thousand Points of Light"—were encouraged to act in the place of a sympathetic state.[3]

This new version of social Darwinism is neatly expressed in the budget proposal of the current Speaker of the House. Paul Ryan's financial plan aims to radically reduce the role of the state in a market-based economy that cannot, by its own design, employ everyone at a respectable, life-sustaining wage. Ryan fears that those who must rely on the government to supplement what a capital-intensive economy cannot provide will, by doing so, take their rest in "a hammock that lulls able-bodied people into lives of dependency and complacency, that drains them of their will and their incentive to make the most of their lives."[4]

If sixteenth-century England relied on its "reserve army of the poor" to fill the ranks of the foot soldier, the modern market society has its standby army of poor and underemployed to sweep the halls, clean the toilets, take out the trash, wash dirty dishes, and so on through the parade of menial tasks that "the worthy" choose to avoid.[5] Coddle this army—read: help them make ends meet, to live another week or month—Ryan reasons, and we risk robbing them of their human proclivity to labor.[6] It is likely easier for those who count their lives successes to embrace the mantle of a radical individualism that elevates autonomy above history.

It is no surprise that the beginning of the twenty-first century varies in important ways from the first few years of the 1900s. History, like capital, is always on the move. Yet each period mirrors, in its own fashion, John Dewey's description of America on the cusp of the Great Depression as a country whose "occupation is acquisition, whose concern is with security, and whose creed is that the established economic regime is peculiarly 'natural' and hence immutable in principle." What San Francisco at the dawn of the twentieth century shares with New Orleans a century later is a dependence on the inexorable logic of the market, and it is this logic that was deployed in both disasters to solve the demanding complexities of recovery.

What both calamities exposed is that always precarious arrangement that hides—stretching Gunnar Myrdal's original idea—America's essential dilemma: race *and* class inequality cloaked in the high drama of "democratic stagecraft."[7]

In the past several chapters, we examined up close the reshuffling of the diverse people whose lives shifted from some reasonable sense that this-would-follow-that to life without such a guarantee. In first-person accounts of human behavior in the wake of catastrophe, we witnessed the human spirit to reach out and help and accept help in return. We looked into the deep roots of the looting myth. There we discerned the ways fictional social kinds—the ghoul, the looter, and more—are fashioned to counter that utopian moment of togetherness and begin the work of re-sorting a jumbled array of disparate peoples, a first step in returning to some semblance of a market-ordered city. We took a concerted look at the complex work to base disaster assistance on a metric loyal to something other than the visceral human need among all who suffer to reclaim the surety that this would, indeed, follow that.

We also examined in some detail the perverse efforts to accumulate valuable urban real estate from vulnerable people who differed in kind from the more powerful and privileged. Shaping and informing the rearrangement of the socio-spatial configuration of the cities, the distribution of relief, and the aggressive attempts to steal from the marginalized was that invisible hand working tirelessly in the service of market interests. A final chapter shifted the unit of concern to the cities themselves, looking all too briefly at their disparate recoveries.

Please note, I am not arguing for some kind of conspiracy or purposeful behavior that recovers inequality. When society bowed to the market, the fact is that most everything became a business deal, including disaster recovery. Each chapter rests on the assumption that those material and symbolic differences necessary for the well-being of a market society were embedded so deeply in the tissue of both 1906 and 2005 America that willful, intentional acts of recovery discrimination were not necessary to re-create durable inequality following the two catastrophes. Indeed, the re-creating of human disparity proceeds apace with recovery, assuming the appearance of the "natural" to an arguably greater effect than the two catastrophes themselves.[8]

Recall chapter 5 for a moment and progressive Edward Devine, Columbia professor of social economy, who, in explaining the task of disaster relief workers in San Francisco, notes, "We pay them to discriminate." His stark message is mirrored in the words of FEMA director Joseph Allbaugh, who, in his testimony to Congress a couple of years before the flooding of New Orleans, expresses his concern that "federal disaster assistance may have evolved into . . . an oversized entitlement program." In each of these statements, we can discern an algorithm of recovery that begins with the seemingly commonsense—read: natural—assumption that a victim of disaster must first be judged worthy, eligible, a proper candidate for relief.

Ralph Waldo Emerson thought a good deal about the natural and nature. Sidney Hook was thinking of the poet of Concord when he wrote, "Nature can run amok [and] the sufferings produced by the mindless intrusions of fire . . . flood and wind in human affairs often dwarf those resulting from human cruelty." There is some truth in Hook's tip of the hat to Emerson. But it is ironic, is it not, that the human labor done in the name of disaster relief too often creates a suffering, a cruelty, that equals or exceeds that wrought by nature?[9] This meanness, and the unself-conscious way it is expressed, is a visible, dramatic portrayal of the mundane, commonplace injustices that pass ignored in routine, day-to-day market life. This ordinary, pedestrian arrangement of class and race disparity is, simply put, thrown into sharp relief in the wake of disaster.[10]

How could it be otherwise in a society where the motive power—the primeval mover—is material, not human, interests? It was inescapable that recovery efforts would work to remake each city in the interests of the market. It is this path dependency that joins these two periods in history, each marked by the concerted efforts of local, state, and federal groups and agencies to achieve something we call "recovery."

## "WHAT IS THE SHELF LIFE OF AN HISTORICAL LESSON?"

Many who watched the flooding of this irreplaceable city at the turn of the twenty-first century saw it as an omen, a sign that things are not well with us as a people.[11] For some, to paraphrase Dostoyevsky, it was reason enough to give back their tickets to the universe. Yet the visceral rage expressed by those who watched this cataclysm and the inhuman treatment of fellow citizens offers modest hope that we could find a more compassionate way to coexist in this America.

A market society, after all, is something we made and did so for a reason. It answered certain questions for us while solving certain problems. But now it is getting in our collective way. It is polarizing us. In the antiseptic words of the Federal Reserve, "Wealth is highly concentrated in the United States, and top shares have been rising in recent decades, raising both normative and macroeconomic policy concerns."[12] It is the "normative," now commonplace ways we adjust our feelings, our actions, our everyday lives to the coarseness of market-driven unfairness that beckon some considered thought.

Some of us hoped that the physical and social decimation of New Orleans was an invitation to imagine a different society, one tilted more toward equality and fellow feelings. But this would require—at a minimum—that we agree to walk away from what Polanyi called a "market society" and toward a more compassionate social contract. Polanyi himself envisioned this move. His "great transformation" was, in one sense, a double entendre. It was meant to describe a momentous shift to a society subservient to the demands of a market economy, on the one hand, and a historic shift away from this arrangement, on the other, toward a more prosocial, compassionate society, one where the pursuit of human well-being replaced the quest for profit.

It is now more than twelve years since the levees fell and the city flooded. There is little evidence to date that we have changed course. As the twenty-first century rolls on, a reality television star with a history of multiple bankruptcies, and a rather perverse need for the admiration of others, occupies the office of the presidency. His proposed budget for 2018 would cut FEMA's funding by $600 million and encourage cities and states to assume more responsibility for the cost of disaster.[13] But extreme weather waits for no inept or adept political leadership, nor does it care a whit for whatever form the market takes at any given historical moment.

### HELLO "HARVEY" AND . . .

As I write on this brisk Sunday, September 10, 2017, parts of Houston, Texas, remain underwater from Hurricane Harvey. Harvey will be remembered as a rain event, dumping during a six-day period an estimated 27 trillion gallons of rain over Texas and Louisiana. To help put this in perspective, that's an average of 4 trillion, 500 million gallons a day, for six days. The sheer magnitude of this catastrophe left people working at the National Weather Service scrambling to cobble together words that adequately conveyed the range and depth of destruction.[14] Harvey wreaked havoc on America's fourth-largest city. The amount of destruction exceeds that wrought by Katrina. Predictably, rebuilding Houston will come with a price tag that far exceeds the cost of rebuilding New Orleans.

I suspect, however, that whatever the cost, the trajectory of recovery in

Houston will be more like that of San Francisco than New Orleans. Similar to San Francisco at the dawn of the twentieth century, Houston in the second decade of the twenty-first century is essential to the stability of a market society. Notably, Mayor Sylvester Turner proclaimed confidently, less than a week after the historic flooding of the city, with several neighborhoods still underwater, "Let me be very, very clear: the City of Houston is open for business."[15] On a final note, Hurricane Irma is just over the horizon, and a second tropical storm is queued up behind Irma. What awaits us?

# NOTES

## FROM WHENCE RECOVERY?

1. Ron Eyerman, 2015, *Is This America? Katrina as Cultural Trauma* (Austin: University of Texas Press).

2. Julia Vitullo-Martin and J. Robert Moskin, 1994, *The Executive's Book of Quotations* (New York: Oxford University Press), 105.

## CHAPTER 1: "THE EARTH DRAGON" AND "MISS KATRINA"

1. Charles Augustus Keeler, ca. 1906, "San Francisco through Earthquake and Fire," Paul Elder, courtesy of the Bancroft Library, University of California, Berkeley.

2. Gordon Thomas and Max Morgan Witts, 1971, *The San Francisco Earthquake* (New York: Stein and Day), 66. See also David Perlman, 2006, "The Great Quake, 1906–2006: The Epicenter," *SFGate*, April 11, sfgate.com/bayarea/article/The-Great-Quake-1906-2006-The-epicenter-2520146.php (accessed March 2015).

3. Fred J. Hewitt, 1906, "Wreck of City's Buildings Awful," Virtual Museum of the City of San Francisco, April 19, sfmuseum.net/1906/ew4.html (accessed March 2015).

4. Helen Hillyer Brown, 1976 [1906], *The Great San Francisco Fire* (San Francisco: Hillside Press), 23.

5. Laurence Yep, 2006, *The Earth Dragon Awakes: The San Francisco Earthquake of 1906* (New York: HarperCollins).

6. The 1906 San Francisco earthquake and firestorms were the first disaster to be photographed. Kodak's first camera was available in 1888 for those who could afford it. By 1900 the Kodak Brownie, a far cheaper model, was widely popular.

7. Christoph Strupp, 2006, "Dealing with Disaster: The San Francisco Earthquake of 1906," Institute of European Studies, paper 060322, University of California, Berkeley, 7–8.

8. Marie Bolton, 1997, "Recovery for Whom? Social Conflict after the San Francisco Earthquake and Fire, 1906–1915" (PhD diss., University of California, Davis).

9. "Jack London and the Great Earthquake and Fire," sfmuseum.org/hist5/jlondon.html (accessed April 2015).

10. Ibid.

11. David McCullough is quoted in the 2006 film *American Experience: The Great San Francisco Earthquake*, pbs.org/wgbh/amex/earthquake/ (accessed April 2015).

12. Nicole Cooley, 2010, *Breach* (Baton Rouge: Louisiana State University Press), 1.

13. Kevin L. Alive, 2005, "Truth Oral History: New Orleans Disaster," Oral History and Memory Project, interviewed September 11, nzdl.org/gsdlmod? (accessed June 2015).

14. Steve Kroll-Smith, Vern Baxter, and Pam Jenkins, 2015, *Left to Chance: A Story of Two New Orleans Neighborhoods* (Austin: University of Texas Press), 5.

15. Dietmar Felber, 2010, "At Lafayette School after Hurricane Katrina: An American Ghost Story," *Mississippi Quarterly*, June 22, thefreelibrary.com/At+Lafayette+School+after+Hurricane+Katrina%3a+an+American+ghost+story.-a02592 96682 (accessed April 2015).

16. Lucien Febvre quoted in Ira Katznelson, 1992, *Marxism and the City* (Oxford: Oxford University Press), 1; Friedrich Nietzsche, 1974, *The Gay Science* (New York: Random House), 218.

17. Jean Baudrillard, 2008, *The Perfect Crime* (London: Verso Press), 64.

18. Howard Zinn finds history anything but well ordered; for him, it is a jungle. "The only thing I am really sure of is that we who plunge into the jungle need to think about what we are doing, because there is somewhere we want to go." Zinn, 1990, *The Politics of History* (Urbana: University of Illinois Press).

19. Elizabeth Clemens, 2007, "Toward a Historicized Sociology: Theorizing Events, Processes, and Emergence," *Annual Review of Sociology* 33: 533; Charles Tilly, 1990, *Coercion, Capital, and European States* (Malden, MA: Blackwell), 35.

20. E. L. Quarantelli, 2006, "Catastrophes Are Different from Disasters: Some Implications for Crisis Planning and Managing Drawn from Katrina," Social Sciences Research Council, June 11, ssrc.org (accessed April 2010); Department of Homeland Security, 2008, "National Response Framework," fema.gov/pdf/emergency/nrf/nrf-core.pdf (accessed February 2015).

21. Dennis Smith, 2006, "The Greatest Fire Alarm in American History," firehouse.com/news/10501077/the-greatest-fire-alarm-in-american-history (accessed March 2016).

22. Dennis Smith, 2005, *San Francisco Is Burning: The Untold Story of the 1906 Earthquake and Fires* (New York: Penguin Press), 47.

23. Andrea Rees Davies, 2012, *Saving San Francisco: Relief and Recovery after the 1906 Disaster* (Philadelphia: Temple University Press), 17.

24. Brian Handwerk, 2005, "New Orleans Levees Not Built for Worst Case Events," *National Geographic News*, September 2, news.nationalgeographic.com/news/2005/09/0902_050902_katrina_levees.html (accessed April 2011); Douglas Brinkley, 2015, "The Broken Promise of the Levees That Failed New Orleans," *Smithsonian Magazine*, September, smithsonianmag.com/smithsonian-institution/broken-promise-levees-failed-new-orleans-180956326/ (accessed October 2009); William Freudenburg et al., 2009, *Catastrophe in the Making: The Engineering of Katrina and the Disasters of Tomorrow* (Washington, DC: Island Press).

25. Friedrich Nietzsche, 1988, "The Drama of Zarathustra," in *Nietzsche's New Seas*, edited by Michael Allen Gillespie and Tracy B. Strong (Chicago: University of Chicago Press), 220–231.

26. See Flyvbjerg's brief, but informative, discussion of types of case studies in Bent Flyvbjerg, 2001, *Making Social Science Matter* (Cambridge: Cambridge University Press), 80.

27. Richard Wright, 2008, "Down by the Riverside," in *Uncle Tom's Children* (New York: HarperCollins), 12–13.

28. W. E. B. DuBois, 1994 [1903], *The Souls of Black Folk* (New York: Dover), 7.

29. Wright, 2008, 13.

30. Clifford Geertz, 1983, *Local Knowledge* (New York: Basic Books), 180. The significance of categorical inequality in understanding how we sort ourselves into groups and classes and vertically rank those sortings into powerful and weak, worthy and unworthy, prized and despised, and so on is forcefully argued in Charles Tilly, 1999, *Durable Inequality* (Berkeley: University of California Press). A category, Tilly offers, is a culturally and socially organized system of distinction: "Bounded categories deserve special attention because they provide clearer evidence for the operation of durable inequality, because their boundaries do crucial organizational work, and because categorical differences actually account for much of what ordinary observers take to be the result of variation in individual talent or effort" (66).

31. DuBois, 1994 [1903], 92.

32. Kenneth Hewitt, 1983, *Interpretations of Calamity* (Boston: Allen and Irwin), 9.

33. Juan Murria, 2004, "Feedback from the Field: A Disaster, by Any Other Name," *International Journal of Mass Emergencies and Disasters* 22(1): 117–129.

34. Samuel Henry Prince, 2011 [1920], *Catastrophe and Social Change: Based upon a Sociological Study of the Halifax Disaster* (Charleston, SC: Nabu Press), 20; Philip Fradkin, 2005, *The Great Earthquake and Firestorms of 1906* (Berkeley: University of California Press), xiii; Rebecca Solnit, 2009, *A Paradise Built in Hell: The Extraordinary Communities That Arise in Disaster* (New York: Penguin Books), 16.

35. David Harvey, 1973, *Social Justice and the City* (Athens: University of Georgia Press), 16.

36. Charles Dickens, 1999 [1859], *A Tale of Two Cities* (Mineola, NY: Dover).

37. Kenneth Burke, 1989, *On Symbols and Society* (Chicago: University of Chicago Press), 70.

38. Eric R. Wolf registered this insight in the literature more than two decades ago: "The arrangements of a society become most visible when they are challenged by crisis." Wolf, 1990, "Distinguished Lecture: Facing Power—Old Insights, New Questions," *American Anthropologist* 92(3): 593.

39. Kroll-Smith, Baxter, and Jenkins, 2015.

## CHAPTER 2: GEOGRAPHIES OF INEQUALITY

1. Morris Birkbeck, 1818, *Notes on a Journey in America from the Coast of Virginia to the Territory of Illinois*, 4th ed. (London: Severn), 66.

2. Tony Williams, 2011, *The Jamestown Experiment: The Remarkable Story of the Enterprising Colony and the Unexpected Results That Shaped America* (Naperville, IL: Sourcebooks), xi–xii, 31–32. American historian Nancy Isenberg writes, "As the English conceived it . . . any land had to be taken out of its natural state and put to commercial use—only then would it be truly owned." See her noteworthy book *White Trash: The 400-Year Untold History of Class in America* (New York: Viking Press), 18.

3. W. E. B. DuBois, 1994 [1903], *The Souls of Black Folk* (New York: Dover), 50.

4. US Geological Survey, 2008, "Bay Area Earthquake Probabilities," earthquake.usgs.gov/regional/nca/ucerf/ (accessed October 2014).

5. William Issel and Robert W. Cherny, 1986, *San Francisco, 1865–1932: Politics, Power, and Urban Development* (Berkeley: University of California Press), 8.

6. James E. Vance Jr., 1964, *Geography and Urban Evolution in the San Francisco Bay Area* (Berkeley: Institute for Government Studies), 3.

7. Gray Brechin, 2006, *Imperial San Francisco: Urban Power, Earthly Ruin* (Berkeley: University of California Press).

8. Simon Winchester, 2005, *A Crack in the Edge of the World* (New York: Harper's), 239.

9. "Proceedings of the 39th Annual Meeting of the National Board of Fire Underwriters, 1905," quoted in Andrea Davies Henderson, 2005, "Reconstructing Home: Gender, Disaster Relief, and Social Life after the San Francisco Earthquake and Fire, 1906–1915" (PhD diss., Stanford University), 37.

10. Hermann Schussler, 1900, "The Water Supply of San Francisco, California: Before, during and after the Earthquake of April 18th, 1906," quoted in Henderson, 2005, 37n59.

11. Ari Kelman, 2003, *A River and Its City: The Nature of Landscape in New Orleans* (Berkeley: University of California Press), 4.

12. Richard Campanella, 2007, "Above-Sea-Level New Orleans: The Residential Capacity of Orleans Parish's Higher Ground," unpublished report, Center for Bioenvironmental Research, April, 3.

13. Lawrence A. Powell, 2012, *The Accidental City: Improvising New Orleans* (Cambridge, MA: Harvard University Press).

14. Earthea Nance, 2009, "Responding to Risk: The Making of Hazard Mitigation Strategy in Post-Katrina New Orleans," *Journal of Contemporary Water Research & Education* 141 (March): 21–30.

15. Deon Roberts, 2008, "Drainage Veteran Calls for Greater Pump Capacity," *New Orleans City Business*.

16. Peirce F. Lewis, 2003, *New Orleans: The Making of an Urban Landscape* (Charlottesville: University Press of Virginia), 19–20; see also Kelman, 2003, 6.

17. Anthony Oliver-Smith captures the social-environmental complexity of disaster in these words: "What really constitutes a disaster . . . is the combination of a destructive agent from the natural and/or man-made environment and a group of

human beings living in a specific local socio-cultural context." Oliver-Smith, 1986, "Disaster Context and Causation: An Overview of Changing Perspectives," in *Natural Disasters and Cultural Responses*, edited by Oliver-Smith, Disaster Studies in Third World Societies (Williamsburg, VA: College of William and Mary), 1–34.

18. Kenneth Hewitt, 1983, *Interpretations of Calamity* (Boston: Allen and Unwin), 9.

19. US Geological Survey, "Earthquake History of the Bay Area," earthquakesafety .com/earthquake-history.html (accessed March 2015); "New Orleans, Louisiana's History with Tropical Storms," hurricanecity.com/city/neworleans.htm (accessed March 2015). See also David Roth, "Louisiana Hurricane History," National Weather Service, Camp Springs, MD, srh.noaa.gov/images/lch/tropical/lahurricanehistory .pdf (accessed March 2015).

20. Lewis, 2003, 10.

21. Andrew Carnegie, 1889, "The Gospel of Wealth," *North American Review*, xroads.virginia.edu/~drbr/wealth.html (accessed May 2015).

22. Issel and Cherny, 1986, 23.

23. Young Chen, 2000, *Chinese San Francisco, 1850–1943* (Stanford, CA: Stanford University Press).

24. Issel and Cherny, 1986, 16.

25. Philip Fradkin, 2005, *The Great Earthquake and Firestorms of 1906* (Berkeley: University of California Press), 33.

26. Marie Bolton, 1997, "Recovery for Whom? Social Conflict after the San Francisco Earthquake and Fire, 1906–1915" (PhD diss., University of California, Davis), 8.

27. Christoph Strupp, 2006, "Dealing with Disaster: The San Francisco Earthquake of 1906," Institute of European Studies, paper 060322, University of California, Berkeley, 14.

28. Michael Kazin, 1989, *The Barons of Labor: The San Francisco Building Trades and Union Power in the Progressive Era* (Urbana: University of Illinois Press), 13.

29. Christopher M. Douty, 1977, *The Economics of Localized Disasters: The San Francisco Catastrophe* (New York: Arno Press), 174. Worth noting, Baker would draw on a markedly different vocabulary—as we will see—to describe the aftermath of the San Francisco earthquake and firestorms.

30. Ibid., 174.

31. Kazin, 1989, 18.

32. From clerical workers to small business owners, the middle class was not monolithic. The concept of an "upper middle class" emerged in the 1890s, and it would take another several decades for the idea of a "lower middle class" to enter the vernacular. Lewis Coser, 2004, *The Dictionary of the History of Ideas* (Charlottesville, VA: Electronic Text Center), 1–21.

33. David Hilfiker, 2006, "A History of Poverty in America," onbeing.org/program/seeing-poverty-after-katrina/extra/history-poverty-america-chapter-4/2156, chap. 4 (accessed April 2015).

34. Thorstein Veblen, 1899, *The Theory of the Leisure Class* (New York: Macmillan).

35. William James, 1992 [1899], "What Makes a Life Significant?," in *On Some of Life's Ideals*, edited by James (New York: Henry Holt), 49–94.

36. Michael E. McGerr, 2003, *A Fierce Discontent: The Rise and Fall of the Progressive Movement in America, 1870–1920* (New York: Free Press), 7.

37. Nell Painter, 2013, *Standing at Armageddon: A Grassroots History of the Progressive Era* (New York: W. W. Norton), xxxiii, 24.

38. Peter R. Decker, 1978, *Fortunes and Failure: White-Collar Mobility in Nineteenth Century San Francisco* (Cambridge, MA: Harvard University Press), 266.

39. Issel and Cherny, 1986, 16.

40. David Harvey, 2005, *A Brief History of Neoliberalism* (Oxford: Oxford University Press), 169.

41. "Margaret Thatcher Wanted to Crush Power of Trade Unions," *Guardian*, July 31, 2013, theguardian.com/uk-news/2013/aug/01/margaret-thatcher-trade-union-reform-national-archives (accessed April 2015).

42. Ronald Reagan, 1981, "Remarks and a Question-and-Answer Session with Reporters on the Air Traffic Controllers Strike," August 3, Ronald Reagan Presidential Library and Museum, reaganlibrary.archives.gov/archives/speeches/1981/80381a.htm (accessed July 2017).

43. *Wikipedia*, s.v. "Largest Cities in the United States," en.wikipedia.org/wiki/Largest_cities_in_the_United_States_by_population_by_decade#1900 (accessed April 2015).

44. "Top Cities in the United States by Population and Rank," infoplease.com/ipa/a0763098.html (accessed on April 2015).

45. "The Black Population: 2000," Census 2000 Brief, census.gov/prod/2001pubs/c2kbr01-5.pdf (accessed April 2015).

46. Bruce Katz, 2006, "Concentrated Poverty in New Orleans and Other American Cities," Brookings Institution, brookings.edu/opinions/concentrated-poverty-in-new-orleans-and-other-american-cities (accessed April 2015).

47. Bruce H. Webster Jr. and Alemayehu Bishaw, 2006, "Income, Earnings, and Poverty Data from the 2005 American Community Survey," US Department of Commerce Economics and Statistics Administration, census.gov/prod/2006pubs/acs-02.pdf (accessed November 2016).

48. Lewis, 2003, 128.

49. Kelman, 2003, 211. Kelman quotes a journalist on the Magnolia curtain: "the Magnolia curtain, that curious combination of indolence and political self-interest that has settled so charmingly over the First Families of New Orleans."

50. Lewis, 2003, 128.

51. Sharon Zukin, 2006, "David Harvey on Cities," in *David Harvey: A Critical Reader*, edited by Noel Castree and Derek Gregory (Malden, MA: Blackwell), 113.

52. Karl Polanyi, 1944, *The Great Transformation: The Political and Economic Origins of Our Time* (New York: Beacon Press), 54.

53. Aristotle, 1916, bk. 4 of *A Treatise on Government*, translated by William Ellis (London: E. P. Dutton), 126.

54. Charles Baudelaire, 2008, *Paris Spleen* (Indianapolis: Hackett), 52–53.

55. Mary Douglas, 2002 [1966], *Purity and Danger* (New York: Routledge).

56. Friedrich Engels, 1895, *Introduction to Karl Marx's "The Class Struggles in France, 1848 to 1850,"* marxists.anu.edu.au/archive/marx/works/1895/03/06.htm (accessed April 2015); Polanyi, 1944, 57.

57. Marianne Weber, 1988, *Max Weber: A Biography* (Piscataway, NJ: Transaction Books), 85–286.

58. Susan T. Fisk and Shelly E. Taylor, 1991, *Social Cognition*, 2nd ed. (New York: McGraw-Hill).

59. Ian Hacking, 1999, *The Social Construction of What?* (Cambridge, MA: Harvard University Press), 126, 125.

60. Robert Park, 1916, "The City: Suggestions for the Investigation of Human Behavior in the Urban Environment," *American Journal of Sociology* 20 (March): 577.

61. Erving Goffman, 1963, *Behavior in Public Places* (New York: Free Press), 10; Harvey Zorbaugh, 1983 [1929], *The Gold Coast and the Slum: A Sociological Study of Chicago's Near North Side* (Chicago: University of Chicago Press), xix; Ira Katznelson, 1992, *Marxism and the City* (Oxford: Oxford University Press), 16–17.

62. Erving Goffman, 1959, *The Presentation of Self in Everyday Life* (New York: Doubleday); Elijah Anderson, 2015, "The White Space," *Sociology of Race and Ethnicity* 1(1): 10–21; Katznelson, 1992, 20.

63. Cindi Katz, 2006, "Messing with the 'Project,'" in *David Harvey*, edited by Castree and Gregory.

64. Friedrich Engels's thick account of the spatial order of Manchester, England, at mid-nineteenth century anticipates the market orders of both San Francisco in 1906 and New Orleans in 2005:

> Owing to the curious lay-out of the town it is quite possible for someone to live for years in Manchester and to travel daily to and from his work without ever seeing a working-class quarter or coming into contact with an artisan . . . mainly because the working-class districts and the middle-class districts are quite distinct. . . . In those areas where the two social groups happen to come into contact with each other the middle classes sanctimoniously ignore the existence of their less fortunate neighbors.

Quoted in Katznelson, 1992, 150.

65. Haitians have played a prominent role in the shaping of New Orleans since their arrival in the late 1700s. See Edward Branley, 2014, "NOLA History: The New Orleans–Haitian Connection," gonola.com/2014/03/24/nola-history-the-new-orleans-haitian-connection.html (accessed May 2017).

66. Sarah Deutsch, 2000, *Women and the City: Gender, Space, and Power in Boston, 1870–1940* (New York: Oxford University Press), 286.

67. Douglas S. Massey and Nancy A. Denton, 1993, *American Apartheid: Segregation and the Making of the Underclass* (Cambridge, MA: Harvard University Press).

## CHAPTER 3: THE GREAT DERANGEMENTS

1. Henry Wadsworth Longfellow, 1995 [1847], *Evangeline: A Tale of Acadie*, verses 4–5, hwlongfellow.org/poems_poem.php?pid=297 (accessed June 2015).

2. Arnold Genthe, 1936, *As I Remember: The Autobiography of Arnold Genthe* (New York: Reynal & Hitchcock), 88.

3. Christiane Charlemaine, 2007, "Personal Perspective of the Author's Experience Pre– and Post–Hurricane Katrina," *Race, Class & Gender* 14(1–2): 145–148.

4. It was the festival, the holiday, the time out of time that Turner connected to communitas. Victor Turner, 1969, *The Ritual Process: Structure and Anti-structure* (Chicago: Aldine).

5. Edith Turner, 2012, *Communitas: The Anthropology of Collective Joy* (New York: Palgrave), 76; Hugh Baxter, 1987, "System and Life-World in Habermas's 'Theory of Communicative Action,'" *Theory and Society* 6(1): 39–86.

6. *Charities and the Commons: A Weekly Journal of Philanthropy and Social Advance*, vol. 16, *April 1906–October 1906* (New York: Charity Organization Society of New York).

7. "Stories in America," September 2005, storiesinamerica.blogspot.com/2005 /09/new-orleans-evacuees-unknowingly-land.html (accessed August 2015).

8. Lynn Weber and Lori Peek edited a remarkable collection of papers on the diverse experiences of people forced from their houses and city by Hurricane Katrina. See Weber and Peek, eds., 2012, *Displaced: Life in the Katrina Diaspora* (Austin: University of Texas Press).

9. Philip Fradkin, 2005, *The Great Earthquake and Firestorms of 1906* (Berkeley: University of California Press), 34.

10. Stephen Tobriner, 2006, "What Really Happened in San Francisco in the Earthquake of 1906," 100th Anniversary Earthquake Conference, April 18–22, 1906eqconf.org/plenarySessions.htm (accessed August 2015).

11. Eric Niderost, 2006, "The Great 1906 San Francisco Earthquake and Fire," History Net, June, historynet.com/the-great-1906-san-francisco-earthquake-and -fire.htm (accessed June 2016). Made land or made ground is land that is shaped by the backfilling of marsh or swamp with natural or man-made materials, refuse, and the like.

12. Selection from the Hooker Family Papers, "Russian Hill Thursday Night," Bancroft Library, University of California, Berkeley, online Archive of California, oac.cdlib.org/view?docId=hb7m3nb5f1;NAAN=13030&doc.view=frames&chunk .id=div00004&toc.depth=1&toc.id=&brand=oac4 (accessed September 2015).

13. "Excerpt from Operation Kaleidoscope: A Melange of Personal Recollec-

tions," Bancroft Library, University of California, Berkeley, online Archive of California, bancroft.berkeley.edu or content.cdlib.org/view?docId=hb2c6004p0&brand =oac4 (accessed September 2015).

14. Quoted in Gladys Hansen, Richard Hansen, and William Blaisdell, 2013, *Earthquake, Fire & Epidemic: Personal Accounts of the 1906 Disaster* (n.p.: Untreed Reads), 52.

15. Earthquake letter from Bertha, Berkeley, to Elsa Billerbeck, Milwaukee, May 13, 1906, Bancroft Library, University of California, Berkeley, online Archive of California, oac.cdlib.org/ark:/13030/hb6z09p1sm/?brand=oac4 (accessed September 2015).

16. Quoted in Charles Keeler, "San Francisco through Earthquake and Fire," Bancroft Library, University of California, Berkeley, online Archive of California, oac .cdlib.org/view?docId=hb0h4nb16n&brand=oac4&doc.view=entire_text (accessed September 2015). The letters describing the immediate aftermath of the earthquake with fires still raging recall the many letters Chicagoans sent their kin and friends describing the travails of that first major American urban conflagration. Chicagoan Francis Test wrote to his mother three days after the Great Chicago Fire of 1871. "I am convinced," he states flatly, "that money will not be the main thought of any people, nor will the poor man have to take a low seat as usual. We are all alike here now, or, as it is expressed, we are all on a level." In her letter Laura Rollins describes how the fire destroyed seemingly impermeable social boundaries: "The tenement families flying clothesless before the flames; the rich of a few hours before not ashamed to mix with them—as the fire of the forest and prairies make animals, commonly enemies, run together as friends." Karen Sawislak, 1995, *Smoldering City: Chicagoans and the Great Fire, 1871–1874* (Chicago: University of Chicago Press), 39, 42.

17. Jack London, 1906, "The Story of an Eyewitness," *Colliers: The National Weekly*, May 5, sfmuseum.net/hist5/jlondon.html (accessed September 2015).

18. Edith H. Rosenshine, "The San Francisco Earthquake of 1906," Bancroft Library, University of California, Berkeley, online Archive of California, oac.cdlib .org/view?docId=hb4k4007s5m&brand=oac4&chunk.id=meta (accessed September 2015).

19. Emma Burke, 1906, *Overlook Magazine*, June 2, sfmuseum.net/1906/ew13 .html (accessed September 2015).

20. Graham Taylor, 1906, "The Earthquake's Emphasis on Human Good," in *Charities and the Commons*, 293.

21. Ray Stannard Baker, 1906–1907, "A Test of Men," *American Magazine* 63: 81. Christoph Strupp echoes Baker's assessment: "For at least a few days, the social hierarchies of the city ceased to exist in the camps and relief stations: rich and poor, white- and blue-collar workers, masters and servants together stood side by side in the bread lines." Strupp, 2006, "Dealing with Disaster: The San Francisco Earthquake of 1906," Institute of European Studies, paper 060322, University of California, Berkeley, 1–45, 25.

22. "A hurricane is categorized by its wind speed using the Saffir-Simpson Hurricane Scale. Category 1: Winds 119–153 km/hr (74–95 mph)—faster than a cheetah. Category 2: Winds 154–177 km/hr (96–110 mph)—as fast or faster than a baseball pitcher's fastball." NASA, nasa.gov/audience/forstudents/5.../what-are-hurricanes-58.html (accessed October 2015).

23. US House, 2005, "A Failure of Initiative: The Final Report of the Select Bipartisan Committee to Investigate the Preparation for and Response to Hurricane Katrina," House Report 109-377, December 6, 102, 2, docplayer.net/12497993-A-failure-of-initiative-final-report-of-the-select-bipartisan-committee-to-investigate-the-preparation-for-and-response-to-hurricane-katrina.html (accessed September 2015).

24. Elizabeth Fussell, 2006, "Leaving New Orleans: Social Stratification, Networks, and Hurricane Evacuation," Social Science Research Council, June 11, under standingkatrina.ssrc.org/Fussell (accessed October 2015).

25. BBC News, 2005, "'Desperate SOS' for New Orleans," September 2, news.bbc.co.uk/2/hi/americas/4206620.stm (accessed September 2015).

26. Cheryl Hayes, 2006, interview by Steve Kroll-Smith and Pam Jenkins, Pontchartrain Park, January 12.

27. Lola Vollen and Chris Young, 2008, *Voices from the Storm* (San Francisco: McSweeny Books), 100–101.

28. Prentiss Polk, "The Katrina Experience: An Oral History Project," the katrinaexperience.net/?p=19 (accessed September 2015).

29. Shelly Darnel, 2006, conversation with Steve Kroll-Smith, Gentilly, October 12.

30. Steve Kroll-Smith, Vern Baxter, and Pam Jenkins, 2015, *Left to Chance: A Story of Two New Orleans Neighborhoods* (Austin: University of Texas Press), 26.

31. "What Really Happened in New Orleans: Denise Moore's Story," *Daily Kos*, September 6, 2005, dailykos.com/story/2005/09/07/146166/-What-REALLY-happened-in-New-Orleans-Denise-Moore-s-story-UPDATED (accessed September 2015).

32. Miss Grace, 2005, interview by Steve Kroll-Smith, Algiers Point, December.

33. Peter Kropotkin, 1995 [1914], *Mutual Aid: A Factor in Evolution* (n.p.: CreateSpace Independent Publishing Platform); Burke, 1906; Baker, 1906–1907, 90. Tellingly, Baker writes, "The period of mutual aide—of 'earthquake love'—lasted about one month; shorter time in some directions of activity; longer in others. But gradually, a little here and a little here, personal greed and private interest began to break through. Men remembered themselves again."

34. Vollen and Young, 2008, 87.

35. Lauren Barsky, Joseph Trainor, and Manuel Torres, 2006, "Disaster Realities in the Aftermath of Hurricane Katrina: Revisiting the Looting Myth," *Quick Response Report: Natural Hazards Center* 184 (February): 4.

36. Rebecca Solnit, 2009, *A Paradise Built in Hell: The Extraordinary Communities That Arise in Disaster* (New York: Penguin Books), 7.

37. Charles E. Fritz, 1961, "Disasters," in *Contemporary Social Problems*, edited by Robert K. Merton and Robert A. Nisbet (New York: Harcourt), 651–694; Allen Barton, 1969, *Communities in Disaster: A Sociological Analysis of Collective Stress Situations* (New York: Doubleday). In a tribute to the evocative importance of the altruistic community to the sociology of disaster, Barton offers seventy-one sociological propositions on the provenance, duration, and context of this curious human display.

38. Liisa Eränen and Karmela Liebkind, 1993, "Coping with Disaster: The Helping Behavior of Communities and Individuals," in *International Handbook of Traumatic Stress Syndromes*, edited by John Wilson and Beverly Raphael (New York: Springer), 958; Henry W. Fischer III, 2008, *Response to Disaster* (Kuala Lumpur: UPA Press), 221–222; Charles Tilly, 1999, *Durable Inequality* (Berkeley: University of California Press).

39. Max Weber, 1968, *Economy and Society: An Outline of Interpretive Sociology*, edited by Gunther Roth and Claus Wittich (Berkeley: University of California Press), 43.

40. Ibid.

41. Baker, 1906–1907, 82.

42. "The present epoch," Michel Foucault suggests, "will perhaps be above all the epoch of space. We are in the epoch of simultaneity . . . of juxtaposition . . . of the near and far, of the side-by-side, of the dispersed. We are at a moment . . . when our experience of the world is less that of a long life developing through time than that of a network that connects points and intersects with its own skein." Unlike spaces, places are meaning-filled geographies. Space is to mundane consciousness as place is to the heart. We are not just in places but inevitably of places. Foucault, 1984, "Of Other Spaces: Utopias and Heterotopias," *Architecture, Mouvement, Continuité* 5: 46. See also Steven Feld and Keith Basso, eds., 1997, *Senses of Place* (Santa Fe, NM: School of American Research Press).


## CHAPTER 4: FASHIONING "THE LOOTER"

1. Thomas A. Spragens Jr., 1973, *The Politics of Motion: The World of Thomas Hobbes* (Lexington: University Press of Kentucky), 153.

2. Maureen Dowd, 2005, "United States of Shame," *New York Times*, September 3, A21, nytimes.com/2005/09/03/opinion/united-states-of-shame.html (accessed February 2016).

3. Joseph R. Chenelly, 2005, *Army Times* 2(1) (September 3), informationclear inghouse.info/article10100.htm (accessed October 2015).

4. US House, 2006, "A Failure of Initiative," House Report 109-377, 248, gpo.gov /fdsys/pkg/CRPT-109hrpt377/pdf/CRPT-109hrpt377.pdf (accessed March 2016). Lurid tales of horrific inhumanity linked to ethnic and racial "others" are common in disaster. Consider this account in the *Altoona (PA) Mirror*, describing what, by

all accounts, were gross miscarriages of justice followed by mythmaking in the wake of the Johnstown, Pennsylvania, flood of 1889:

Early Sunday morning two Italians were caught with their fingers in their pockets upon which were rings, and were shot dead. One Hungarian, perfect in his greed, was caught in the act of separating a finger from a woman's hand. He was hung on the Kernville hillside. . . . A colored man detected in suspicious acts was saved with difficulty from lynching. The public pulse is too outraged to consider a single moment for inquiring and four other foreigners were run to swift justice yesterday afternoon because of the jewelry found on them.

Quoted in Jane Gray and Elizabeth Wilson, 1984, "Looting in Disaster: A General Profile of Victimization," DRC Working Paper 71, Disaster Research Center, Ohio State University, dspace.udel.edu/bitstream/handle/19716/1295/WP71.pdf?sequence =1 (accessed August 2015).

5. Doug Mataconis, 2010, "New Orleans Police Were Ordered to Shoot Looters after Katrina," August 26, outsidethebeltway.com/new-orleans-police-were-or dered-to-shoot-looters-after-katrina/ (accessed July 2015).

6. Jamie Omar Yassin, 2005, "Demonizing the Victims of Katrina: Extra!," November–December, fair.org/index.php?page=2793 (accessed February 2016).

7. Ashley Katherine Farmer, 2011, "A Call to Arms: The Militarization of Natural Disasters in the United States" (master's thesis, Eastern Kentucky University), 20.

8. "Earthquake and Fire: San Francisco in Ruins," joint edition of the *Call-Chronicle-Examiner*, April 19, 1906, 1, chroniclingamerica.loc.gov/lccn/sn820157 32/1906-04-19/ed-1/seq-1/ (accessed July 2015).

9. Thomas S. Duke, 1910, "Synopsis of the San Francisco Police and Municipal Records of the Greatest Catastrophe in American History," sfmuseum.org/1906 /06pd1.html (accessed July 2015).

10. Brigadier General Frederick Funston, 1906, "How the Army Worked to Save San Francisco," *Cosmopolitan*, July, parks.ca.gov/pages/24204/files/funston_re port_earthquake_cosmopolitan_july_1906.pdf (accessed August 2015).

11. In the Great Chicago Fire of 1871, Mayor R. B. Mason placed the city under martial law. In recounting this historical moment, Karen Sawislak writes:

To a large degree, the [military] occupation aimed to reestablish the social and spatial barriers that had been lost to the disordering force of disaster. In essence the general made sure that the people of Chicago remained in their more ordinary places, or at least did not stray where they normally did not belong. . . . All of Sheridan's men were authorized to fire immediately upon any person who refused to obey an order.

Sawislak, 1995, *Smoldering City: Chicagoans and the Great Fire, 1871–1874* (Chicago: University of Chicago Press), 57.

12. Havidán Rodríguez, Joseph Trainor, and Enrico L. Quarantelli, 2006, "Rising

to the Challenges of a Catastrophe: The Emergent and Prosocial Behavior Following Hurricane Katrina," *Annals of the American Academy of Political and Social Science* 604: 99.

13. Spike Lee, 2006, *When the Levees Broke: A Requiem in Four Acts* (HBO).

14. Lisa Grow Sun, 2011, "Disaster Mythology and the Law," *Cornell Law Review* 96(5): 1134.

15. Henry Morse Stephens, 1908, "How the History of the Disaster Is Being Made," sfmuseum.org/1906/morse.html (accessed August 2015); Philip Fradkin, 2005, *The Great Earthquake and Firestorms of 1906* (Berkeley: University of California Press), 68. Reporting on Hurricane Sandy, Katy Welter writes, "Looting—opportunistic burglary—has been minimal in cities struck hardest by Sandy. New York City's crime rate reportedly fell by a third following the storm." Welter, 2012, "The Myth of Disaster Looting," *Next City*, November 5, nextcity.org/daily/entry/the-myth-of-disaster-looting (accessed September 2015).

16. Krista Zala, 2005, "100 Years after America's Deadliest Quake, Evidence Gone and Questions Remain," *Stanford Report*, October, news.stanford.edu/news/2005/october5/starr-100505.html (accessed July 2015).

17. Fradkin, 2005, 15.

18. The idea of the civic and military temper is taken from William James, 1972 [1907], *The Moral Equivalent of War* (New York: Harper).

19. A debate in a 2007 edition of the journal *Natural Hazards Observer* offers a glimpse of the typical argument among disaster researchers. Scholars Enrico Quarantelli and Kelly Frailing argue for and against the evidence of looting after disasters, with Quarantelli arguing that a lack of evidence exists to prove its prevalence and Frailing retorting that such evidence exists, citing her work with colleague Dee Wood Harper. Using crime statistics for burglary rates in the aftermath of Hurricanes Betsy and Katrina as a proxy for post-disaster looting in New Orleans, Frailing and Harper note, however, that the property crimes in New Orleans "were already substantially higher than the pre- and post-storm rates for the comparable storms." Considering these preexisting crime rates, they suggest that the city's "historically evolving socio-economic conditions," compounded with the delayed presence of the US Army and National Guard, played a major role in the increased burglary, and therefore looting, rates post–Hurricane Katrina. While there may have been increased burglary rates post-Katrina, the use of this statistic as a proxy for looting seems insufficient to support the claim that high rates of post-disaster looting are not a myth. Frailing and Harper, in fact, acknowledge the debate among disaster scholars, noting that Quarantelli and colleague Russell Dynes's long insistence on the looting myth is supported by "a review of natural disasters done by the Disaster Research Center at Ohio State University that found extremely low verifiable rates of looting after 40 natural disasters in the United States." "Looting after Disaster: Myth or Reality?," 2007, *Natural Hazards Observer* 31(4) (March): 1–4.

20. Sigmund Freud identified a wellspring of human aggression in the emergence of private wealth: "In abolishing private property we deprive the human love

of aggression of one of its instruments." Freud, 1962 [1927], *Civilization and Its Discontents* (New York: W. W. Norton), 60.

21. Erich Goode and Nachman Ben-Yehuda, 1994, *Moral Panics: The Social Construction of Deviance* (New York: Wiley Blackwell), 7; Lee Clarke and Caron Chess, 2008, "Elites and Panic: More to Fear than Fear Itself," *Social Forces* 87(2): 993–1014. See also Rebecca Solnit, 2009, *A Paradise Built in Hell: The Extraordinary Communities That Arise in Disaster* (New York: Penguin Books).

22. Fradkin, 2005, 15.

23. Sawislak, 1995, 52.

24. Fradkin, 2005, 15.

25. "Special Report: Historic Tornado Outbreak of April 27, 2011," *Quantum Research International*, special ed., May 2011, groundcontrol.com/Satellite_VSAT _Equipment/Quantum_Newsletter_SpecialEdition_May2011.pdf (accessed September 2015).

26. "Cultivating a State of Readiness: Our Response to April 27, 2011," January 2012, 63, ema.alabama.gov/filelibrary/TRAC_Report.pdf (accessed June 2016).

27. Janet French, 2016, "Looting Not a Problem in Fort McMurray, Police Say," *Edmonton Sun*, May 6, edmontonsun.com/2016/05/06/looting-not-a-problem-in -fort-mcmurray-police-say (accessed May 2016). In a more recent disaster, the October 2016 flooding of thirty-four rural counties in North Carolina from severe rainfall, a remnant of Hurricane Matthew, looting was, again, conspicuously absent. Kyle DeHaven, the Greene County manager, reports that while curfews were set to protect people from driving on flooded roads at night, "There was no looting to my knowledge" (from an interview with Janie Phelps, who serves in the National Guard and interviewed DeHaven a couple weeks after the floodwaters receded as part of a research project for a class I coteach, "Disaster, Self, and Society").

28. Lauren Barsky, Joseph Trainor, and Manuel Torres, 2006, "Disaster Realities in the Aftermath of Hurricane Katrina: Revisiting the Looting Myth," *Quick Response Report: Natural Hazards Center* 184 (February): 4, 2–3, udspace.udel.edu /handle/19716/2367 (accessed June 2016).

29. Georg Simmel, 1969, "The Metropolis and Mental Life," in *Classic Essays on the Culture of the Cities*, edited by Richard Sennett (Englewood Cliffs, NJ: Prentice Hall), 49.

30. Fradkin, 2005, 69.

31. Quoted in Michael I. Niman, 2005, "Katrina's America: Failure, Racism, and Profiteering," *Humanist* 65(6), thefreelibrary.com/Katrina's+America%3A+failure ,+racism,+and+profiteering.-a0138537037 (accessed May 2016).

32. Felicity Barringer and Jere Longman, 2005, "Police and Owners Begin to Challenge Looters," *New York Times*, September 1, nytimes.com/2005/09/01/us /nationalspecial/police-and-owners-begin-tochallenge-looters.html?_r=0 (accessed May 2016).

33. Gray and Wilson, 1984.

34. Quoted in Russell Dynes and E. L. Quarantelli, 1968, "What Looting in Civil Disturbances Really Means," *Trans-action* 5(6): 9–14.

35. Barringer and Longman, 2005.

36. Jim Dwyer and Christopher Drew, 2005, "Fear Exceeded Crime's Reality in New Orleans," *New York Times*, September 29, A1, nytimes.com/2005/09/29/us/na tionalspecial/fear-exceeded-crimes-reality-in-new-orleans.html (accessed April 2016).

37. *English Oxford Living Dictionaries*, s.v. "loot," en.oxforddictionaries.com /definition/loot (accessed March 2016).

38. By the mid-seventeenth century, the German word *plündern*, literally "rob of household goods," was in common use. See google.com/search?safe=active&q =origin+of+word+plunderer (accessed March 2016). For "bandit," see en.oxford dictionaries.com/definition/bandit (accessed March 2016). For "looter," see en.ox forddictionaries.com/definition/us/looter (accessed March 2016).

39. See *Merriam-Webster's*, s.v. "looting," merriam-webster.com/dictionary /looting (accessed March 2016).

40. Friedrich Nietzsche, 1974 [1887], *The Gay Science* (New York: Vintage Books), 58; Hobbes quoted in Ian Hacking, 2002, *Historical Ontology* (Cambridge, MA: Harvard University Press), 105.

41. Ian Hacking, 1999, *The Social Construction of What?* (Cambridge, MA: Harvard University Press), 131; Hacking, 2002, 111.

42. Hacking, 1999, 131.

43. Dan Kurzman, 2001, *Disaster! The Great San Francisco Earthquake and Fire of 1906* (New York: HarperCollins), 86.

44. Fradkin, 2005, 138, 139.

45. Ibid., 7.

46. Kurzman, 2001, 132.

47. Kevin J. Mullen, 2005, "The Dark Days after the 1906 Earthquake: New Orleans' Chaos Echoes S.F. Violence," *SFGate*, September 11, sfgate.com/opinion /article/The-dark-days-after-the-1906-earthquake-New-2569826.php (accessed March 2016).

48. "Operation Kaleidoscope: Chapter 28. A City in Ruins," Bancroft Library, University of California, Berkeley, BANC MSS 73/194c, oac.cdlib.org/view?docId =hb2c6004p0&brand=oac4&doc.view=entire_text (accessed April 2016).

49. Gordon Thomas and Max Morgan Witts, 1971, *The San Francisco Earthquake* (New York: Stein and Day), 147.

50. Fradkin, 2005, 65.

51. Ibid., 68.

52. Charles Morris, 2002 [1906], *The San Francisco Calamity by Earthquake and Fire* (Urbana: University of Illinois Press), 125.

53. Fradkin, 2005, 293.

54. Ibid., 68, 293 (emphasis added).

55.	It is worth noting that the National Archives chose the header "Souvenir Hunters" for the photo. The demographics of the people in the photo did not match the social kind of the looter.

56. Carol Nolte, 2006, "The Great Quake, 1906–2006: The Last Stand," *SFGate*, April 15, sfgate.com/news/article/The-Great-Quake-1906-2006-The-last-stand-A2 537403.php#photo-2363827 (accessed May 2016).

57. Fradkin, 2005, 68.

58. Ibid., 143, 137, 143 (emphases added).

59. US War Department, cited in ibid., 135.

60. James B. Stetson, cited in ibid., 100–101.

61. Zala, 2005.

62. Kathleen Tierney and Christine A. Bevc, 2005, "Disaster as War: Militarism and the Social Construction of Disaster in New Orleans," in *The Sociology of Katrina: Perspectives on a Modern Catastrophe*, edited by David Brunsma, David Overfelt, and Steve Picou (Lanham, MD: Rowman & Littlefield), 46.

63. Andrew Bynum, 2015, "In the Wake of Katrina: A Story of Post-disaster Militarization, Blackwater, and Profit" (honors research paper, University of North Carolina at Greensboro).

64. Jeremy Scahill, 2005, "Blackwater Down," *Nation*, October, thenation.com /article/blackwater-down (accessed April 2016); Ed Lavandera, 2015, "'Legend' of American Sniper Chris Kyle Looms over Murder Trial," *CNN News*, February 25, cnn.com/2015/02/09/us/chris-kyle-american-sniper (accessed April 2016).

65. Jeffrey H. Jackson, 2010, *Paris under Water: How the City of Light Survived the Great Flood of 1910* (New York: Palgrave), 247.

66. "How Citizens Turned into Saviors after Katrina Struck," 2015, *CBS News*, August 29, cbsnews.com/news/remembering-the-cajun-navy-10-years-after-hurri cane-katrina/ (accessed March 2015).

67. Aaron Kinney, 2005, "'Looting' or 'Finding'?," *Salon*, September 2, salon.com /2005/09/02/photo_controversy (emphases added) (accessed March 2015). Worth noting as well is that the two white "finders" are identified as "residents," not so the black man. The likelihood, of course, is the white people are tourists; the black "looter" is the more likely "resident." To view this image, see web.ics.purdue .edu/~natt/lootingphoto.htm.

68. Hacking, 1999, 51.

69. Niman, 2005, 12.

70. Adam Cohen, 2002, "Editorial Observer: Justice Rehnquist's Ominous History of Wartime Freedom," *New York Times*, September 22, nytimes.com/2002/09/ 22/opinion/editorial-observer-justice-rehnquist-s-ominous-history-of-wartime -freedom.html (accessed April 2015). More than a decade after the city flooded, five former New Orleans police officers pleaded guilty "to conspiracy, obstruction of justice and civil rights charges," stemming from the shooting of unarmed citizens in the anarchy of disaster. The plea agreements resulted in three- to twelve-year prison sentences for the defendants. Campbell Robertson, 2016, "New Orleans

Police Officers Plead Guilty in Shooting of Civilians," *New York Times*, April 20, nytimes.com/2016/04/21/us/hurricane-katrina-new-orleans-danziger-bridge -shootings.html (accessed March 2015).

71. Kate Zernike, 2005, "In Hunt for Life's Necessities, Rumors Fly and Lines Crawl," *New York Times*, September 2, nytimes.com/2005/09/02/national/national special/02scavenge.html (accessed February 2014).

72. Gaia Pianigiani and Sewell Chan, 2016, "Food Theft by Italy's Homeless and Hungry May Not Be a Crime, Court Says," *New York Times*, May 4, A4.

73. This reasoning plot is taken from Nietzsche. See Alexander Nehamas, 1987, *Nietzsche: Life as Literature* (Cambridge, MA: Harvard University Press), 45.

74. If we can make up people, we can also try to unmake them. In numerous ways and using various venues, we can see how mea culpas from leading newspapers that questioned their own sensational stories of looting, reliable academic research on the looting myth, and denouements by once vocal supporters are all attempts to unmake "the looter." But once this social kind is made in historical context, it is almost impossible to unmake it.

75. Simmel, 1969, 51.

76. Ibid., 52.

77. Ray Stannard Baker, 1906–1907, "A Test of Men," *American Magazine* 63: 82.


## CHAPTER 5: DISASTER RELIEF

1. Selections from the James D. Phelan Papers, "Committees, Clubs and Organizations; Articles 1906: Rise of the New San Francisco," Bancroft Library, University of California, Berkeley, BANC MSS C-B 800, Carton 18:16, oac.cdlib.org/view?doc Id=hb1t1nb1vr&brand=oac4&doc.view=entire_text (accessed May 2014).

2. Quoted in Marc Morial, 2015, "Hurricane Katrina: A Decade of Recovery and Rebuilding," *To Be Equal* 33 (August 25), nul.iamempowered.com/content/tbe33 -hurricane-katrina-decade-recovery-and-rebuilding (accessed May 2014).

3. Jack Hirshleifer, 2008, *The Concise Encyclopedia of Economics*, s.v. "Disaster and Recovery," econlib.org/library/Enc/DisasterandRecovery (accessed May 2014).

4. Marie Bolton, 1997, "Recovery for Whom? Social Conflict after the San Francisco Earthquake and Fire, 1906–1915" (PhD diss., University of California, Davis), 107–108.

5. Second Amended Complaint-Class Action for Injunctive and Declaratory Relief, Civil No. 05-5488, SRD, November 10, 2005, 16–17, news.findlaw.com/hdocs /docs/fema/mcwfema111005cmp.pdf (accessed May 2014).

6. Human character, the ethical and moral qualities of a person, plays an outsize role in the administration of disaster relief. It recalls the distinction sometimes drawn between the Shakespearean tragedy of character and the Greek tragedy of circumstance. See Michael Roemer, 1995, *Telling Stories* (Lanham, MD: Rowman & Littlefield), 16.

7. The Laws of the United States, Private Acts of the First Congress, Statute 2, June 14, 1790, 2, legisworks.org/congress/1/private-1.pdf (accessed May 2014).

8. Ibid., 3.

9. Vincanne Adams, 2013, *Markets of Sorrow, Labors of Faith* (Durham, NC: Duke University Press), 39.

10. Michele L. Landis, 1999, "Fate, Responsibility, and 'Natural' Disaster Relief: Narrating the American Welfare State," *Law & Society Review* 33(2): 266. See also Michele Landis Dauber, 2013, *The Sympathetic State: Disaster Relief and the Origins of the American Welfare State* (Chicago: University of Chicago Press).

11. Dauber, 2013, 395–396.

12. Louis A. Wiltz, 2010, *The Great Mississippi Flood of 1874: Its Extent, Duration and Effects*, ebook, gutenberg.polytechnic.edu.na/3/1/8/8/31889/31889-h/31889-h .htm (accessed May 2014).

13. Landis, 1999, 271.

14. Tom Baker, 1996, "On the Genealogy of Moral Hazard," *Texas Law Review* 75(2): 250.

15. Tom Baker, 2000, "Insuring Morality," University of Connecticut School of Law Articles and Working Papers, no. 2, lsr.nellco.org/uconn_wps/2 (accessed April 2014).

16. Max Weber, 2001 [1905], *The Protestant Ethic and Spirit of Capitalism* (London: Routledge), 120, 19.

17. Mark Twain and Charles Dudley Warner, 2001 [1873], *The Gilded Age: A Tale of Today* (New York: Penguin Books).

18. Horatio Alger Jr., 1868, *Ragged Dick; or, Street Life in New York with the Boot Black* (New York: A. K. Loring).

19. Sydney E. Ahlstrom, 2004, *A Religious History of the American People* (New Haven, CT: Yale University Press).

20. Weber, 2001 [1905], 120.

21. With passage of the Disaster Relief Act in 1950, Washington assumed primary responsibility for assisting local and state governments in their disaster-response efforts. Anna Marie Baca, 2008, "History of Disaster Legislation," *FEMA on Call: Disaster Reserve Workforce News*, September, 1, fema.gov/pdf/dae/200809 .pdf (accessed April 2014). "It is the intent of Congress," the law reads,

> to provide an orderly and continuing means of assistance by the Federal Government to States and local governments in carrying out their responsibilities 1) to alleviate suffering and damage resulting from major disasters, 2) to repair essential public facilities in major disasters, and 3) to foster the development of such State organizations and plans to cope with major disasters as may be necessary.

William C. Nicholson, 2013, *Emergency Response and Emergency Management Law* (Springfield, IL: Charles C. Thomas), 352.

22. Inflation calculator, 2016, in2013dollars.com/1906-dollars-in-2016 (accessed March 2016).

23. Philip Fradkin, 2005, *The Great Earthquake and Firestorms of 1906* (Berkeley: University of California Press), 186.

24. Andrea Rees Davies, 2012, *Saving San Francisco: Relief and Recovery after the 1906 Disaster* (Philadelphia: Temple University Press), 73–74.

25. Inflation calculator, 2016.

26. Davies, 2012, 74.

27. "Forecasting the Verdict of November Fifth," *Literary Digest*, October 5, 1912, 549; Davies, 2012, 74.

28. "Measuring Worth," 2014, measuringworth.com (accessed April 2014).

29. Fradkin, 2005, 198.

30. Davies, 2012, 43.

31. "Measuring Worth," 2014.

32. Schmitz would be convicted of graft in 1907. His conviction was later overturned. His deputy Abraham Reuf did not fare as well. He would serve his sentence in San Quentin. Davies, 2012, 170.

33. William Issel and Robert W. Cherny, 1986, *San Francisco, 1865–1932: Politics, Power and Urban Development* (Berkeley: University of California Press), 39.

34. Fradkin, 2005, 81.

35. Issel and Cherny, 1986, 39.

36. Ernest Bicknell, 1935, *Pioneering with the Red Cross* (New York: Macmillan), 14; Roosevelt quoted in Marian Moser Jones, 2008, "Confronting Calamity: The American Red Cross and the Politics of Disaster Relief, 1881–1939" (PhD diss., Columbia University), 252.

37. Davies, 2012, 54.

38. Fradkin, 2005, 198–199.

39. Ibid., 199.

40. Jones, 2008, 282; Christoph Strupp, 2006, "Dealing with Disaster: The San Francisco Earthquake of 1906," Institute of European Studies, paper 060322, University of California, Berkeley, 24.

41. Michael E. McGerr, 2003, *A Fierce Discontent: The Rise and Fall of the Progressive Movement in America, 1870–1920* (New York: Free Press), 3–40.

42. Shelly Brown-Jeffy and Steve Kroll-Smith, 2009, "Recovering Inequality: Democracy, the Market Economy, and the 1906 San Francisco Earthquake and Fire," in *The Political Economy of Hazards and Disasters*, edited by Eric C. Jones and Arthur D. Murphy (Lanham, MD: Altimira Press), 92–93.

43. Bolton, 1997, 4. In her memorable book on the Great Chicago Fire of 1871, Karen Sawislak describes a quite similar sorting process in organizing aid: "In the end, the elite directors of the Relief and Aid Society created a set of rules and regulations that sought to fit the experience of diverse individuals into categories that were largely a product of their own perceptions of class ethnic difference." Sawislak,

1995, *Smoldering City: Chicagoans and the Great Fire, 1871–1874* (Chicago: University of Chicago Press), 119.

44. Bolton, 1997. See also Kevin L. Rozario, 1997, "Nature's Evil Dreams: Disaster and America, 1871–1906" (PhD diss., Yale University).

45. Bolton, 1997, 103–108.

46. Russell Sage Foundation, 1913, *San Francisco Relief Survey: The Organization and Methods of Relief Used after the Earthquake and Fire of April 18, 1906*, compiled from studies by Charles J. O'Connor, Francis H. McLean, Helen Swett Artieda, James Marvin Motely, Jessica Peixotto, and Mary Roberts Coolidge (New York: Survey Associates), 293.

47. Ibid., 297.

48. Ibid., 115.

49. Ibid., 113. Karen Sawislak describes the work of the "Chicago Relief and Aid Society" in terms that would foreshadow the relief efforts in San Francisco more than three decades later: "No one received aid without investigation. A professional staff sought to fit potential recipients into one of two categories within an inflexible typology: honest, hard-working, but a victim of ill luck; or deceitful, lazy, and the architects of their own wretched state." Sawislak, 1995, 90.

50. Russell Sage Foundation, 1913, 114, 116, 147.

51. Ibid., 116.

52. Ibid., 338.

53. Jones, 2008, 270.

54. San Francisco City Guides, 2013, "1906 Train and Ferry Evacuation," in *Guidelines*, sfcityguides.org/public_guidelines.html?article=1519&submitted=TRUE&srch_text=&submitted2=&topic=Earthquakes (accessed March 2015).

55. Russell Sage Foundation, 1913, 128.

56. Ray Stannard Baker, 1906–1907, "A Test of Men," *American Magazine* 63: 82.

57. Bolton, 1997, 108.

58. Davies, 2012, 59.

59. Ibid.

60. Ibid., 60.

61. Ibid.

62. Bolton, 1997, 55; Strupp, 2006, 32. The goal of demixing was also a part of the recovery of Chicago in the aftermath of its devastating conflagration in 1871. Sawislak writes in her history of the blaze: "By sheer vigilance, and so drastically limiting travel and access across the city, the general [Philip Sheridan] thus began to reverse the stunning mixture of people set in motion by the Great Fire." Sawislak, 1995, 58.

63. Davies, 2012, 85–111.

64. The class distinctions in the camps and food lines are a theme that threads its way throughout Russell Sage Foundation, 1913, 29, 50, 69–70, and more.

65. Ibid., 237.

66. Ibid., 49.

67. Bolton, 1997, 61.

68. J. B. Deacon, 1918, *Disasters and the American Red Cross in Disaster Relief* (New York: Russell Sage Foundation), 238.

69. Baker quoted in F. W. Fitzpatrick, 1907, "January Ruminations," *Fireproof Magazine* 10: 15.

70. Dauber, 2013.

71. Upton Sinclair, 2001 [1906], *The Jungle* (Mineola, NY: Dover).

72. Susan Sterett, 2009, "New Orleans Everywhere: Bureaucratic Accountability and Housing Policy after Katrina," in *Catastrophe, Law, Politics, and the Humanitarian Impulse*, edited by Austin Sarat and Javier Lezaun (Amherst: University of Massachusetts Press), 83–115.

73. The six acts are the following: Disaster Relief Act of 1950, Disaster Relief Act of 1970, Disaster Relief Act of 1974, Disaster Relief Act of 1974, Stafford Disaster Relief and Emergency Assistance Act of 1988, and Homeland Security Act of 2002.

74. "Katrina Timeline," 2005, *ThinkProgress*, September 6, thinkprogress.org /katrina-timeline-90ec8a71fb99#.2h5milvjd (accessed April 2014).

75. Ibid.

76. "Reimbursement Procedure for FEMA Public Assistance," in.gov/dhs/files /reimbursement_procedures.pdf (accessed February 2016). See also "Assistance to Individuals and Households Fact Sheet," fema.gov/recovery-directorate/assistance -individuals-and-households-fact-sheet (accessed February 2016).

77. Sterett, 2009, 94.

78. Ibid., 106.

79. Donald R. Kelley and Todd G. Shields, 2013, *Taking the Measure: The Presidency of George W. Bush* (College Station: Texas A&M University Press), 122.

80. Ezra Klein, 2012, "Romney's Theory of the 'Taker Class,' and Why It Matters," *Washington Post*, September 17, washingtonpost.com/news/wonk/wp/2012/09/17 /romneys-theory-of-the-taker-class-and-why-it-matters (accessed May 2016).

81. Reagan did not coin the term *welfare queen*. Its origin is unclear. It first appeared either in a 1974 article by George Bliss in the *Chicago Tribune* or in *Jet*. Neither publication cites the other in their "welfare queen" stories of that year. Rhea Boyd, 2014, "The Myth of the Entitled Single Mother Remains as Relevant as Ever," *Medpage Today's Kevin MD*, February 28, kevinmd.com/blog/2014/02/myth -entitled-single-mother-remains-relevant.html (accessed July 2016).

82. Recall the words of William Graham Sumner, who writes a facsimile of the entitlement hazard into his 1883 book, *What the Social Classes Owe Each Other*:

> The man who has done nothing to raise himself above poverty finds that the social doctors flock about him, bringing the capital which they have collected from the other class, and promising him the aid of the State to give him what the other had to work for. In all these schemes and projects the organized intervention of society through the State is either planned or hoped for, and the State is thus made to become the protector and guardian of certain classes.

Sumner, 1974 [1883], *What the Social Classes Owe Each Other* (Caldwell, ID: Claxton), 21.

83. Joel Bleifuss and Brian Cook, 2005, "Unnatural Disaster: How Policy Decisions Doomed New Orleans," *In These Times*, September 2, inthesetimes.com/article /2310 (accessed August 2016).

84. Shaila Dewan, 2012, "Moral Hazard: A Tempest-Tossed Idea," *New York Times*, February 26, 1B.

85. The entitlement hazard is not limited to disaster relief. It has made its way into the record of the Supreme Court decision in the *Shelby County v. Holder* case to gut the Voting Rights Act of 1965. In his remarks to the solicitor general arguing the case for the federal government, the late justice Antonin Scalia railed against what he called the "perpetuation of racial entitlement," noting that "whenever a society adopts racial entitlements, it is very difficult to get out of them through the normal political processes." Quoted in Linda Greenhouse, 2016, "Resetting the Post-Scalia Supreme Court," *New York Times*, February 18, 21.

86. "New Orleans after the Storm: Lessons from the Past, a Plan for the Future," Brookings Institution Metropolitan Policy Program, October 2005, 4, brookings .edu/wp-content/uploads/2016/06/20051012_NewOrleans.pdf (accessed January 2016).

87. *McWaters v. FEMA*, 408 F. Supp. 2d 221, 230–231 (see also 6); Second Amended Complaint-Class Action for Injunctive and Declaratory Relief, 16–17.

88. Davida Finger, 2008, "Stranded and Squandered: Lost on the Road Home," *Seattle Journal for Social Justice* 7(1): 59–100.

89. David Schrayer, 2007, "New Orleans Affordable Housing Assessment: Lessons Learned, a Report on the Responses to Hurricanes Katrina, Rita and Wilma and Their Effects on the State of Housing," presented to Mercy Corps, July, preventionweb.net/files/9061_file11862041251.pdf (accessed March 2016).

90. John Moreno Gonzales, 2008, "Katrina Victims Complain about Red Tape," *USA Today*, March 3, usatoday.com/news/nation/2008-03-13-4205913428_x.htm (accessed January 2009).

91. For a history of heir property in the United States, see Heather K. Way, 2009, "Informal Homeownership in the United States and the Law," *Saint Louis University Public Law Review* 29(13): 116–191.

92. Richard Kluckow, 2014, "The Impact of Heir Property on Post-Katrina Housing Recovery in New Orleans" (master's thesis, Colorado State University), 26.

93. Ibid., 68–69.

94. Steve Kroll-Smith, Vern Baxter, and Pam Jenkins, 2015, *Left to Chance: A Story of Two New Orleans Neighborhoods* (Austin: University of Texas Press), 96.

95. Finger, 2008, 70.

96. Gary Rivlin, 2015, *Katrina after the Flood* (New York: Simon & Schuster), 379.

97. Sterett, 2009, 97; Joel Warner, 2015, "The Long Road Home," *International*

*Business Times*, August 15, ibtimes.com/long-road-home-2062255 (accessed March 2014).

98. Jonathan P. Hooks and Trisha B. Miller, 2006, "The Continuing Storm: How Disaster Recovery Excludes Those Most in Need," *California Western Law Review* 43(1): 21–73 (emphasis in the original), 41.

99. Davies, 2012, 142.

## CHAPTER 6: SPATIAL ACCUMULATION BY DISPOSSESSION

1. David Harvey, 2010, *The Enigma of Capital* (Oxford: Oxford University Press), 57; Karl Polanyi, 1944, *The Great Transformation* (Boston: Beacon Press), 34.

2. Polanyi, 1944, 35; E. P. Thompson, 1991, *The Making of the English Working Class* (New York: Penguin), 237.

3. Joseph A. Schumpeter, 1950, *Capitalism, Socialism and Democracy* (New York: Harper's), 83. I am indebted to Kevin Rozario, 2002, *The Culture of Calamity* (Chicago: University of Chicago Press), for linking disaster to Schumpeter's characterization of the market economy as a "gale of creative destruction."

4. David Harvey, 2005, *A Brief History of Neoliberalism* (Oxford: Oxford University Press), 43.

5. Naomi Klein, 2007, *The Shock Doctrine: The Rise of Disaster Capitalism* (New York: Henry Holt). See also Shelly Brown-Jeffy and Steve Kroll-Smith, 2009, "Recovering Inequality: Democracy, the Market Economy, and the 1906 San Francisco Earthquake and Fire," in *The Political Economy of Hazards and Disasters*, edited by Eric C. Jones and Arthur D. Murphy (Lanham, MD: Altimira Press), 42–64.

6. Rozario, 2002, 85.

7. Quoted in Philip Fradkin, 2005, *The Great Earthquake and Firestorms of 1906* (Berkeley: University of California Press), 294.

8. See Ralph Henn, 2016, "Chinatown in Hunters Point?," *San Francisco Magazine* (1970), familyhenn.com/RWHenn/quake.htm (accessed May 2016).

9. Editorial, 1906, *Argonaut*, April 28, 7.

10. Quoted in Fradkin, 2005, 295–296.

11. Editorial, 1906, *New York Times*, August 8, 6.

12. *Chinese-Western Daily*, April 27, 1906, quoted in Young Chen, 2000, *Chinese San Francisco, 1850–1943* (Stanford, CA: Stanford University Press), 146.

13. Erica Y. Z. Pan, 1995, *The Impact of the 1906 Earthquake on San Francisco's Chinatown* (New York: Peter Lang), 63.

14. Quoted in *San Francisco Examiner*, April 30, 1906, 1.

15. Pan, 1995, 38.

16. Jerome A. Hart, 1909, "The New Chinatown in San Francisco," *Bohemian Magazine* 16(5): 593.

17. Charles Babington, 2005, "Some GOP Legislators Hit Jarring Notes in Addressing Katrina," *Washington Post*, September 10, A4.

18. Eric Berger, 2006, "New Orleans Says It Won't Give Free Ride," *Houston Chronicle*, February 22, chron.com/disp/story.mpl/front/3676263.html (accessed January 2011).

19. David Brooks, 2005, "Katrina's Silver Lining," *New York Times*, September 8, nytimes.com/2005/09/08/opinion/katrinas-silver-lining.html?_r=0 (accessed April 2016).

20. Bob Walsh, 2006, "Only 'Best Residents' to Be Allowed Back in St. Thomas Complex," *New Orleans Times-Picayune*, April 25, 1.

21. William P. Quigley, 2008, *Storms Still Raging* (Charleston, SC: BookSurge), 124.

22. Brown-Jeffy and Kroll-Smith, 2009, 54.

23. "New Orleans after the Storm: Lessons from the Past, a Plan for the Future," Brookings Institution Metropolitan Policy Program, October 2005, brookings.edu/wp-content/uploads/2016/06/20051012_NewOrleans.pdf (accessed January 2016).

24. Pan, 1995, 5.

25. Ibid., 19.

26. Pardee Lowe, 1943, *Father and Glorious Descendant* (New York: Little, Brown), 143.

27. Andrew Gyory, 1998, *Closing the Gate: Race, Politics and the Chinese Exclusion Act* (Chapel Hill: University of North Carolina Press), 57.

28. Pan, 1995, 7.

29. Gyory, 1998, 58.

30. Pan, 1995, 12.

31. Charles McClain, 1996, *In Search of Equality* (Berkeley: University of California Press), 85.

32. Editorial, 1853, *Daily Alta California*, January 5.

33. Fradkin, 2005, 32.

34. Pan, 1995, 27.

35. Robert Barde, 2004, "The Plague in San Francisco: An Essay Review," *Journal of the History of Medicine and Allied Sciences* 59(3): 464.

36. Fradkin, 2005, 36.

37. Chen, 2000, 146.

38. Simon Winchester, 2005, *A Crack in the Edge of the World* (New York: Harper's), 239.

39. Quoted in Pan, 1995, 33.

40. Laurence Yep, 2008, *The Earth Dragon Awakes* (New York: HarperCollins). Approximately twenty thousand Chinese inhabited Chinatown at the time of the disaster. More than fifteen thousand were forced from their homes by the fires. See historynet.com/the-great-1906-san-francisco-earthquake-and-fire.htm (accessed June 2012).

41. H. V. Cather, 1932, "The History of San Francisco's Chinatown" (master's thesis, University of California, Berkeley).

42. Steeped in the Teutonic thought of late-nineteenth- and early-twentieth-

century social thought, Theodore Roosevelt embraced the theme of racial expansion. In his book *The Winning of the West*, he concluded that peace in the West would not be won without the extermination of the Indians. Roosevelt, 2010 [1889], *The Winning of the West*, vol. 4 (Ann Arbor: University of Michigan Press).

43. Chen, 2000, 148–149. See also Delber L. McKee, 1977, *Chinese Exclusion versus the Open Door Policy, 1900–1906* (Detroit: Wayne State University Press). The Sino-American Treaty, also known as the Gresham-Yang Treaty, suspended immigration of Chinese laborers to the United States for ten years but allowed conditional readmission of immigrants who were visiting China. This act did away with the terms of the Scott Act of 1888 and placed exclusion and registration laws passed since 1882 on a proper treaty basis. Proposed renewal of the treaty caused China to call for a boycott of American goods and the US Congress to extend exclusion indefinitely.

44. Ibid., 153.

45. Chen, 2000, 48–149.

46. Quoted in McKee, 1977, 192–193. See also Pan, 1995, 78.

47. Chen, 2000, 165.

48. Winchester, 2005, 331.

49. Gladys Hansen and Emmet Condon, 1989, *The Denial of Disaster* (San Francisco: Cameron), 114.

50. Quoted in Pan, 1995, 61.

51. Ibid., 74.

52. Ibid., 15–16.

53. Inflation calculator, 2017, in2013dollars.com/1906-dollars-in-2017?amount =300000 (accessed September 2017).

54. Cather, 1932, 30.

55. Businessman quoted in Pan, 1995, 80; Chuen Hung quoted in Fradkin, 2005, 295.

56. "The Race Problem—an Autobiography: A Southern Colored Woman," *Independent*, March 17, 1904, 589.

57. Quoted in Pan, 1995, 66.

58. Editorial, 1908, "San Francisco's New Chinatown," *New York Times*, February 11, A6.

59. Christoph Strupp, 2006, "Dealing with Disaster: The San Francisco Earthquake of 1906," Institute of European Studies, paper 060322, University of California, Berkeley, 33. See also Fradkin, 2005.

60. Charles Fritz, 1961, "Disaster," in *Contemporary Social Problems*, edited by Robert K. Merton and Robert A. Nisbet (New York: Harcourt), 651–694.

61. "75th Anniversary of the Wagner-Steagall Housing Act of 1937," FDR Presidential Library and Museum, FDR and Housing Legislation, fdrlibrary.org/housing (accessed March 2015).

62. Peirce F. Lewis, 2003, *New Orleans: The Making of an Urban Landscape* (Charlottesville: University Press of Virginia), 133.

63. Margaret C. Gonzalez-Perez, 2003, "A House Divided: Public Housing Policy in New Orleans," *Louisiana History* 44(4): 451.

64. Alexis de Tocqueville, 2007, *Democracy in America* (New York: Penguin Books).

65. Lewis, 2003, 133.

66. US Department of Housing and Urban Development, "About HOPE VI," portal.hud.gov/hudportal/HUD?src=/program_offices/public_indian_housing /programs/ph/hope6 (accessed February 2016).

67. Andrew Cuomo, 1999, "HOPE VI: Building Communities, Transforming Lives," US Department of Housing and Urban Development, December, huduser .org/publications/pdf/hope.pdf (accessed August 2010).

68. Quigley, 2008, 67.

69. C. C. Campbell-Rock, 2006, "The Katrina Reader: Whitewashing New Orleans," cwsworkshop.org/katrinareader/node/440.

70. Quigley, 2008, 68.

71. Quoted in CNN, 2005, "New Orleans Braces for Monster Hurricane," August 28, cnn.com/2005/WEATHER/08/28/hurricane.katrina (accessed September 2009).

72. Steve Kroll-Smith and Shelly Brown-Jeffy, 2013, "A Tale of Two American Cities: Disaster, Class and Citizenship in San Francisco, 1906, and New Orleans, 2005," *Journal of Historical Sociology* 26(4): 540.

73. Housing and Urban Development Hearing, house.gov/financialservices /hearing110/htnagino22207.pdf (accessed October 2010).

74. Nicolai Ouroussoff, 2007, "History vs. Homogeneity in New Orleans Housing Fight," *New York Times*, February 22, nytimes.com/2007/02/22/arts/design/22hous .html (accessed October 2010).

75. Quigley, 2008, 85.

76. Bill Quigley and Sara H. Godchaux, 2015, "Locked Out and Torn Down: Public Housing Post Katrina," Social Justice Advocacy, billquigley.wordpress.com/2015 /06/08/locked-out-and-torn-down-public-housing-post-katrina-by-bill-quigley -and-sara-h-godchaux (accessed March 2015).

77. Gwen Filosa, 2007, "Mayor Applauds Council Vote," *New Orleans Times-Picayune*, December 20, 1.

78. Quigley, 2008, 69.

79. Bill Quigley, 2007, "HUD Sends New Orleans Bulldozers and $400,000 Apartments for the Holidays," Institute for Southern Studies, mail.southernstudies .org/2007/12/hud-sends-new-orleans-bulldozers-and-400000-apartments-for -the-holidays.html (accessed March 2009).

80. Letter posted on website of the National Economic and Social Rights Initiative, 2008, habitants.org/zero_evictions_campaign/stop_the_demolitions_and _corruption_in_new_orleans (accessed January 2011).

81. United Nations Report, "Guiding Principles on Internal Displacement," unhcr

.org/en-us/protection/idps/43ce1cff2/guiding-principles-internal-displacement
.html (accessed January 2017).

82. Kroll-Smith and Brown-Jeffy, 2013, 543.

83. Quoted in John Moreno Gonzales, 2008, "UN Experts Criticize New Orleans Housing," *Common Dreams: Breaking News & Views for the Progressive Community*, February 29, commondreams.org/news/2008/02/29/un-experts-criticize-new
-orleans-housing# (accessed April 2016).

84. UN Human Rights, Office of the High Commissioner for Human Rights, 2008, Committee on the Elimination of Racial Discrimination, *Special Procedures Bulletin* 8 (March), www2.ohchr.org/english/bodies/chr/special/docs/Issue8th31 March2008.pdf (accessed March 2011).

85. Reuters, 2009, "Goldman Sachs Announces Investment in New Orleans Mixed-Income Housing Project," January 7, goldmansachs.com/media-relations /press-releases/archived/2009/new-orleans-mixed-income.html (accessed April 2015); Goldman Sachs, 2011, "Rebuilding an Entire Community in New Orleans," *New York Times*, May 11, A17.

86. Peter Drier, 2008, "HUD Secretary Alphonso Jackson's Resignation," *Huffington Post*, April 10, huffingtonpost.com/peter-dreier/hud-secretary-alphonso-ja _b_94787.html (accessed February 2010).

87. Editors, 2015, "10 Years after Katrina, Many New Orleans Residents Permanently Displaced," Amnesty International, Human Rights Now, September 1, blog.amnestyusa.org/us/10-years-after-katrina-many-new-orleans-residents-per manently-displaced (accessed April 2016).

88. In a sardonic twist on history, during the 1927 Great Mississippi Flood, white plantation owners watched as their black tenant workers began migrating north to the hopefully more humane environs of the cities and away from what DuBois called "the second slavery." To stanch this out-migration of labor, black tenant farmers were swept up and ferried to the many small islands that poked up from the floodwaters. Here they were kept until the water receded and work could begin again. As the tenant system began to break down, many of these black laborers migrated to New Orleans. By 2005, of course, black labor was, by and large, dispensable. Hurricane Katrina was an opportunity to rid the city of a low-income black population, many of whose ancestors were once considered indispensable to the southern economy.

89. Friedrich Engels, 1954, *The Housing Question: A Pamphlet* (Ann Arbor: University of Michigan Press).

90. E. Franklin Frazier, 1962, *The Black Bourgeoisie* (New York: Collier's Books); William Julius Wilson, 1980, *The Declining Significance of Race: Blacks and Changing American Institutions* (Chicago: University of Chicago Press), 1.

91. Adolph Reed Jr., 2006, introduction to *Unnatural Disaster: The Nation on Hurricane Katrina*, edited by Betsy Reed (New York: Nation Books), 6.

92. Eugene Robinson, 2011, *Disintegration: The Splintering of Black America*

(New York: Anchor Books), chap. 5. For a critical take on how race has been fashioned over time in America, see Michael Omi and Howard Winant's *Racial Formation in the United States*. The authors make a convincing case for understanding "race as an unstable and 'decentered' complex of social meanings constantly being transformed by political struggle." Omi and Howard, 2015, *Racial Formation in the United States* (New York: Routledge Press), 55.

93. Wendell Pierce, 2015, "Rebuilding Pontchartrain Park," *Slate*, September 15, slate.com/articles/news_and_politics/history/2015/09/wendell_pierce_s_efforts_to _rebuild_pontchartrain_park_after_katrina_battling.html (accessed April 2016).

94. Wai Chee Dimcock, 2009, "World History according to Katrina," in *States of Emergency*, edited by Russ Castronovo and Susan Gillman (Chapel Hill: University of North Carolina Press), 144; Bob Dylan, 1976, "Shelter from the Storm," bobdylan .com/songs/shelter-storm/ (accessed April 2016).

## CHAPTER 7: ONE CITY NECESSARY, ONE CITY EXPENDABLE

1. For a close-up look at the Marx family's travails in London and Engels's experiences in Manchester, see Mary Gabriel, 2011, *Love and Capital: Karl and Jenny Marx and the Birth of a Revolution* (New York: Little, Brown). Both Marx and Engels also knew that the spaces of capitalism are anything but fixed. They are forever mutating, adapting to the demands of history and the market's insatiable search for gain. "The circulation of money as capital is an end in itself," Karl Marx wrote, "for the valorization of value takes place only within this constantly renewed movement. The movement of capital is therefore limitless." Marx, 2007 [1909], *Capital: A Critique of Political Economy*, vol. 2, *The Process of Circulation of Capital* (New York: Evergreen Review), 253.

2. Sharon Zukin, 2006, "David Harvey on Cities," in *David Harvey: A Critical Reader*, edited by Noel Castree and Derek Gregory (Malden, MA: Blackwell), 110. See also David Harvey, 2008, *Spaces of Global Capitalism* (London: Verso), 89.

3. "Katrina Timeline," 2005, *Think Progress*, September 6, thinkprogress.org /katrina-timeline-90ec8a71fb99#.7u9kb6iee (accessed June 2014).

4. Jon Ponder, 2010, "Worst Presidential Vacation Ever: 5 Years Ago, Bush Took Time Out to Politick While New Orleans Drowned," *Pensito Review*, pensitoreview .com/2010/08/27/worst-presidential-vacation-ever-5-years-ago-bush-took-time -out-to-politick-while-new-orleans-drowned (accessed June 2014).

5. "Katrina Timeline," Bush Legacy Tour, americansunitedforchange.org/page /content/katrinatimeline (accessed June 2014).

6. Ibid.

7. "Roosevelt Offers Aid; Sends Telegrams of Sympathy to Gov. Pardee and Mayor Schmitz," *New York Times*, April 19, 1906, 1, query.nytimes.com/gst/abstract .html?res=990DE7DA113EE733A2575AC1A9629C946797D6CF&legacy=true (accessed June 2016).

8. Philip Fradkin, 2005, *The Great Earthquake and Firestorms of 1906* (Berkeley: University of California Press), 5, 83.

9. Adolph Reed Jr., 2006, introduction to *Unnatural Disaster: The Nation on Hurricane Katrina*, edited by Betsy Reed (New York: Nation Books), 29.

10. Parker Brown Willis, 1937, *The Federal Reserve Bank of San Francisco: A Study in American Central Banking* (New York: Columbia University Press).

11. William Issel and Robert W. Cherny, 1986, *San Francisco, 1865–1932: Power, Politics and Urban Development* (Berkeley: University of California Press), 51.

12. Richard Walker, 1996, "San Francisco at Center of Globalization: Historical Essay" (originally written for the journal *Urban Geography*), foundsf.org/index.php?title=San_Francisco_at_Center_of_Globalization (accessed April 2016).

13. Hayden Perry, n.d., "Labor Politics in Action, 1901–1911: The Union Labor Party of San Francisco," Solidarity, solidarity-us.org/node/1726 (accessed May 2016); Robert E. L. Knight, 1960, *Industrial Relations in the San Francisco Bay Area, 1900–1918* (Berkeley: University of California Press), 371.

14. Andrea Rees Davies, 2012, *Saving San Francisco: Relief and Recovery after the 1906 Disaster* (Philadelphia: Temple University Press), 118–120.

15. Ibid., 117.

16. Fradkin, 2005, 344, 196.

17. Ibid., 342.

18. Laura A. Ackley, 2014, *San Francisco's Jewel City: The Panama-Pacific International Exposition of 1915* (Berkeley: Heyday Press), 3.

19. Davies, 2012, 140.

20. Willard Worden, 2015, "When San Francisco Became the Jewel City," *Economist*, August 11, economist.com/blogs/prospero/2015/08/willard-worden (accessed on June 2016).

21. Anthony Oliver-Smith, 1996, "Anthropological Research on Hazards and Disasters," *Annual Review of Anthropology* 25: 313.

22. Steve Ingersoll, 2004, "New Orleans—'The City That Care Forgot' and Other Nicknames: A Preliminary Investigation," Louisiana Division Fact Finder, March, nutrias.org/facts/careforgot.htm (accessed May 2016).

23. New Orleans Convention and Visitors Bureau, 2015, "New Orleans Achieves 9.52 Million Visitors and Record-Breaking Visitor Spend in 2014," March 9, neworleansonline.com/pr/releases/releases/2014%20Visitation%20Release.pdf (accessed June 2016).

24. "Top Cities in the U.S. by Population and Rank," Infoplease, infoplease.com/ipa/a0763098.html (accessed on June 2016).

25. Eric Arnesen, 1994, *Waterfront Workers of New Orleans: Race, Class, and Politics, 1863–1923* (Urbana: University of Illinois Press), 212.

26. Quoted in Justin A. Nystrom, 2014, "The Vanished World of the New Orleans Longshoreman," *Southern Spaces*, March 5, southernspaces.org/2014/vanished-world-new-orleans-longshoreman (accessed June 2016).

27. Ibid.

28. William Julius Wilson, n.d., "White Flight," datacenterresearch.org/pre-katrina/tertiary/white.html (accessed June 2016).

29. Pamela Engel and Rob Wile, 2013, "11 American Cities That Are Shells of Their Former Selves," *Business Insider*, June 26, businessinsider.com/american-cities-in-decline-2013-6 (accessed June 2016).

30. Richard Thompson, 2014, "As Work Winds Down at Avondale, Shipyard's Future Remains Cloudy; Projects Expected to Dry Up in Oct.," *New Orleans Advocate*, October 1, theadvocate.com/new_orleans/news/business/article_fee0ad4b-05e2-507a-adaa-7ffd58735670.html (accessed November 2016).

31. Sharon Zukin connects the shift to a postmodern urban architecture with the decline of the working class, noting, "Postmodern design aestheticized a city's industrial past—while making it clear that the urban working class was obsolete." Zukin, 2006, 116.

32. Joe Vetter, 2009, "The Decline of New Orleans," International Communist League, October 23, icl-fi.org/english/wv/945/neworleans.html (accessed June 2016).

33. Griselda Nevarez, 2015, "Latino Workers Helped Rebuild New Orleans, but Many Weren't Paid," *NBC News*, August 28, nbcnews.com/storyline/hurricane-katrina-anniversary/latino-workers-helped-rebuild-new-orleans-many-werent-paid-n417571 (accessed November 2016).

34. Kevin Fox Gotham and Miriam Greenberg, 2014, *Crisis Cities* (New York: Oxford University Press), 189. For an engaging history of tourism in New Orleans, see Mark J. Souther, 2013, *New Orleans on Parade: Tourism and the Transformation of the Crescent City*, Making the Modern South (Baton Rouge: Louisiana State University Press).

35. Melanie K. Smith, 2007, introduction to *Tourism, Culture and Regeneration*, edited by Smith (Cambridge, MA: CABI), xv.

36. Leslie Eaton and Cameron McWhirter, 2015, "New Orleans's Uneven Revival in Decade after Katrina," *Wall Street Journal*, August 26, wsj.com/articles/the-new-orleans-economy-ten-years-after-katrina-1440628953 (accessed May 2016).

37. Smith, 2007, 177.

38. Colleen Curry, 2012, "Joplin, New Orleans Benefit from 'Disaster Tourism,'" *ABC News*, January 19, abcnews.go.com/US/disaster-tourism-booms-hurricanes-tornados/story?id=15389166 (accessed May 2016).

39. Roberto E. Barrios, 2016, "Hurricane Katrina's Forgotten Survivors," Sapiens, May 12, sapiens.org/culture/hurricane-katrina-lower-9th-ward (accessed May 2016).

40. Lauren Zanolli, 2015, "New Orleans Transforms Access to Health Care, but Major Concerns Remain," *Aljazeera America*, August 31, america.aljazeera.com/articles/2015/8/31/new-orleans-health-care-woes.html (accessed January 2017).

41. Gary Rivlin, 2015, *Katrina after the Flood* (New York: Simon & Schuster), 368.

42. Engel and Wile, 2013; New Orleans Data Center, datacenterresearch.org/data-resources/population-by-parish (accessed June 2016); Robert McClendon, 2015, "New Orleans Is 2nd Worst for Income Inequality in the US, Roughly on Par

with Zambia, Report Says," *New Orleans Times-Picayune*, August 26, nola.com /politics/index.ssf/2014/08/new_orleans_is_2nd_worst_for_i.html (accessed June 2016); Marla Nelson, Laura Wolf-Powers, and Jessica Fish, 2015, "Persistent Low Wages in New Orleans' Economic Resurgence: Policies for Improving Earnings for the Working Poor," *New Orleans Index at Ten*, New Orleans Data Center research report, 1, s3.amazonaws.com/gnocdc/reports/TheDataCenter_PersistentLowWag esinNewOrleans.pdf (accessed November 2015).

43. Eugen Neuhaus, 2015, *The Art of the Exposition: Personal Impressions of the Architecture, Sculpture, Mural Decorations, Color Scheme & Other Aesthetic Aspects of the Panama-Pacific Exposition* (San Francisco: Paul Elder), 87; Bruce Alpert, 2015, "President Obama: New Orleans Rebuilt Not as 'It Had Been,' but Better," *New Orleans Times-Picayune*, August 27, nola.com/katrina/index.ssf/2015/08/obama _says_new_orleans_rebuilt.html (accessed May 2016).

44. Allison Plyer, 2016, "Facts for Features: Katrina Impact," New Orleans Data Center, August 26, datacenterresearch.org/data-resources/katrina/facts-for-impact (accessed December 2016).

45. Bryn Mickle, 2016, "Flint, Michigan: Welcome to America's Forgotten City," *M Live Michigan*, March 4, mlive.com/news/flint/index.ssf/2016/03/welcome_to _flint_michigan_were.html (accessed June 2016).

46. Quoted in Lawrence J. Vale and Thomas J. Campanella, 2005, "Conclusion: Axioms of Resilience," in *The Resilient City: How Modern Cities Recover from Disaster*, edited by Vale and Campanella (Oxford: Oxford University Press), 346.


### BY WAY OF CLOSING


1. Ruth Anna Putnam, 1997, *The Cambridge Companion to William James* (Cambridge: Cambridge University Press), 372.

2. The phrase "There is no alternative to market logic," or TINA, begins with a speech by Margaret Thatcher and echoes in many and varied literatures on markets and inequality. See, for example, Manfred Steger, Paul Battersby, and Joseph Siracusa, 2014, *The Sage Handbook of Globalization* (Thousand Oaks, CA: Sage), 30.

3. Ronald Reagan, 1981, "Remarks at the Annual Meeting of the National Alliance of Business," October 5, reaganlibrary.archives.gov/archives/speeches/1981/100581a .htm (accessed June 2016); George Bush, 1989, "Presidential Inaugural Address," American Presidency Project, January 20, presidency.ucsb.edu/ws/?pid=16610 (accessed December 2016).

4. Noah Smith, 2015, "Does the Social Safety Net Make Us Lazy?," *Bloomberg News*, January 26, bloomberg.com/view/articles/2015-01-26/social-safety-net-busi ness-startups-and-risk-aversion (accessed August 2016).

5. Nancy Isenberg, 2016, *White Trash: The 400-Year Untold History of Class in America* (New York: Viking Press), 315.

6. In an interview on Sirius XM Radio in May 2017, Ben Carson, President

Trump's secretary of the Department of Housing and Urban Development, grants the underemployed and poor more agency than Ryan. For Carson, poverty "is to a large extent . . . a state of mind." The secretary's message is one of positive thinking. Think you have food in the fridge. Think you have a life-sustaining wage. Think you have . . . and so on through the palliative mantra of mind over matter. Jose A. DelReal, 2017, "Ben Carson Calls Poverty 'a State of Mind' during Interview," *Washington Post*, May 17, washingtonpost.com/people/jose-a-delreal/?utm_term=.cd46 44e0228a (accessed May 2017).

7. Dewey cited in Richard Hofstadter, 1944, *Social Darwinism in American Thought* (New York: Beacon Press), 123; Gunnar Myrdal, 1995, *An American Dilemma: The Negro Problem and Modern Democracy* (Piscataway, NJ: Transaction Press); Isenberg, 2016, 315.

8. In his genealogy of market culture in early modern Britain, Jean-Christophe Agnew writes, "A money medium can imbue itself with life . . . a recurrent anticipation of gain and loss that lends to all social intercourse a pointed, transactional quality." Agnew, 1986, *The Market and the Theatre in Anglo-American Thought, 1550–1770* (New York: Cambridge University Press), 4.

9. Sidney Hook, 1974, *Pragmatism and the Tragic Sense of Life* (New York: Basic Books), 48.

10. The deep structure of a society, notes Eric R. Wolf, is likely to "become most visible when . . . challenged by crisis." Wolf, 1990, "Distinguished Lecture: Facing Power—Old Insights, New Questions," *American Anthropologist* 92(3): 593.

11. The subheading title is from Judith A. Howard and Ernest Zebrowski Jr., 2007, *Category 5: The Story of Camille, Lessons Unlearned from America's Most Violent Hurricane* (Ann Arbor: University of Michigan Press), 236.

12. Jesse Bricker et al., 2015, "The Increase in Wealth Concentration, 1989–2013," Board of Governors of the Federal Reserve System, June, federalreserve .gov/econresdata/notes/feds-notes/2015/increase-in-wealth-concentration-1989 -2013-20150605.html (accessed October 2016).

13. Ron Nixon, 2017, "Popular Choice to Lead FEMA, but Challenges Await," *New York Times*, July 22, A8.

14. Christine Hauseraug, 2017, "As Harvey Raged, Meteorologists Grasped for Words to Describe It," *New York Times*, August 29, nytimes.com/2017/08/29/us /hurricane-harvey-warnings-unprecedented.html?mcubz=0 (accessed September 2017).

15. Emily Tillett, 2017, "Houston Mayor Sylvester Turner Says City Is 'Open for Business,'" *CBS News*, September 3, cbsnews.com/news/houston-mayor-sylvester -turner-says-city-is-open-for-business/ (accessed September 2017).

# INDEX

Page numbers in *italics* represent photographs.